Kazuo Ishiguro

Contemporary Critical Perspectives
Series Editors: Jeannette Baxter, Sebastian Groes and Sean Matthews
Consultant Editor: Dominic Head

Guides in the *Contemporary Critical Perspectives* series provide companions to reading and studying major contemporary authors. They include new critical essays combining textual readings, cultural analysis and discussion of key critical and theoretical issues in a clear, accessible style. Each guide also includes a preface by a major contemporary writer, a new interview with the author, discussion of film and TV adaptation and guidance on further reading.

Titles in the series include:

J. G. Ballard edited by Jeannette Baxter
Ian McEwan edited by Sebastian Groes

KAZUO ISHIGURO

Contemporary Critical Perspectives

Edited by
Sean Matthews and Sebastian Groes

continuum

Continuum International Publishing Group

The Tower Building　　　　　　80 Maiden Lane
11 York Road　　　　　　　　　Suite 704
London SE1 7NX　　　　　　　　New York, NY 10038

www.continuumbooks.com

British Library Cataloguing-in-Publication Data
A catalogue record for this book is available from the British Library.

ISBN:　978-0-8264-9723-9 (hardback)
　　　　978-0-8264-9724-6 (paperback)

Library of Congress Cataloging-in-Publication Data
A catalog record for this book is available from the Library of Congress.

Typeset by Newgen Imaging Systems Pvt Ltd, Chennai, India
Printed and bound in Great Britain by MPG Books Group

Contents

On Having a Contemporary Like Kazuo Ishiguro

Haruki Murakami

There are some writers who, when one of their new novels comes out, send me running down to the bookstore to buy a copy; then I put aside whatever else I am reading and bury myself in their work. These days, only a handful of writers have this effect on me, and Kazuo Ishiguro is one of them.

I think Ishiguro's most outstanding feature is that all of his novels are so different; from one to the next, they are put together in different ways, and point in different directions. In structure and style, each is clearly meant to stand apart from the others. Yet each also bears Ishiguro's unmistakable imprint, and each forms a small yet wonderfully distinct universe in itself.

But that is not all. When all those little universes are brought together (of course this only happens in the reader's head), a far broader universe – the sum of all of Ishiguro's novels – takes vivid shape. In this sense, his novels occupy both a vertical, diachronic dimension and a horizontal, synchronic dimension at once. It is this aspect of Ishiguro that strikes me most powerfully. Each of his novels may mark a step forward in an evolutionary process (excuse me, of course they *are* evolving). Yet the specifics of whether that process exists, or what it may or may not involve, interests me far less than the manner in which all the works are bound together. That, I feel, is what makes Ishiguro so special, and so unlike most other writers.

In all my years reading Ishiguro, he has never disappointed me or left me doubting him. All I feel is a deep admiration for the infallible skill with which he has piled all these different worlds on top of one another. Of course I have my personal preferences when it comes to his work; work A, let's say, may suit my tastes better than work B. Compared to other writers, though, Ishiguro's fictional world makes this question of comparison relatively unimportant. What strikes me as much more significant is the way that each of his works complements and supports the others. Just like molecules bonding together.

Clearly only a very few writers are capable of creating this sort of composite universe. It is not just a matter of coming up with a great novel every so often. Rather, Ishiguro has a certain vision, a master plan, that shapes his work – each new novel that he writes constitutes another step in the construction of this larger macro-narrative. This, at least, is how I feel about his work.

Perhaps I can make my point more clearly this way. Ishiguro is like a painter working on an immense painting. The massive, sprawling sort of painting that might cover the ceiling or walls of a cathedral. It is lonely work, which involves huge amounts of time, and vast stores of energy. A lifetime job. Every few years, he completes a section of this painting and shows it to us. Together, we gaze on the expanding domain of his universe as, stage by stage, it unfolds. This is both a thrilling and an extremely private experience. But we have yet to gain a bird's-eye view of the total work. We can only guess what images may appear in the completed painting, and how they may move and excite us.

As a reader of novels, it is a joy to be blessed with a contemporary like Kazuo Ishiguro. And as a novelist, it is a great encouragement. To picture what his new novels may look like is to picture my yet unwritten work as well.

Translated by Ted Goossen

Series Editors' Preface

The readership for contemporary fiction has never been greater. The explosion of reading groups and literary blogs, of university courses and school curricula, and even the apparent rude health of the literary marketplace, indicate an ever-growing appetite for new work, for writing which responds to the complex, changing and challenging times in which we live. At the same time, readers seem ever more eager to engage in conversations about their reading, to devour the review pages, to pack the sessions at literary festivals and author events. Reading is an increasingly social activity, as we seek to share and refine our experience of the book, to clarify and extend our understanding.

It is this tremendous enthusiasm for contemporary fiction to which the *Contemporary Critical Perspectives* series responds. Our ambition is to offer readers of current fiction a comprehensive critical account of each author's work, presenting original, specially commissioned analyses of all aspects of their career, from a variety of different angles and approaches, as well as directions towards further reading and research. Our brief to the contributors is to be scholarly, to draw on the latest thinking about narrative, or philosophy, or psychology, indeed whatever seemed to them most significant in drawing out the meanings and force of the texts in question, but also to focus closely on the words on the page, the stories and scenarios and forms which all of us meet first when we open a book. We insisted that these essays be accessible to that mythical beast the Common Reader, who might just as readily be spotted at the Lowdham Book Festival as in a college seminar. In this way, we hope to have presented critical assessments of our writers in such a way as to contribute something to both of those environments, and also to have done something to bring together the most important qualities of each of them.

Jeannette Baxter, Sebastian Groes and Sean Matthews

Acknowledgements

The editors and publishers would like to thank Kazuo Ishiguro for his generous and continued support of this project.

This collection derives in part from the conference 'Kazuo Ishiguro and the International Novel', which was held at Liverpool Hope University in June 2007. We would like to thank Liverpool Hope University for their generous support of the event, and of the *Contemporary Critical Perspectives* series.

Special thanks are due to Haruki Murakami, whose Foreword provides a fascinating insight into the significance of Ishiguro's achievement from the perspective of a fellow contemporary writer and also his translator, Ted Goossen.

Thanks also to our fellow series editor, Jeannette Baxter, and the consultant editor, Dominic Head. We especially thank Anna Fleming and Colleen Coalter for patience far beyond the call of duty in the long process of bringing this text into being.

Chapter Two draws on materials from Motoyuki Shibata's essay 'Lost and Found: On the Japanese Translations of Kazuo Ishiguro', published in *In Other Words*, 30, 32–39.

Daniel Lewis was a great help in compiling the Further Reading section. We are especially grateful to Pat Fitzgerald for help with proofreading and the index.

Sebastian Groes would like to thank Ish for the lively conversation that made that post-conference drive back to London fly by. He also thanks José Lapré, for her encouragement and support.

SG/SM
London/Nottingham, June 2009

Contributors

Justine Baillie is Senior Lecturer in English at the University of Greenwich. Her primary research interests are in critical theory, postcolonial literature and women's writing. She has published studies of African American women's writing and is currently working on a critical study of Toni Morrison's fiction.

Mark Currie is Professor of English Literature at the University of East Anglia. His research interests are in literary theory, narrative theory and contemporary fiction. His recent work has been concerned with time and narrative, and particularly with forms of knowledge about time that have developed in contemporary fiction. His publications include *Metafiction* (Longman, 1995), *Postmodern Narrative Theory* (Palgrave, 1997), *Difference* (Routledge, 2004) and *About Time: Narrative, Fiction and the Philosophy of Time* (Edinburgh University Press, 2007). He is currently working on a new study, *The Unexpected*, which explores issues of anticipation and prolepsis in relation to contemporary fiction and the philosophy of time.

Ted Goossen is Professor of Japanese Literature and Culture at York University, Canada.

Sebastian Groes is Lecturer in English Literature at Roehampton University. He specializes in modern and contemporary culture and literature, and representations of cities. He is the author of two forthcoming works, *British Fiction of the Sixties* (Continuum, 2010) and *The Making of London: London's Textual Lives from Thatcher to New Labour* (Palgrave, 2010), and editor of *Ian McEwan: Contemporary Critical Perspectives* (Continuum, 2009).

David James is Lecturer in Nineteenth and Twentieth-century Literature at the University of Nottingham. His work focuses on the relationship between narrative form, aesthetics and cultural geography. His most recent publication is *Contemporary British Fiction and the Artistry of Space: Style, Landscape, Perception* (Continuum, 2008), and he is the co-editor of the collection *New Versions of Pastoral: Post-Romantic, Modern, and Contemporary Responses to the Tradition* (Fairleigh Dickinson University Press, 2009). He is a regular contributor to *Textual Practice*.

Hélène Machinal is Senior Lecturer in English Literature at Université de Bretagne Occidentale. She has published a monograph titled *Conan*

Doyle, de Sherlock Holmes au Professeur Challenger (Presses Universitaires de Rennes, 2004), and essays on contemporary British writers including Graham Swift, Patrick McGrath, and on authors of Gothic and fantastic fiction, including Robert Louis Stevenson and Bram Stoker.

Sean Matthews is the Director of the D. H. Lawrence Research Centre at the University of Nottingham, where he teaches modern and contemporary literature and theory, and convenes the Contemporary Fiction Reading Group. His most recent publications include articles on Ian McEwan, Richard Hoggart, Raymond Williams, the Chatterley Trial, the journal *Scrutiny* and a polemic on contemporary literary criticism and theory. His study of Raymond Williams is forthcoming in the Routledge Critical Thinkers Series.

John Mullan is Professor of English Literature at University College London. His books include *Sentiment and Sociability. The Language of Feeling in the Eighteenth Century* (Oxford University Press, 1988), *How Novels Work* (Oxford University Press, 2006), *Lives of the Great Romantics by Their Contemporaries: Shelley* (Pickering and Chatto, 1996), and *Eighteenth-Century Popular Culture. A Selection* (Oxford University Press, 2000). He contributes reviews and a weekly column to *The Guardian*.

Haruki Murakami is a Japanese writer and translator whose work includes numerous short stories, the novels *Norwegian Wood* (Harvill, 1987; 2000), *The Wind-up Bird Chronicle* (Harvill, 1995; 1997) and *Kafka on the Shore* (Harvill, 2002; 2005) and the non-fiction book on the Sarin gas attack on the Tokyo subway, *Underground* (Harvill, 1998; 2000). His work has been translated into more than thirty languages and has received many prizes. His latest book is the memoir *What I Talk About When I Talk About Running* (Harvill, 2007; 2008).

Richard Robinson is Lecturer in English Literature at the University of Swansea. He works in twentieth-century fiction, comparing narratives drawn from Anglophone and European literatures. His most recent work, *Narratives of the European Border: A History of Nowhere* (Palgrave Macmillan, 2007), analyzes the representation of borders in modernist and postmodernist writing.

Brian W. Shaffer is Professor of English and Dean of Academic Affairs for faculty development at Rhodes College, in Memphis, Tennessee. He is the author of several books, including *Reading the Novel in English, 1950–2000* (Wiley-Blackwell, 2006), *Understanding Kazuo Ishiguro* (University Press of Mississippi, 1998) and *The Blinding Torch: Modern British Fiction and the Discourse of Civilization* (University of Massachusetts Press, 1993). He has (co-)edited *Conversations with Kazuo Ishiguro* (University Press of Mississippi, 2008).

Motoko Sugano is a doctoral student of Waseda University's Graduate School of Letters, Arts and Sciences in Tokyo. Her research interests include the representation of imperialism in Kazuo Ishiguro's work and (post)colonial literatures in English by writers from South East Asian countries.

Motoyuki Shibata is Professor of American Literature at the University of Tokyo. He has written widely on contemporary literature in English, including essays on Paul Auster and Kazuo Ishiguro. He has translated many novels by contemporary American authors, including Paul Auster, Steve Erickson, Steven Millhauser, Richard Powers and Stuart Dybek. He was winner of the 27th Suntory Prize for Social Sciences and Humanities for *American Narushisu* (American Narcissus, University of Tokyo Press, 2005). He is a regular contributor to the Japanese magazines *Coyote* and *Monkey Business*.

Paul-Daniel Veyret is Senior Lecturer in English Literature at Michel de Montaigne-Bordeaux 3. His research interests range from contemporary British writers such as Alex Garland, Timothy Mo and Kazuo Ishiguro to diasporic Indian literature, cinema and theory. His first book was a full-length study of Kazuo Ishiguro, *Kazuo Ishiguro: L'encre de la mémoire* (Presses Universitaires de Bordeaux, 2005). He is the co-founder, with Prof. Jean-François Baillon, of DESI (Diasporas: Etudes des Singularités Indiennes), a research group focused on the Indian diaspora. His new book focuses on the diasporic imagination in the works of Salman Rushdie, Amitav Ghosh and Rohinton Mistry.

Chronology of Kazuo Ishiguro's Life

1954   Born on 8 November in Nagasaki, Japan, to the oceanographer Shigeo Ishiguro and Shizuko Ishiguro (née Michida).

1960   The Ishiguro family (including his elder sister Fumiko) moves to Guildford, Surrey. Younger sister Yoko born in the UK.

1960–1966   Educated at Stoughton Primary School. Later becomes head chorister.

1966–1973   Educated at Woking County Grammar School for Boys, Surrey.

1973   Works in a variety of jobs, including grouse beater for the Queen Mother at Balmoral Castle, Aberdeen (Scotland).

1974   Travels to USA and Canada, keeps journal and attempts to establish himself as a musician by sending out demo tapes.

1974–1978   Studies English and Philosophy at the University of Kent (BA with Honours).

1975   Postpones postgraduate degree to write fiction

1976   Works as a community worker at Renfrew Social Works Department, Renfrew (Scotland).

1979–1980   Works as a resettlement worker with homeless people at West London Cyrenians (Notting Hill). Meets Lorna Anne MacDougal, his future wife.

1979   Summer: writes four short stories at a farmhouse in Cornwall.

1979–1980   Enrols for the MA in Creative Writing at the University of East Anglia, mentored by Malcolm Bradbury and Angela Carter.

1980   Moves to Cardiff, Wales. *Granta*'s Bill Buford publishes the short story 'A Strange and Sometimes Sadness' in magazine *Bananas*.

1981   Move to Sydenham, South London. Short stories 'A Strange and Sometimes Sadness', 'Getting Poisoned' and 'Waiting for J' published in *Introduction 7: Stories by New Writers*. Buford commissions first novel.

1982   *A Pale View of Hills* published in Britain and America. Becomes British subject. Commissioned to write two plays for television by Channel 4.

1983   Royal Society of Literature awards the Winifred Holtby Prize for *A Pale View of Hills*. 'A Family Supper' published in *Firebird 2*. Included in *Granta's* 'Best Young British Novelists' edition.

1984   Channel 4 broadcasts *A Profile of Arthur J. Mason*, winning the Golden Plaque for Best Short Film at the Chicago Film Festival. Arts Council Britain offers him a writer's bursary.

1986   *An Artist of the Floating World* published in Britain and America, winning the Whitbread Book of the Year Award, and shortlisted for the Booker Prize. Marries MacDougal. Channel 4 broadcasts *The Gourmet*. Travels to Singapore and Malaysia.

1987   Reprint of 'A Family Supper' in *The Penguin Book of Modern Short Stories*, Malcolm Bradbury (ed.).

1989   *The Remains of the Day* published in Britain and America, and awarded the Booker Prize. Visits Japan for the first time in thirty years.

1990   University of Kent, Canterbury, awards Honorary D.Litt. Reprint of 'A Family Supper' in *Esquire*. Special guest at the Houston International Festival.

1992   Daughter Naomi born.

1993   Again included in *Granta's* 'Best Young British Novelists' edition. The film adaptation of *The Remains of the Day* is released, nominated for eight Oscars and wins numerous awards.

1994   Member of Cannes Film Festival Jury chaired by his childhood hero Clint Eastwood.

1995   *The Unconsoled* published, winning the Cheltenham Prize, shortlisted for the Booker Prize. Awarded OBE (Order of the British Empire) for services to literature. Awarded the Italian Premio Scanno prize.

1998   Attends British State Banquet held in honour of Japanese Emperor Akihito. Awarded the French honour of 'Chevalier dans l'Ordre des Arts et Lettres'.

2000   *When We Were Orphans* published in Britain and America, shortlisted for the Booker Prize and the Whitbread Award in 2001.

2003   Attends colloquium on his work in Paris; proceedings later published in *Études britanniques contemporaines*.

2004   Film of *The Saddest Music in the World* (dir. Guy Maddin) released; original screenplay by Ishiguro rewritten by Maddin and George Toles.

2005   *Never Let Me Go* published in Britain and America, shortlisted for the Booker Prize, the 2006 Arthur C. Clarke Award and the 2005 National Book Critics Circle Award.

2006   Film of *The White Countess* (dir. James Ivory) released in the UK after premiering at American Two River Festival in 2005.

2007   Attends International Conference, 'Kazuo Ishiguro and the International Novel', held in June at Liverpool Hope University.

2009   *Nocturnes: Fives Stories of Music and Nightfall* published in Britain and America.

'Your Words Open Windows for Me': The Art of Kazuo Ishiguro

SEAN MATTHEWS AND SEBASTIAN GROES

The work of Kazuo Ishiguro occupies an important place in our contemporary cultures. Haruki Murakami's declaration, in the 'Foreword' to this volume, that the publication of an Ishiguro novel is an *event*, an occasion to rush to the bookstore to buy a copy and then to set aside all distractions in order to read it, describes a reaction that is shared by many readers around the world. The wide, admiring readership this body of work has generated, not to mention the catalogue of prizes and awards it has received and the wealth of interpretation and criticism it has sustained, is proof of the unusual resonance, and the international significance, of Ishiguro's art. After *The Remains of the Day* (1989) was successfully turned into a critically acclaimed Hollywood blockbuster, the adaptation of *Never Let Me Go* (2005) for the big screen is another confirmation of Ishiguro's status as a serious novelist who is also a major figure within the popular imagination.

One measure of an author's importance is the way in which well-known texts continue to offer up new and suggestive critical readings even as they settle into the canon of serious literary fiction, and the contributions to this volume demonstrate how thoroughly Ishiguro's work fulfils this criterion. Although we may be hesitant or actively resistant these days to the pronouncement of critical principles upon which a canon might be constructed, and even more wary of sticking our necks out, as F. R. Leavis so famously did in *The Great Tradition* (1948), in order 'to insist on the pre-eminent few' (Leavis 1948: 3), Ishiguro's work has an evident claim to being considered in such company.

We are nowadays extremely conscious of the vagaries of publishing fashion, of the difficulties of translation, and of the arbitrariness of critical attention, and we are exceedingly cautious about making value claims about contemporary authors (or any author at all), but thinking in such Leavisian terms for just a moment does facilitate a better placing and understanding of Ishiguro's distinctive achievement. Leavis maintained that the major novelists 'not only change the possibilities of art for practitioners and readers' but also that 'they are significant in terms of the human awareness they promote; awareness of the possibilities of life' (Leavis 1948: 2). Again, such critical terms and objectives are at some distance from the prevailing academic discourse of literary criticism, even if they more readily resonate with readers outside the classroom than many other scholarly readings, but they do seem appropriate and helpful when considering this particular writer. Such statements focus our attention on that preoccupation with the interrelations of art and life, of aesthetics and ethics, which is so central to Ishiguro's vision. John Mullan's 'Afterword' to this volume, which draws on the responses of members of the *Guardian*'s Book Club to the novel, shows how such issues continue to frame the majority of readers' reactions to Ishiguro. In the interview later in this volume, Ishiguro reiterates his own sense of his role as a 'writer who has a serious purpose [. . .] talking about the serious things in life, about what makes our life worthwhile' (p. 116), and – modestly but insistently – relates this creative ambition to the example of such classic authors as 'Dickens, Dostoevsky, Jane Austen and, yes, Tolstoy' (p. 117).

The most telling thing, first of all, about Ishiguro's invocation of these authors is that he situates himself in relation to a range of writers from such diverse national backgrounds – elsewhere in the interview he talks of Mishima, Kawabata, and Murakami; of Calvino and Levi; of Nemirovsky, and he has paid strong tribute to the example of Chekhov and Kafka while also praising Pat Barker, Beryl Bainbridge, and Penelope Fitzgerald for their move away from the historical novel in favour of more personal work. Whereas Leavis was concerned specifically and programmatically with the Anglophone tradition of the English novel (one that nevertheless famously, and provocatively, included Henry James and Joseph Conrad), Ishiguro makes a feature of his eclectic, cosmopolitan heritage, even to the extent of offering a wry apology for the fact that 'you have to set a novel somewhere' (p. 118), on the grounds that *any* location may have the effect of introducing incidental local issues and meanings to a story that might distract the reader from the significance of human existence in any place at any given point in time.

In relationship to this tradition Ishiguro's invocation of the 'international novel' (Oe and Ishiguro 1991: 109–122; Wong and Ishiguro 2008: 178–180) as a description of his works, or, rather, artistic ambition is telling. Categories such as the postcolonial novel, new writing or world literature are 'closed' in the sense that they clearly delineate forms that derive their meaning from opposition to and correction of a colonial context and experience, and challenge the Eurocentric Humanist values that underpin the imperial project. In contrast, Ishiguro's engagement with the international novel is in the form of writing which, despite its specificity in time and place, reaches beyond national and linguistic boundaries. His work celebrates openness and tolerance, addressing readers of all places and times without falling into cultural relativity. Ishiguro never plays the 'identity card' – he felt the urge to move away from Japanese subject matter after being co-opted by critics as a Japanese writer by Western critics (see Chapter Two), and he acts increasingly as a contemporary Everyman. In Ishiguro's work Otherness is not a function of identity, but rooted in a deeply moral imagination. *The Remains of the Day* deals with British appeasement of the Nazis, but it is also a subtle indictment of the failures of the international community during the inter-war period. *Never Let Me Go* seems to be about the ethical dilemmas presented to us by cloning, but it is first of all an analysis of the complexities of human relationships, and cloning itself may be read as a metaphor for any number of modes of exclusion. *Nocturnes* (2009) is not a collection of stories about musicians but more a meditation on the ability of music to connect human beings via that elusive human faculty, the imagination.

There is another aspect to Ishiguro's hesitancy with regard to the function of *place* in his fictions that should give us pause, which also relates both to his 'internationalism' and to his admiration for the classic authors. The necessity of setting demands a level of responsibility or fidelity towards locale and history with which he openly professes discomfort. There is a paradox here: Ishiguro is rightly recognized as a master of the precise representation of specific places and historical circumstances, but those places and histories are, nevertheless, often only obliquely or hauntingly present in the narration itself – Stevens goes on his journey in the week of the Suez crisis, but those events are never mentioned; Banks seems remarkably unconcerned by the fall of Shanghai that is taking place around him; Kathy H. and the other clones are wholly inattentive to the routines and politics of the world. The manner in which Ishiguro's narratives are deeply embedded in their historical moments, but also set at significant tangents or angles to those histories, is a formal and thematic characteristic of his work that many readers have explored, and the critics in this volume are no exception. On the whole, such readings tend, quite properly, to work to recover that historical specificity, the relation to occluded events and attitudes, in order primarily to elucidate the extent of the narrators' or protagonists' self-deception and emotional, moral, and political accountability, or else to expose something about the nature of the wider collective or national responsibility for the course of events. Retrieving the historical context of these narratives is a necessary and illuminating task, which chimes with the powerful and predominant mode of criticism of our time. In this volume, for instance, Sean Matthews and Justine Baillie demonstrate the corrosive impact of Nagasaki's destruction upon Etsuko's understanding of motherhood in *A Pale View of Hills* (1982). Sebastian Groes and Paul Veyret suggest that a teleplay such as *The Gourmet*'s (1993) appropriation and reworking of the Gothic genre should be read as a direct reaction to and criticism of the erosion of the social fabric in Thatcher's Britain. Hélène Machinal analyses the ways in which attention to the classic detective novel in its golden age and the geopolitics of the late 1930s provide an illuminating context for understanding *When We Were Orphans* (2000).

Although these essays pay attention to genre, and the relationship between form and subject matter, the careful re-inscription of these characters and stories into the texture of their historical moment does, however, run several risks. Once the work of re-contextualization has been done, the 'proper' historical co-ordinates identified, there is a danger that the process of reading has been short-circuited, that the heart of the novel has been exposed – short of finding ever more histori- cal detail, the work of the critic is complete. There is also the danger that such criticism adopts what E. P. Thompson called 'the enormous condescension of posterity' (Thompson 1968: 13), taking for granted a master-narrative of history that gives priority to ideological or moral perspectives unavailable to those it most concerns. Certainly such a reading might ultimately partially *excuse*, or even *explain* an Ono, a Stevens, or a Banks on the grounds of their historically or ideologically determined false consciousness, but it will thus necessarily relegate the micro-narrative to secondary status. Such readings overlook the ways Ishiguro asks us to consider how these stories evoke themes that are in some senses universal, and even timeless, which might benefit pre- cisely from being seen *less* historically:

> There's always a tension between the setting you choose and the fact that you want to use that location for universal metaphors, for stories that can be applied to all sorts of human situations. You've got to say to your readers that the novel is set in a particular time and place, but hopefully they'll be able to see that it's also about things that are happening over and over again. The balance is quite difficult, but it is why great books can yield so many different kinds of readings. (p. 119)

It is for this reason that Leavis is such a telling point of reference. He insists on the *form* of the work, on its extension of 'the possibilities of art', and also in relation to the problematic but powerful category of 'life' (Leavis 1948: 3). Leavis comments elsewhere that '[i]t is one of the diffi- culties of criticism that the critic has to use such phrases' (Leavis 1955: 74), but these emphases nonetheless remind us that we must be equally attentive to what is *within* the text, in terms of its structure and style, its 'rhetoric' (Wayne C. Booth's term which both David James and John Mullan use in their essays), as to the local and historical context. It is a commonplace clever-cleverly to deconstruct tensions between form and content, but it is important – above all else in reading Ishiguro – that the critic achieves a balanced account of this relation. In this volume, Mark Currie's elucidation of the patterns of hermeneutic challenge and temporal difficulty in Kathy H.'s narrative mode (especially in relation to her patterning of the remembered past, the connections between narrative time and the time of narrated events) is a fine example of the peculiar fruitfulness of such a critical mode, resulting in a reading that, from a close attention to tense and structure, opens out the questions of social freedom and responsibility that are the burden of the tale. Similarly, David James's reading of *The Remains of the Day* concentrates on the nuance of Stevens's voice in order to examine the range of demands the narrative makes of its readers, how quiet but sophisticated is Ishiguro's extension of 'the possibilities of art'.

Art truly matters in Ishiguro's work. His characters' experience of music, painting or writing consistently brings into focus the moral, emotional or political questions they face. Art is often the determining feature of his characters' self-conception: one thinks of Ono's painting in *An Artist of the Floating World* (1986); Ryder's piano playing in *The Unconsoled* (1995); the clones' work for Madame's gallery in *Never Let Me Go*; the musicianship of the characters who populate the recent collection of short stories, *Nocturnes*; or even Jackson's conception of his bar as a piece of performance art in *The White Countess* (2005). At another level, incidents concerning a particular character's relation to art, which might appear delicately, if deceptively, subsidiary to the main narrative, frequently provide the most telling indices of that character's inner condition: Etsuko's refusal to play her violin in *A Pale View of Hills*, for example, or Stevens's struggle to conceal his book from Miss Kenton in *The Remains of the Day*, both expose important aspects of the characters' personalities and states of mind.

On another level the tracing of the intertextual relations of Ishiguro's writing to music, film, the novel or the visual arts commonly serves to open up the meanings of his work. The exploration of the tropes of detective fiction, for instance, allows us to understand more fully the nature and behaviour of the narrator of *When We Were Orphans*. Still more tellingly, as Motoyuki Shibata and Motoko Sugano show in their contribution to this collection, allusions to the films of Yasujiro Ozu, in particular, but also a range of period Japanese fiction and film, help to structure the representation of place and relationships in the early 'Japanese' fictions. Shibata and Sugano also historicize the early work by investigating its critical reception in Japan, showing that the problems of translation have sometimes had a curious effect in the representation of Japan and its history, cultural traditions and military traumas – and that there clearly are limits to Ishiguro's 'international' ambitions. In Chapter Six, Richard Robinson's erudite exploration of the play of naming and anonymity in *The Unconsoled*, of the use of proper nouns, above all those relating to film and football, is one aspect of a process of reading that re-enacts Ryder's experience of disorientation. Robinson's account of the novel opens up the questions about life, fate, and contingency that are central to Ishiguro's artistic project, through a rigorous analysis of one strategy of the work. Over and above the many stylistic and formal characteristics that distinguish Ishiguro's *oeuvre*, it is clear that his writing offers a sustained, fundamental exploration of the functions of art, of the interrelations of aesthetics and ethics, in the modern world.

But why does art matter? And what is its 'function', if there is one at all, according to Ishiguro? Isn't it enough for art 'just' to be beautiful? Ishiguro's contemporary Ian McEwan has said, provocatively, that 'we know in our hearts that the very best art is entirely and splendidly useless' (McEwan 2005). It is instructive to turn to *Never Let Me Go*, which contains some evidence of Ishiguro's thinking about the importance and the uses of art. The clones are asked to produce art for Madame's gallery without knowing why, but during their encounter with Madame and Miss Emily later in the novel, when Hailsham has long vanished, Tommy hints at the significance of their work, and Miss Emily explains:

> You said it was because your art would reveal what you were like. What you were like inside. [. . .] Well, you weren't far wrong about that. We took away your art because we thought it would reveal your souls. Or to put it more finely, we did it to *prove you had souls at all*. (Ishiguro 2005: 255; emphasis in the original)

The wider point Emily makes is not so much that art might reveal the existence of the soul through the expression of some essence, but to try to protect the clones against reductive treatment by those in the outside world. Emily shows that the context in which the Hailsham clones, and we, Ishiguro's readers, grow up has a direct effect on the richness of their, and our, mental life and well-being. Art needs the world to reflect the 'real' through which we live, and the world needs art to reflect on, and understand, itself.

The chapters that make up this volume say a great deal about how *we* as readers respond to the art of an author so concerned with art. It is now axiomatic that each critical reading tells us as much about the nature and priorities of our own reading practice, of our critical discipline and discourse, as it does about the textual object it addresses. Readings of Ishiguro in this volume of *Contemporary Critical Perspectives* are particularly revealing in this regard. Justine Baillie and Sean Matthews offer an account of *A Pale View of Hills* that examines the formation of Etsuko's identity in the light of theoretical work in the fields of gender studies, trauma theory, and postmodern narrative. They too attempt to find a new critical balance by suggesting that the answers to the universal questions raised by Ishiguro's first novel can be generated only if the historical context and the gendered nature of identity are taken into account. The impact of World War II, and in particular the atom bombs, on the consciousness of Japanese women is, curiously, a force of both destruction and creation that results in a wholly ambivalent attitude towards motherhood, which, although formerly associated with a duty towards the nation, now becomes a possibility of forging a newfound selfhood. Brian W. Shaffer reassesses the standing of two of the early stories, the Beckettian 'Waiting for J' (1981) and 'Getting Poisoned' (1981), showing how these short studies of psychological despair are not negligible experiments but organically connected to later, fabulist novels such as *The Unconsoled* and *When We Were Orphans*. Indeed, these short stories are autonomous pieces of considerable literary merit that force us to re-evaluate Ishiguro's own pronouncement that he is primarily a novelist and not a short story writer. The critical and popular success of Ishiguro's *Nocturnes* also supports the idea that Ishiguro can easily cross over into different genres, which he also demonstrated in his lyrics for jazz singer Stacey Kent's album *Breakfast on the Morning Tram* (2007), which have a strong affiliation with the later novels. The complex composition of the story collection as an interrelated series of works transcends the traditional singularity of the short story, bringing to mind James Joyce's *Dubliners* (1914), while the description of *Nocturnes* as an album in which specific musical motifs and themes recur seems even more apt.

Besides his engagement with music, Ishiguro has a long-standing interest in two other art forms which have shaped the twentieth century consciousness: film and television. In Chapter Three Paul Veyret and Sebastian Groes explore Ishiguro's engagement with the screen by exploring his tele- and screenplays. In *The Gourmet*, a short television film, they uncover Ishiguro as a writer whose adventure in another genre has, at least temporarily, allowed him to discard his humanist roots and to act as a witty contributor to the mid-eighties moment of high postmodernism. An examination of Ishiguro's two films, *The Saddest Music in the World* (2003) and *The White Countess* (2005), elucidates his interest in thinking about utopias. In both films, however, the artistic spaces only temporarily manage to create harmony between different nations before collapsing under the dead weight of History and the violence of war.

At the heart of Ishiguro's work is a series of grand, dialectical oppositions: between History and the Present; Objectivity and Subjectivity; Reality and Imagination; Individual and Collective; Contingency and Universality; Realism and Surrealism. A curious paradox operates within the texts. The writing, which seems so sure of itself and never puts a foot wrong, leads the reader away from certainties rather than affirms them. The role of language is important within this process: it is both a source with which to construct reality while its very constructedness leads us away from any notion of 'authenticity' of that reality. Indeed, despite the clarity of Ishiguro's texts, the language sometimes becomes overstrained and constructed to the point of collapse, so that 'reality' too gives way to possibilities that are dangerous and contingent. In this respect, Ishiguro's work resembles not that of the great, classic writers of the humanist tradition but rather the modernists, whose questioning of everything, from time and space to established knowledge itself, continues to haunt us. In 'The Ideology of Modernism' (1957), the Hungarian literary critic Georg Lukács's attack on the negation of outward reality and the disintegration of personality in the work of modernist writers such as Kafka, James Joyce, T. S. Eliot, and Samuel Beckett, he quotes the Austrian writer Robert Musil, who noted of his unfinished masterpiece *The Man without Qualities* (1930):

> 'I have not, I must insist, written a historical novel. I am not concerned with actual events . . . Events, anyhow, are interchangeable. I am interested in what is typical, in what one might call the ghostly aspect of reality.' [Lukács continues:] The word 'ghostly' is interesting. It points to a major tendency in modernist literature: the attenuation of actuality. In Kafka, the descriptive detail is of an extraordinary immediacy and authenticity. But Kafka's artistic ingenuity is really directed towards substituting his *angst*-ridden vision of the world for objective reality. The realistic detail is the expression of a ghostly un-reality, of a nightmare world, whose function is to evoke *angst*. (Lukács 1957: 148)

Musil and Lukács bring to the fore a key tension present in Ishiguro's work as well, namely, the idea that we as individuals are not proper, rounded subjects but merely ghostly actors and performers inhabiting roles that are allocated to us randomly by the context in which we find ourselves. In *The Remains of the Day*, Miss Kenton asks: '"Why, Mr. Stevens, why, why do you always have to pretend?"' (Ishiguro 1989: 154), and Miss Emily notes that clones are 'simply pawns in a game' (Ishiguro 2005: 261). We are doomed to enact narratives over which we, if we think of the pianist Ryder and the detective Christopher Banks, have little control, or, as in the case of the butler Stevens or carer Kathy H., do not even want any control. At our more fragile and less rational moments, we understand this. It frightens us and imbues everything in the world with a sense of loss that we can only recuperate through forging, nursing, and celebrating brittle human relationships. It is a high-quality and above all *human* writer such as Ishiguro who shows us how to do this, and in the act returns to us a degree of agency, hope, and comfort. In the final story, 'Cellists', in *Nocturnes*, a promising young cello player, Tibor, is taken on by a self-proclaimed cello virtuoso who turns out to not be able to actually play the instrument at all. It is their relationship that forms an analogy for the relationship between writer, text and reader: 'You suggest verbally, then I play. That way, it's not like I copy, copy, copy. Your words open windows for me' (Ishiguro 2009: 208).

CHAPTER ONE

'Somewhere Just Beneath the Surface of Things': Kazuo Ishiguro's Short Fiction

BRIAN W. SHAFFER

Chapter Summary: Kazuo Ishiguro's six published works of short fiction have been dismissed as amateur experiments or as mere preliminary sketches for the author's novels. This chapter reassesses the standing of two early short stories, 'Waiting for J' (1981) and 'Getting Poisoned' (1981), in terms of their importance to an understanding of Ishiguro's consistent concern for the representation of psychological trauma. It shows how the seeds of *The Unconsoled* (1995) and the later, more fabulist novels are to be found in these early stories, but also that the author's earlier and later fictions are organically connected in ways not generally recognized.

Kazuo Ishiguro is known primarily as the author of six critically acclaimed, award-winning novels published over the past quarter century, but his first published works were short stories. 'A Strange and Sometimes Sadness', 'Waiting for J', and 'Getting Poisoned', all appeared in *Introduction 7: Stories by New Writers* (1981); 'The Summer After the War' (1983) in *Granta 7*; 'A Family Supper' (1983) in *Firebird 2*; and, most recently, 'A Village After Dark' (2001) came out in *The New Yorker* after first appearing in France in a French translation. These stories, in part because they represent Ishiguro's earliest work, have often been dismissed by author and critics alike as juvenilia or as amateur experiments that merit attention only as sketches towards the more mature and accomplished novels. Paul Vlitos's assessment of Ishiguro's earliest stories as providing 'a useful window onto Ishiguro's early attempts to deal with themes that would preoccupy his later work' (Vlitos 2003: 178) sums up the prevailing view. I would like to suggest, however, that the seeds of *The Unconsoled* (1995) and the later, more fabulist novels are to be found in the earliest of Ishiguro's fictions, and that the author's earlier and later works are far more organically connected, in particular in their exploration of trauma, than is generally recognized. More specifically, I reassess the standing of two of the early stories, 'Waiting for J' and 'Getting Poisoned', arguing for their importance in helping us

understand Ishiguro's later representations of trauma in the more celebrated novels.

It is not surprising that many readers view the stories as sketches
or studies that anticipate the plots, intellectual terrain, and narrative
devices of one or more of the novels. 'A Strange and Sometimes Sadness',
for example, written during Ishiguro's first term in the creative writing
program at the University of East Anglia, explores such subjects as the
dropping of the atomic bomb on Nagasaki, a troublesome pregnancy,
and the trauma of geographical displacement (between Japan and
England), subjects later honed and developed in *A Pale View of Hills*
(1982). 'The Summer After the War', written between the composition of
Ishiguro's first and second novels, clearly anticipates *An Artist of the
Floating World* (1986) in its treatment, among other things, of a Japanese
painter whose earlier propagandistic, wartime artwork supported the
now discredited fascist-imperialist cause, and who for this reason seeks
to remake his past life, both in his own eyes and in the eyes of his
grandson.

'A Family Supper', perhaps the most accomplished and autonomous
of the three Japanese stories, was written towards the end of Ishiguro's
year at East Anglia, while he was drafting *A Pale View of Hills*. Wai Chew
Sim (Sim 2005: 81) has praised this story for demonstrating Ishiguro's
skill at building dramatic tension and exploring the familial and genera-
tional tensions played out against the backdrop of Japanese wartime
and post-war trauma that are further elucidated in Ishiguro's first two
novels. More a vignette than a story, 'A Family Supper' is Chekhovian
in its economy, subtlety, and power; it explores the ways in which well-
intentioned fathers, literally or figuratively, murder their wives and
children. 'A Family Supper' also concerns the trauma of geographical
displacement explored in *A Pale View of Hills* and *When We Were Orphans*
(2000), and employs a number of interlocking motifs (suicide, ghosts,
and poison, among others) that recur in *A Pale View of Hills*.

What unites these three Japanese stories, and indeed Ishiguro's
first three novels, is thus their shared focus on the unsaid, on matters
that lie 'somewhere just beneath the surface of things' (Ishiguro
1981a: 21). Mark Kamine has observed, alluding to the repressed nature
of Ishiguro's protagonist-narrators, 'Few writers dare to say so little of
what they mean as Ishiguro' (Kamine 1989: 22). These works are also
united in being narrated by self-deceiving first-person protagonists
who seek to hide painful memories from themselves (and from their
readers) and who attempt, unsuccessfully, to remake themselves in the
light of what they fear were shameful, even damning, past decisions.
Bruce King's remarks on the characteristic Ishiguro narrator aptly
describe this quality: 'Each story uses a monologue to reveal more
about the speaker then the person intends. In each, the precise facts
of what happened are not clear as the reader can only piece together
what has been said by seeing through the narration to a different story'
(King 2004: 165).

Unlike these three fictions, Ishiguro's fourth story, 'A Village After Dark', was never intended by the author to be an autonomous story. Rather, as Ishiguro explained in personal communication with me, it was written as an experiment geared towards working out certain narrative techniques he was exploring while writing *The Unconsoled*. Indeed, it is impossible *not* to think of Ryder, the protagonist of that novel, when encountering Fletcher, the protagonist of 'A Village After Dark', who arrives in a generic English village to accomplish an unspecific but urgent and important task, and whose controversial (and perhaps guilty) past life in the village he (and we) can only vaguely infer and never clearly recall.

While it is understandable, even if reductive, that many readers would view the earlier mentioned four stories as working studies of the later novels, the same cannot be said of the remaining two, 'Waiting for J' and 'Getting Poisoned', which demand scrutiny for reasons beyond the light they shed on the genesis of the novels. These two stories, among the very first Ishiguro wrote, are experimental *tours de force* that approach the interest, if not the depth and subtlety, of the novels. They merit the attention of all serious readers of Ishiguro both as intriguing and adept independent fictions and for the light they shed on the connection between the more finely chiselled, superficially realistic earlier novels (*A Pale View of Hills*, *An Artist of the Floating World*, *The Remains of the Day* (1989)) and the more fabulist, experimental, or avant-garde later novels (*The Unconsoled*, *When We Were Orphans*, *Never Let Me Go* (2005)). These two stories help us to see that the seeds of *The Unconsoled* and the later novels are to be found in the earliest of Ishiguro's works, and that the earlier and later works are far more organically connected, in particular in their exploration of trauma, than is generally recognized.

Ironically, of the six Ishiguro stories, 'Waiting for J' and 'Getting Poisoned' are held in the lowest critical regard. Clive Sinclair and Barry Lewis, for example, dismiss these tales, when compared with Ishiguro's early novels, as derivative and lacking in brilliance (Sinclair 1985: 36; Lewis 2000: 130). Ishiguro himself is equally dismissive, deeming the latter story a juvenile experiment on such 'vogue subjects' as 'adolescent sex and violence' (Sexton 1987: 16). The following readings of 'Waiting for J' and 'Getting Poisoned' therefore reassess the standing of these stories in the author's corpus and counter the benign neglect with which these misunderstood tales of trauma have been received.

'Waiting for J' is in many ways altogether different from the Japanese stories and novels that were to follow. It may be said instead to resemble and anticipate far more strongly *The Unconsoled* with its pervasive dream-like atmosphere, its troublingly self-destructive protagonist-narrator, its subtle use of character doubling, and its paranoia-inducing Kafkaesque and Beckett-like qualities. Alluding to works by Samuel Beckett and Franz Kafka in its title, 'Waiting for J' is a quirky and enigmatic psychological intrigue. Yet the story also explores issues common to many of Ishiguro's works, such as narratorial self-deception and repression, and interrogation of the sources and goals of the artistic life. The story also presents us with an unreliable narrator, an untrustworthy and self-undercutting narrative voice. As in all of Ishiguro's works, here too 'outer' narrative layers need to be stripped away in order to grasp the essence of the story at which the protagonist only reluctantly hints.

'Waiting for J' tells of a nameless, isolated, sexually repressed, and voyeuristic narrator who, on his fortieth birthday, waits for 'J', a childhood friend four years his senior, to appear and murder him (the precise significance of the initial 'J' and this particular birthday remain as much a mystery at the story's end as at its beginning). The agreement between the two originates in a childhood agreement to murder each other when each turns forty so as to avoid old age, a turn of events that, incidentally, anticipates the plotline of Ian McEwan's *Amsterdam* (1998). Despite the narrator's 'dread' of J, he masochistically feels 'a curious excitement in anticipation' of seeing his old friend again (Ishiguro 1981b: 32). The story is shrouded in uncertainty (qualifying phrases such as 'quite probably' and 'I cannot be sure' abound), particularly as to the events surrounding the improbable childhood murder pact and its even more improbable execution. The narrator, four years earlier and after twenty years without seeing his friend, had visited J's apartment on J's own fortieth birthday, as promised, and murdered him with an ornamental knife. Just before the narrator commenced the murder of his friend, the two appear to agree that the ghost of J will also keep up his end of the bargain, killing the narrator in his turn on his fortieth birthday. And this is where the story ends, precisely where it began, with the protagonist awaiting J's arrival: 'I feel an odd mixture of relief and disappointment each time I find J is not standing there behind me. He will come, of that I am certain. The futility of that triumph [the narrator's murder of J] four years ago seems embarrassingly obvious to me now' (Ishiguro 1981b: 37). Like Beckett's enigmatic *Waiting for Godot, waiting* is the central dramatic action of the work. Also like Beckett's play, we seem no closer to grasping the significance of the work's events at the end than at the beginning. It is perhaps for these reasons that critics have generally ignored this tale, which so resolutely resists interpretive closure.

'Waiting for J' might initially appear as an amateurish murder mystery or ghost story with psychotic overtones. Indeed, there is no way to know for certain whether it is a supernatural element or the protagonist's mental illness that determines the tale's outcome. However, this would be to take the story, and what the obviously troubled narrator tells us, at face value, something experienced readers of Ishiguro know to resist. A careful study of the tale affords a far different interpretation, one lacking any supernatural or chronologically inconceivable suicide pact. Indeed, such a reading of the story reveals that the narrator's life is utterly *unlike* the one he presents to us. For example, the narrator portrays himself as a leading scholar, stressing that 'it is acknowledged that

I am as well acquainted with my particular field as anyone in the country', and as a popular teacher: 'Last week [. . .] two of my students dropped in to borrow a chess set' (Ishiguro 1981b: 29), who frowns on 'self-deception' (Ishiguro 1981b: 32). Yet it slowly becomes obvious that the narrator is altogether self-deceived and may even possess delusions of grandeur. For example, J's disappointing position as the 'supervisor in a warehouse' (Ishiguro 1981b: 34), appears to undermine the protagonist's own status as a world-class scholar; just as the revelation that J's 'friends' are in fact merely 'acquaintances' seems to comment on the narrator's apparent reclusive streak, and lack of friends – the visiting, chess-playing students, the narrator observes revealingly, stay 'for over half an hour' (Ishiguro 1981b: 29).

The emerging similarities between the two characters, in turn, lead to the recognition that J and the narrator are surely one and the same individual, and that the story is thus a Gothic tale of the Double. In this case, a fantasy self, the successful, well-to-do, celebrated art scholar, seeks to kill off his actual self, the impoverished, unpopular, defeated warehouse supervisor. Seen in this light, 'Waiting for J' rather than being a ghost story or murder mystery is a latter-day *Strange Case of Dr. Jekyll and Mr. Hyde* (1886), in which a fantasy self and a quotidian self battle it out for survival. What Freud writes of character doubling in his 1907 lecture 'Creative Writers and Daydreaming' is germane to the protagonist's presentation of J in this story: 'The psychological novel in general no doubt owes its special nature to the inclination of the modern writer to split up his ego [. . .] into many part-egos, and, in consequence, to personify the conflicting currents of his own mental life in several heroes' (Freud 1989: 654). What Freud argues of 'the uncanny' is also relevant to the story, particularly to its vague or disorienting qualities. Freud associates the uncanny with a state of spatial disorientation: the uncanny is always 'something one does not know one's way about in' (Freud 1955: 221). Uncanny works typically 'keep us in the dark for a long time about the precise nature' (Freud 1955: 251) of the worlds they depict. This quality is certainly true of 'Waiting for J' and later of *The Unconsoled*.

That the two friends should be read as character doubles, two sides of the same ego, is hinted at frequently in the story. Sometimes it is even made explicit, such as when J tells the narrator, 'You come to haunt me, old fellow. Like a conscience' (Ishiguro 1981b: 34). Other explicit references to this psychological doubling take place when it is noted, even after twenty years without contact, that 'J recognized me immediately' (Ishiguro 1981b: 33), and that 'The light from the kitchen lit up one side of [J's] face,' while, 'the other half of the face was in shadow' (Ishiguro 1981b: 36). At other times this doubling is more implied than revealed. We learn, for example, that both the protagonist and J have endured a 'fortnight' of gloominess and dreariness, anxiety and sleeplessness, in part due to the mysterious and disturbing 'footsteps' in the halls of their respective apartments (Ishiguro 1981b: 28; 29; 34; 35). Both characters are sculptors of sorts, using knives to carve wood or stone. Each injures or considers injuring himself with his sculpting knife (Ishiguro 1981b: 28; 32; 33; 36). And both take a sadistic and aesthetic interest in the suffering of others or of themselves. As younger men, they both watched in emotionless, aloof fascination while J mutilated the head of an injured rabbit, 'as if crafting something out of stone' (Ishiguro 1981b: 31), just as the two greet the narrator's 'murder' of J with the same emotionless, sadomasochistic interest (Ishiguro 1981b: 36).

There is yet further evidence to suggest that J, a failure of whom the narrator is ashamed, is the narrator's quotidian self, while the other self, the famous scholar, is the stuff merely of projection and fantasy. For example, the narrator's and J's apartments perfectly mirror each other, but at opposite ends of the social spectrum. The narrator's London apartment looks down on the mews below; his living room is done up in 'fashionable' furniture and contains a striking 'glass coffee table' (Ishiguro 1981b: 28) in its centre. By contrast, J's dimly lit apartment, which is in a 'gloomy building', perhaps a shabby mews, is 'unremarkable other than for its starkness. There was little to distract the eye from the worn-looking armchairs or the drab little coffee table' (Ishiguro 1981b: 33–34). Similarly, their careers are mirror images of each other: J had grand aspirations to leave his childhood village for London, and then make his way to Turkey. 'He told me that to stay in that village was like living in a shell,' the narrator remembers J saying; 'He made me promise several times that when the time came [. . .] I would follow his example and travel the world' (Ishiguro 1981b: 32). J's goals, apparently, were realized by the narrator instead, while J became a manual labourer and was forced to abandon his travel plans and other 'childish' (Ishiguro 1981b: 34) ambitions. Disappointingly, he remained behind in the village, enclosed in his 'shell' (Ishiguro 1981b: 32). Later, J attends the narrator's scholarly lecture on Turkish architecture and insists that 'After all [. . .] our fields are hardly unrelated' (Ishiguro 1981b: 35) because both warehouse and catalogue objects. At last we understand that J, who is trapped in the shell that was his own worst nightmare, is the actual person the narrator has become. His fantasy life, the projected self of the successful art scholar, must annihilate J, psychically if not physically, in order to survive – or he will himself be destroyed by J.

Ishiguro's comment on *A Pale View of Hills* is equally relevant to this story: '[T]he whole narrative strategy of the book was about how someone ends up talking about things they cannot face directly through other people's stories. I was trying to explore [. . .] how people use the language of self-deception and self-protection' (Mason 1989: 337). Although in certain regards derivatively Gothic, this absurdist, uncanny psychological thriller also provides a narrative and critical context for better understanding Ishiguro's later novel *The Unconsoled*, which, despite announcing a significant departure in fictional orientation for the author – a shift away from the terrain, tone, and temperament of the first three novels – clearly has its roots in the uncanny, absurdist, dream-like story from fourteen years earlier.

Like 'Waiting for J', 'Getting Poisoned' is a profound study of psychological despair, the failure to face reality, and homicidal agony. Similarly distinct from the author's Japanese concerns, 'Getting Poisoned', written in a diary form (in twenty-two instalments over a five-week period), nevertheless sheds light on *A Pale View Of Hills* in using cats to explore child abuse and infanticide, and in using wider socio-historical currents as a means of exploring and revealing character dynamics. Like 'The Summer After the War', this story is narrated by a boy; like 'A Family Supper', poison figures prominently. Like all of Ishiguro's fiction it is narrated by an unreliable protagonist who tells a story that greatly differs, and disturbingly so, from the one he thinks he is telling. 'Getting Poisoned' is a tale of child abuse narrated by a boy who is unaware of his own victimhood. Like Ian McEwan's early story 'Conversation with the Cupboard Man' (McEwan 1975), and novel *The Cement Garden* (McEwan 1978), it is also the story of a series of dysfunctional sexual power relationships played out against the backdrop of a violent, misogynistic, sexually repressed culture.

Ishiguro is a master at constructing narratives with subtle and uncanny parallels. 'Getting Poisoned' is no exception. The tale explores a series of interlocking and abusive sexual/power relationships and parent–child relationships that echo or mirror one another. An unnamed boy narrator lives with his mother, who is involved with an abusive boyfriend, John. The boy's father is out of the picture, having died or having abandoned them. John abuses the boy's mother, both physically and verbally; the two fight and curse each other openly and the mother frequently cries because of John. She nevertheless repeatedly goes back for more, in a classic (and masochistic) abuse dynamic, begging for affection even though, according to the boy, John screams at her as if she were 'a dog or something' (Ishiguro 1981c: 46).

The mother pays increasing attention to John, which translates into neglecting her son. 'She never comes home till late,' the boy notes, 'and she doesn't mind what I do now' (Ishiguro 1981b: 39). Domestic order deteriorates; the boy begins to sleep until noon; he is left unattended and unmonitored for vast stretches of time. The mother now appears all but indifferent to her son's fate, while John looks '"like he's waiting for me to do something so he can shout at me"' (Ishiguro 1981b: 45). The boy's treatment at home shocks him less than it might; presumably, it mirrors his abusive reception at the hands of the society at large; he is, for example, 'used to getting beaten up' (Ishiguro 1981b: 39) at school.

The parental neglect of the boy is mirrored in the boy's treatment of his cat, Naomi, who is figured initially as an abandoned infant found 'down the lane, wrapped in that bit of newspaper' (Ishiguro 1981b: 39). The boy at first plays the role of caregiver to Naomi, feeding and playing with the cat, but then begins to mistreat her. Imagining that the cat is ignoring him, he stops feeding her, 'just to see how she likes it' (Ishiguro 1981b: 39): 'I haven't fed Naomi all day today. She keeps coming to me but I don't pay her any attention. It serves her right. She shouldn't take me for granted. If it wasn't for me, she'd still be down the lane wrapped up in some newspaper' (Ishiguro 1981b: 39–40). Next the boy makes up a 'game' to play with Naomi:

> What I do is tie a bit of string to her collar. Then I put some food out in her bowl, and when she goes to get the food I hold her by the string so she can't quite reach it. She starts to make a lot of noises then. After a while I usually put the food away in the fridge. (Ishiguro 1981b: 40)

At one point, when Naomi is able to get the food anyway, the boy 'punishes' her by picking her up by the string, until she is 'sort of hanging' (Ishiguro 1981b: 42), virtually strangling the pet. The next day the boy takes poison, 'weed-killer stuff' (Ishiguro 1981b: 42) he finds in the junkroom of his home, and mixes it into Naomi's food. The cat's eyes, which unnerved him the day before when he almost hanged her, now, following her poisoning, add to the boy's feeling of guilt: 'I thought they were looking at me' (Ishiguro 1981b: 43–44). Naomi dies and the boy proceeds to dump her body 'in the lane' (Ishiguro 1981b: 44), where she was found. Clearly, the boy's relationship with the cat mirrors that between the boy and his mother and between the mother and her boyfriend, and presumably the father before him.

The boy's abusive 'parenting' style is not the only thing he learns from his mother and John. He also learns from them, and apparently from the society at large, a sadomasochistic model and understanding of male–female relationships. He learns from the big brother of his friend Edie that girls are properly understood as the objects of male sexual desire, but that sexual contact with them may lead to getting 'poisoned' (Ishiguro 1981c: 38), and to the sickening of the male genitals; Edie's brother, we learn, has 'got the clap'. Indeed, because women are 'dirty', because sexual contact with 'cunts' (the boy's hostile synecdoche for females at large, not merely their genitalia) is a risky business that can lead to 'the clap' and even to death, the boy takes to examining his 'prick very carefully' on a regular basis (Ishiguro 1981c: 38). The boy's attitude towards the risks of sexual contact is best summed up in his diary entry of 11 August: 'I'm not sure I want to have sex. You never know if you're going to get poisoned. It's like picking mushrooms. It's dangerous picking mushrooms and just eating them because some of them are toadstools and you get poisoned' (Ishiguro 1981c: 41).

The boy confuses an imaginary female sex poison with another kind of poison, the 'weed-killer stuff' (Ishiguro 1981c: 42) that he discovers in a locked junkroom at home. This unfrequented room, which seems mainly to contain his father's old possessions, represents the repressed or hidden family past or memory as well as the father's continuing, if indirect, influence upon the boy. In this same room the boy also finds his father's abandoned pornographic magazines, which he proceeds to 'read' repeatedly, without fear of getting poisoned:

> The magazines are pretty good, even though they don't show cunts. I wonder if any of the girls have got the clap [. . .] Some of them must have, because they must all be prostitutes and strippers and things like that. They don't look like they've got it, but [. . .] [i]t takes a bit of time for the poison to start working on you. (Ishiguro 1981c: 40)

The boy's repetition of and emphasis on 'must' suggests the received, prejudicial, and stereotypical nature of his knowledge of females, who threateningly prey on male sexual desire.

The boy's understanding of both the allure of and mortal threat posed by siren-like women informs his relationship with John's 16-year-old daughter, Carol, who moves into the house about midway through the narrative and becomes the boy's first lover. The boy views Carol in much the same spirit as he views the women in the pornographic magazines: as an arousing sex-object. He voyeuristically reads the porn magazines in his room or in the back garden, just as he watches Carol sun-bathe in this same garden from his bedroom window: 'If I stand a little bit back there's no way she can tell I'm looking at her [. . .] Her tits are quite big, though probably not as big as some of the girls in the magazines' (Ishiguro 1981c: 45). When reading the magazines becomes 'boring', watching Carol becomes more interesting; indeed, being flesh and blood rather than an image, she soon looks 'a lot better than all those prostitutes in the magazines' (Ishiguro 1981c: 49).

Carol is also associated with the boy's cat, Naomi, for whose murder the boy clearly feels guilt but denies all responsibility. The parallels between girl and cat are unmistakable. Naomi is 'thin and black, a beautiful cat' (Ishiguro 1981c: 39), just as Carol has:

> long black hair, and [is] quite skinny. But I don't like her face, it gives me the creeps. She wears these little round glasses all the time, even when she's sunbathing. And she sticks her nose up a bit, like she's being snooty [. . .] It's just her face, I don't like looking at it. Because it reminds me. Because I've seen it before. (Ishiguro 1981c: 44)

Carol's eyes remind the boy of Naomi's eyes, the 'round slabs of light' (Ishiguro 1981c: 49) of the girl's eyes recalling Naomi's 'two slabs of glass' (Ishiguro 1981c: 42), and the 'little round glasses' above, as if the girl were somehow the ghost of the murdered cat. The repetition of 'because' suggests that this is an uncanny moment of recognition, similar to that found in 'Waiting for J' between the narrator and J. Carol even asks the boy about his former cat, to which he responds by denying that he ever had one. The boy's guilt, as well as his lust, is aroused by Carol: 'She's watching me all the time, through her little round glasses. I felt cold all over' (Ishiguro 1981c: 47). The boy's 'cold' feeling is also attributable to the power reversal implicit in the reverse gaze: it is now Carol who gazes at, who objectifies, the boy.

Like the boy and Naomi, the boy and Carol also take to playing a 'game', although the game, like that between the mother and John, is sexual in nature, as well as tinged with sadomasochistic violence. Carol lets the boy 'touch her all over her body. I sort of stroke her very lightly, because she likes me doing that' (Ishiguro 1981c: 47). When the boy goes slightly too far, she accuses him of being 'naughty' and threatens to 'get' him back. Like a cat, Carol has nails that can 'dig into my stomach' (Ishiguro 1981c: 48).

The story's climax depicts the boy and Carol's first sexual encounter, following his bringing her a poisoned cup of coffee (presumably it is the same poison, found in dad's junkroom, with which he murders Naomi). During this climactic sexual encounter the boy conflates the female poison and the weed-killer, imagining: 'all the poison going round in [Carol's] body, going round and round, round and round, and I try to pull away but she holds me tighter and presses herself on me and I can feel the poison running stronger and stronger all the time' (Ishiguro 1981c: 50). For the boy, literally, as for the other male characters in the story, figuratively, death is precisely what women, who mortally threaten males, deserve. Men must poison or be poisoned by them. The boy's comment, 'I don't want to think about things too much' (Ishiguro 1981c: 51), reveals the extent to which it is the boy's repression that is first and foremost at issue, as it is in so many early Ishiguro works. The title of the story at last comes into focus: it is less Naomi and Carol than the traumatized, ignorant boy narrator himself, whose mind has been 'poisoned' by his parents, friends, and by his violent and misogynistic culture at large, that is the true subject of Ishiguro's story.

'Waiting for J' and 'Getting Poisoned' not only make clear the organic connection between the author's earlier work and his later novels. They reveal something about Ishiguro's fictional orientation at large, his obsession with trauma – psychological, familial, and historical – that is all too often viewed in historical and political terms alone. Although Ishiguro's novels and stories of course engage with historical and political realities, history and politics are explored primarily in order to plumb the characters' emotional and psychological landscapes and only secondarily to explore, say, post-bomb Nagasaki, Japanese fascism and imperialism of the inter-war years, the English policy of appeasement prior to World War II, or the war-torn, besieged Shanghai of the 1930s. As the author himself remarks of the genesis of his novels: 'I would look for moments in history that would best serve my purposes [. . .] I was conscious that I wasn't so interested in history *per se*, that I was using British history or Japanese history to illustrate something that was preoccupying me' (Oe and Ishiguro 1991: 115). In an interview with Gregory Mason from about the same time, Ishiguro commented further: 'I'm not overwhelmingly interested in what really did happen. What's important is the emotional aspect, the [. . .] position the characters take up at different points in the story, and why they need to take up these positions' (Mason 1989: 342).

Like all of Ishiguro's fictions of the past quarter century, 'Waiting for J' and 'Getting Poisoned' reveal the ways in which traumatized protagonists absorb the stories of others into their own narratives, often manipulating them beyond recognition to serve their private needs, fears, and desires. These stories are not negligible experiments so much as works of considerable interest that provide a key to understanding the psychological trauma, one that lies 'somewhere just beneath the surface of things' (Ishiguro 1981a: 21), at the heart of all Ishiguro narratives.

CHAPTER TWO

Strange Reads: Kazuo Ishiguro's *A Pale View of Hills* and *An Artist of the Floating World* in Japan

MOTOYUKI SHIBATA AND MOTOKO SUGANO

Chapter Summary: Kazuo Ishiguro's work has a wide international readership, and he has frequently commented on how self-conscious this has made him as a writer. Many traces of local and cultural particularity are excised during the process of composition, but nonetheless the process of translation reveals much of the cultural singularity of his writing, bringing to the fore the technical and linguistic issues that are explored in this chapter. The translation and reception of the early works in Japan has further significance because the choices made by Ishiguro and his translators, and their subtle but important alterations to the content of the novels, reveal much about the 'Japanese' qualities of these texts, and, ultimately, about the limits of the 'international novel'.

Introduction: There's a Translator in My Head

Kazuo Ishiguro has often spoken of his writing as means of engaging in dialogue with an audience that spans the entire globe. In the interview in this book, for instance, Ishiguro emphasizes his aspiration to be an author whose work is not constrained by linguistic and cultural borders. He states: '[W]hen I'm writing in my study, I often find myself addressing a particular Norwegian in my head because at some point I know I will have to explain this book to a Norwegian, and many cultural references would not survive the Norwegian translation' (see pp. 114–15). Ishiguro is clearly unusually aware, even at the point of writing, of the range of issues relating to the translation and transmission of texts, of his work's transposition into other languages and frames of reference, of the problems presented by different social and cultural contexts of reading. As he writes, he imagines not simply readers, but the translators who will mediate his work. He elaborated further on the effects of this self-consciousness with regard to translation in an interview with Claire Hamilton:

> You know you are going to be translated, so it is a bit hazardous to write things you know will not survive translation. I suppose it's also just my personal thing: I'm never a big one for puns, I just find them a bit tiresome. I don't find anything special about a pun. It's like seeing two cars of the same make passing in the street, it's just a linguistic coincidence as far as I'm concerned. It's not something I can get wildly excited about anyway. But these things can be a practical barrier sometimes to communication with your larger audience. It's not so much the odd pun in the sentence, but sometimes the whole concept of a novel might be too local, because you haven't really thought beyond your local audience, and it doesn't make sense to people in Norway, or America, even, and it won't make sense here in ten years time either. It's that sort of thing I try to avoid. (Hamilton 2007)

Ishiguro's ambition to grapple with universal and timeless themes in this manner affects his writing at all levels, from the shaping of plot to the framing of sentences and choices of vocabulary, although it is also the case that there remains a sophisticated level of textual allusion, particularly to other films and that most universal of arts, music, but also to literature, which seems predicated on a supra-national canon of classic works.

Despite Ishiguro's best efforts, however, in translation to any language there will be gains and losses of nuance and tone. An instructive instance, for thinking about the Japanese context, takes place in the Japanese translation of *The Remains of the Day* (1989). Consider this passage, in which Stevens has briefly relieved himself of his duties at Darlington Hall in order to attend to his sick father:

> My father opened his eyes, turned his head a little on the pillow, and looked at me.
>
> 'I hope Father is feeling better now,' I said.
>
> He went on gazing at me for a moment, then asked: 'Everything in hand downstairs?'
>
> 'The situation is rather volatile. It is just after six o'clock, so Father can well imagine the atmosphere in the kitchen at this moment.'
>
> An impatient look crossed my father's face. 'But is everything in hand?' he said again.
>
> 'Yes, I dare say you can rest assured on that. I'm very glad Father is feeling better.'
>
> With some deliberation, he withdrew his arms from under the bedclothes and gazed tiredly at the backs of his hands. He continued to do this for some time.
>
> 'I'm glad Father is feeling so much better,' I said again eventually. 'Now really, I'd best be getting back. As I say, the situation is rather volatile.'

He went on looking at his hands for a moment. Then he said slowly:
'I hope I've been a good father to you.'

I laughed a little and said: 'I'm so glad you're feeling better now.' (Ishiguro 1996: 101)

Stevens's repeatedly formal, and capitalized, third-person address to his father as 'Father' (as opposed to 'you'), despite his presence before him, captures the characters' emotional distance from each other, or, more precisely, the repressive sense of propriety that forces them to maintain such a distance. The 'you' he uses in the last line, almost touching in its directness, serves only to reveal the limited sense of intimacy he feels he can afford.

The problem this passage generates for the Japanese translator Masao Tsuchiya lies in the fact that it is not possible to translate 'Father' as *Father*, and 'you' as *you* because something awkward happens. Although we Japanese are often accused of thinking that our culture is unique when it is not, the use of the second person in the Japanese language is indeed rather unusual, and is certainly substantially different from the English. The Japanese do not use the word(s) equivalent to 'you' anywhere near as often as anglophone speakers, and often avoid the second-person pronoun altogether. In conversation, we often grope for a way to address the person we are talking to without directly using 'you', a habit that is particularly maddening, as you might imagine, when someone's name is unknown. For a Japanese person it would be completely normal to address one's father as 'Father' face to face: it would not sound as if they thought this created an appropriate and respectful distance, it would sound entirely normal.

In short, the Japanese translator faces the problem of rendering the distinction between an informal and almost exaggeratedly formal address in a language that only knows the latter. Perhaps unavoidably, Tsuchiya translated 'Father' simply as *Father*, thus rendering Stevens's unusual way of talking to his father much less unusual. The son's inability to display emotional closeness to his father is to a great extent *lost in translation*.

Ishiguro's polite-speaking narrators, of course, are doomed to distance themselves from their readers, from other characters, from the past, and from themselves – this is a characteristic of his work. These distances are on the whole wonderfully reproduced in the Japanese translations through Tsuchiya's use of the polite form. In fact, this multiple sense of distance is often even more conspicuously rendered in the Japanese translations. And in spite of all these distances, or possibly *because of* them, we are moved. Ishiguro's characters' very inability to connect emotionally with others or with themselves makes *The Remains of the Day* emotionally powerful, and this is just as beautifully conveyed through the polite language spoken by the Japanese-speaking Stevens as it is by his English original.

However, as this example demonstrates, the translation of works written in English brings to the fore representational problems that are exacerbated when the story is set in Japan itself. Indeed, it was, ironically perhaps, in his native country that his early, 'Japanese', work presented most problems to critics and readers, and Ishiguro and his translators therefore had an important role in shaping the critical and public reception. The particularity of translation into the Japanese language of a text set in Japan, with familiar (for Japanese readers) cultural and historical points of reference, offers an interesting test case for thinking about 'Ishiguro in translation' generally, but also about the socio-cultural and political specificity of the early 'Japanese' works. Our discussion will therefore focus on the problematic translation and reception of Ishiguro's first two 'Japanese' novels, *A Pale View of Hills* (1982) and *An Artist of the Floating World* (1986).

Unlike in Britain, where Ishiguro's fiction brought him prestigious literary prizes and literary acclaim from the very beginning of his career, the translations of Ishiguro's work were less enthusiastically received in Japan. The novels, for instance, presented the primary problem of translational 're-import', that is, the idea that the translation of these novels into the Japanese language demands some kind of translation 'back' into an original context and language, even though they are actually in all senses originally English.

Jay Rubin, the principal translator of Haruki Murakami, has commented helpfully on these specific representational problems, from the other direction. Murakami's love of American culture would, one would have thought, make it easier to translate the work because of its cultural overlap, but the opposite is true. Rubin argues:

> Even in something so apparently straightforward as our example, much of which consists of a list of salad ingredients, there is no question of doing anything that could remotely be called a 'literal' translation. Written in a special syllabary used for foreign words, some of the ingredients have a tantalizingly foreign sound and *look* in the Japanese text, but they inevitably lose this quality when they are translated 'back' into English and are surrounded by other English words [. . .] Paradoxically, then, the *closeness* of Murakami's style to English can itself pose problems for a translator trying to translate it 'back' into English: the single most important quality that makes his style fresh and enjoyable in Japanese is what is lost in translation. (Rubin 2002: 288–289)

A banal English cliché like 'bed of roses', Rubin notes, though refreshing when literally translated and embedded into Murakami's original Japanese text, becomes nothing but a worn-out cliché again if it is translated 'back' into English.

Ishiguro's Japanese translators face similar technical and linguistic problems, but these difficulties are further complicated at the level of the subject matter of the work. *A Pale View of Hills* and *An Artist of the Floating World* also raise sensitive issues about the country's militarism and nationalism in the 1930s and 1940s, its imperial history, and the country's responsibility for war crimes during the 1939–1945 War, issues that even today remain politically and ethically difficult topics in Japan – controversy is regularly ignited, for instance, around how to narrate the events in Nanking of December 1937 for school textbooks. These are questions of continuing contemporary significance for many Japanese – and Chinese – people. These technical and cultural challenges do, however, give us distinctive and illuminating critical perspective on Ishiguro's 'Japanese' works, and the lengths and limits of his engagement with the Japanese culture and consciousness, while also raising questions about Ishiguro's aspiration towards the writing of international novels.

Exoticism in Exchange for Mild Nostalgia: *A Pale View of Hills*

Takeshi Onodera's Japanese translation of *A Pale View of Hills* brings into close focus the issues we have raised about translation and Ishiguro's goal of a form of 'international writing'. Consider the following passage, describing Nagasaki in the period directly following the war:

> In those days, returning to the Nakagawa district still provoked in me mixed emotions of sadness and pleasure. It is a hilly area, and climbing again those steep narrow streets between the clusters of houses never failed to fill me with a deep sense of loss. Though not a place I visited on casual impulse, I was unable to stay away for long.
>
> Calling on Mrs Fujiwara aroused in me much the same mixture of feelings; for she had been amongst my mother's closest friends, a kindly woman with hair that was by then turning grey. Her noodle shop was situated in a busy sidestreet; it had a concrete forecourt under the cover of an extended roof and it was there her customers ate, at the wooden tables and benches. She did a lot of trade with office workers during their lunch breaks and on their way home, but at other times of the day the clientele became sparse. (Ishiguro 1991: 23)

We can assume that the 'steep narrow streets between the clusters of houses' and the 'noodle shop [. . .] situated in a busy sidestreet' would feel somewhat exotic to English-speaking readers, if not overly unfamiliar. Naturally, this is not how the passage will strike Japanese readers. The small eatery with its wooden tables and benches, where 'salarymen' drop in for a quick bowl of *udon* or *ramen*, traditional Japanese fast food, will be entirely familiar to them, and there would be nothing exotic about it at all.

In other respects, however, responses will vary among Japanese readers, depending especially on their age, particularly whether or not they

experienced this immediate post-war period firsthand will be a significant factor, and their familiarity with Nagasaki. Yet, even though the
city of Nagasaki is as hilly today as it was after the war, most of those
tiny houses had been replaced by concrete apartment buildings by the
time *A Pale View of Hills* first appeared; the *udon* diners (or *yatai*) are
still as numerous as ever in Nagasaki, but most of them have been
taken over by chains instead of being independently run by once
prosperous middle-aged women. In short, the passage will evoke a feeling of nostalgia in the Japanese readers' minds to which the English-
speaking audience does not have access. Thus, subtly but definitely, for
the Japanese reader the carefully cultivated exoticism of the cultural
context is replaced by a form of mild nostalgia.

To further complicate this exchange, the critical reception of the
Japanese translation of *A Pale View of Hills* did not really make comparisons between the novel's evocation of the time and place with the
actual Japan of the late 1940s, but rather to the Japanese films depicting
those times, and especially the films of Yasujiro Ozu, which had a significant influence on the formation of Ishiguro's imagination during
his twenties. Taking their cue from the author's own admiration of that
cinematic master chronicler of traditional (and transitional) Japanese
families and marriages in the post-war period, more than one reviewer
evoked Ozu's name for a shorthand description of the novel's atmosphere. Ishiguro, they argued, did not recover the Japan he knew as a
small child, but rather re-invented or re-imagined a Japan he (almost)
never knew, using Japanese films and novels as his chief raw materials
of inspiration.

It is therefore not surprising that Ishiguro himself did not require a
'faithful' translation of *A Pale View of Hills*. According to the translator's
Afterword, Ishiguro specifically asked the translator to avoid using a
certain *kanji* for a certain character (Onodera 1984: 278). *Kanji* are the
Chinese characters used for all sorts of concepts and things that, when
used in Japanese names, have a highly symbolic resonance, and are
therefore crucial tools for characterization because they (can) contain
several meanings at once: there are, for example, a number of possible
kanji to represent the name of *Sachiko*. The use of such ideographs does,
however, have the effect of weakening the 'foreign-ness' of the story,
which is particularly relevant when a narrative is set in Japan. Ishiguro
therefore intervened in order to ensure that this element of the original
was not distorted in translation by the accretion of additional significance associated with the choice of *kanji*. Under normal circumstances,
the translator would select *kanji* for each character, which would import
information and codes not included in the original, instead of using
katakana (a distinct syllabary used only for the representation of foreign
loan-words or borrowed terms or proper names), the usual option for
writing names in novels written in English. Ishiguro's concern not to
allow supplementary meanings to attach to the names of the characters
(*kanji* are inherently allusive, each carrying particular symbolic or

historical tones) underscores his ambition to keep the names 'neutral', indeed 'foreign'. The translation of *A Pale View of Hills* was, then, inevitably affected by the context of Japanese culture, and, in contrast to the overwhelming critical and popular success of the novel in Britain, this contributed to the relatively quiet reception in Japan.

An Artist of the Floating World: 'In the Best of Faith'?

Ishiguro's second publication in Japan, *Ukiyo no Gaka* (1988), Shigeo Tobita's translation of *An Artist of the Floating World*, was received equally quietly by Japanese critics and readers. The novel was reviewed by only one major Japanese newspaper and a number of women's magazines, and only a first impression was printed. This reception suggests that Japanese critics and readers had again stumbled onto difficulties in appreciating the novel. It must be acknowledged that reasons for the reluctance to embrace Ishiguro include the fact that translations of serious foreign novels generally struggle in the Japanese market, but it is also the case that Ishiguro's representation of Japan is considered 'strange' by Japanese readers, that Japanese readers were unfamiliar with Ishiguro's distinctive style of fiction writing (in particular the weight of the unsaid, or of the narrator's nuanced unreliability). However, more than anything the difficulty for Japanese readers of *An Artist of the Floating World* lies in its problematic representation of war and militarism in the 1930s and early 1940s. These difficulties were anticipated by the translator, who together with Ishiguro, endeavoured to bridge the gap between the author and his Japanese readers, which led, needless to say, to a further set of challenges.

Tobita translated the title as *Ukiyo no Gaka*, a literal transposition from the English into Japanese; yet this generates multiple meanings in the Japanese mind. In particular, the word *uki-yo* creates ambivalence. First, the title evokes the impression that the story is about worldliness. According to *Koji-en*, one of the standard dictionaries of the Japanese language, the sound of the word *uki* both refers to the word that means 'to float' as well as to the word that means 'to suffer' (Sim 2006: 77). The word *yo* means 'the world'. Both words thus signify human responses to worldliness. Therefore, the title *Ukiyo no Gaka* extends the meaning of the singular English title to allude more broadly to the life of an artist troubled by the worldliness of the world we live in, rather than to just the 'floating world', itself a signifier of the exotic and the oriental, defined as 'the night-time world of pleasure, entertainment and drink' (Ishiguro 1986: 145) in the English text. Second, the translated title's emphasis on the existent, mythical 'floating world' evokes an archetypal, perhaps even stereotypical image of an exotic Japan that is now far removed from contemporary Japanese society's experience of itself (and indeed our conception of the 'pleasure districts' of major cities).

Nevertheless, the title does have the effect of arousing the Japanese interest in what could be perceived to be a mock-Orientalist novel written by an author with a Japanese-sounding name to whom *ukiyo-e* represents the imaginative potential of exotic arts produced by the Other.

This multiplicity of meanings in the title alone already suggests that translating Japanese subject matter into Japanese affects the representation of that which the translation renders. Indeed, immediately after the publication of *Ukiyo no Gaka*, the translation of Japanese subject matter in English written by an 'outsider' became a topic of debate in Japan. The issue centred on where the fidelity of the translator should reside: should the Japanese translator be faithful to the target culture and Japanese readers, or to the source text? The latter option begs a compromise on the part of translators, who are forced to make their translation somehow 'inauthentic' to Japanese readers, which raises the difficult, if not impossible, dilemma of what might be considered 'inauthentic' by a Japanese audience whose make up is extremely diverse, but whose cultural consciousness is only too aware of the external perception of the country through fictional material such as novels, cinema, and other cultural output.

In an attempt to secure an experience of authenticity, of recognition, for Japanese readers, Tobita structured his translation according to the way in which Japanese works by adjusting two linguistic characteristics of the Japanese language. First, as in the case of *A Pale View of Hills*, Tobita used Chinese ideographs for the names of the characters and the names of the places, which is, as we noted earlier, an unconventional practice in relation to foreign works translated into Japanese because the names lose their sense of 'foreignness'. Tobita explained that his first concern was the readability of the translated texts: writing the characters' names in *katakana* characters hinders readability, generating an *excessive* foreignness (Tobita 1988: 317–18). As a consequence, *Ukiyo no Gaka* does become more readable but the translation also feels *excessively* Japanese and thus 'inauthentic' for a novel translated from another language. Second, Tobita supplies conventions of speech and inflections to recreate the dialogue in Japanese, which also contribute to the sustained sense of 'Japaneseness' of the text, reflecting – as vernacular Japanese is exceptionally well able to do – the characters' gender, age, and social standing far more explicitly and precisely. The dialogue thus sounds slightly politer, and rather more reserved and perhaps lacking in local colour to the contemporary readers in Japan, as though watching Ozu films of the time. The use of speech inflections thus reinforces Japaneseness in the translation, but it is a Japaneseness constructed through the fictional and cinematic worlds provided by Ozu and Akiro Kurosawa.

Tobita's translation also confronted significant difficulties in the translation of elements of the content of the novel. In a review entitled 'Interrogating the "faith" during the war' (1988), the Japanese critic

Masashi Miura writes that Ishiguro's unconventional treatment of Japanese subject matter in *Ukiyo no Gaka* puzzled him and left him unsure of how to respond to the book:

> This novel leaves us with puzzlement and oddity. [. . .] The story tentatively ends with Noriko's marriage but the narrative terminates without providing any responses for the questions that it presents. Near the end of the book, Ono recollects the past saying 'we [Ono and his mentor Matsuda] have the satisfaction of knowing that whatever we did, we did at the time in the best of faith'. But the real problem is what kind of faith they have. [. . .] There are some descriptions of Japanese paintings that read strangely when it is translated into Japanese, but probably this is how they look to the eyes of the outside world. [. . .] Here in Japan, the artists' responsibility for producing war propaganda paintings has long ceased to be an issue but the situation looks different from the outside. (Miura 1988: 12; our translation)

Miura's review is insightful for a number of reasons. His unease about the novel rings through in his avoidance of any reference to Ono's continuing faith in the New Japan Spirit, a *fictional* political ideology promoting strong army control and imperial expansion to China, which is nonetheless similar to the restoration movement of the 1930s (McLeod 1998: 132–134). Miura is well aware that Ishiguro's representation of Japan is addressed to the Western audience, where historical accuracy in this specific matter is arguably of less importance, although there are significant ethical questions nonetheless. Miura is, then, ambivalent with regard to the treatment of the topic of war responsibility for *Japanese* readers and the novel's treatment of Ono's ideological position. Other reviewers of *Ukiyo no Gaka* are similarly silent with regard to the disturbing nature of Ono's convictions. Instead, they praise Ishiguro's skill in the *characterization* of Ono, as a proudly self-righteous if flawed individual, and in his application of the formal convention of the unreliable narrator to create ambiguity and hesitancy around the very issue for which there is no easy solution (Fujikawa 1988: 244; Tobita 1988 and 1992). The general unease towards Ono's occluded political views serves, ironically, to accentuate the success of Ishiguro's complex, recurrent address to issues concerning the dialectics of individual and collective responsibility generally, as much as specifically in terms of Japan.

Another ambiguity brought to the fore by Miura concerns judgements about Japanese artists' agency and accountability with regard to World War II. On the surface, Miura appears to feel awkward about the representation in the novel of a form of Japanese art that does not, in fact, conform to any of the practices or genres of fine art in Japan. However, Miura does relate the issues of Japan's responsibility in relationship to World War II in *An Artist of the Floating World* to the actual history of Japan. He mentions, and characterizes as resolved, debates about artists' responsibility for war propaganda that were topical in the late 1940s and early 1950s, after which the controversy gradually dissipated. He suggests that Ishiguro's novel is returning to these issues in order to express his own unease at the way they continue to haunt post-war Japan, but perhaps even more so because of the problematic ambivalences and uncertainties inherent in the novel's representation of these questions. This issue is, indeed, the primary critical crux in analyses of the novel, with many critics expressing frustration at the novel's engagement with the topic. Edward Costigan, for instance, writes that Ishiguro is guilty of intentionally 'blurring' the central issue of 'choice and responsibility' (Costigan 1991: 29).

It is interesting to view the changes and shifts embedded in the Japanese text of the novel in the light of these debates. In his Afterword to the translation, Tobita states that he implemented, after consultation with the author, some 'revisions' (Tobita 1988: 286). He notes that these amendments included Ishiguro's request to change 'the statue of Emperor Taisho' to 'the statue of Mayor Yamaguchi' (Tobita 1992: 318). The effect of this change is significant: it transforms the historical context of the Takami garden from a space associated with imperial commemoration to the memorial site of a former mayor with an uncertain political career. More importantly, the change effaces the novel's potential direct address to Japan's role in and responsibility for World War II: a statue of Taisho would, for Japanese readers, have a controversial resonance similar to that of the Yasukuni shrine in Tokyo, a memorial to those who died in war and also, for many, a monument to militarism and Japanese imperialism.

There are still further alterations, however, that are not specified in the translator's Afterword. Despite the abrupt termination of his artistic career due to his support for the China campaign propaganda, Ono seems to sustain his faith in militarism and considers his winning of the Shigeta Foundation Award as the crowning achievement of his career. In the original publication, the section that Miura refers to in his review reads as follows:

> But even as he uttered such words, there remained something in Matsuda's manner that afternoon to suggest he was anything but a disillusioned man. [. . .] He may indeed have looked back over his life and seen certain flaws, but surely he would have recognized also those aspects he could feel proud of. For, as he pointed out himself, the likes of him and me, we have the satisfaction of knowing that whatever we did, we did at the time in the best of faith. Of course, we took some bold steps and often did things with much single-mindedness; but this is surely preferable to never putting one's convictions to the test, for lack of will or courage. When one holds convictions deeply enough, there surely comes a point when it is despicable to prevaricate further. (Ishiguro 1986: 201–202)

In the Japanese translation, translated back into English, this reads as follows:

> But on that day, even as he uttered these words, there remained something in him saying self-doubt was not for him. [. . .] He may indeed have looked back on his life and seen some hurt, but at the same time he should also have seen some aspects that made him proud. For, as he himself was saying, the likes of Matsuda and I are aware that, whatever it was, we acted in accordance with faith, and take satisfaction in that fact. Of course, we at times did adventurous things, and too often charged ahead like carriage horses. But our attitude was far better than that of those who never even try to act on their convictions because they lack enough will and courage. When one's conviction runs deep enough, one should realise that it is shameful to hesitate any further. (Ishiguro 1988: 272–273; our translation)

The Japanese translation of this section tends to suppress the militarist implications of the original. In the first sentence, the ideological implication concerning Matsuda's political advocacy has been replaced with the implication of a loss of self-confidence. The sentence to which Miura refers has several important alterations. First, the Japanese translation changes the phrase 'whatever we did' to 'whatever it was', which alters the degree of complicity in the position that Ono and Matsuda took in relationship to the New Japan Spirit. Second, the phrase 'the best of' in 'in the best of faith' is left untranslated, thus occluding any retrospective indication of their degree of commitment. In the next sentence, military slogans are softened and the meaning of Ishiguro's original substantially altered: the phrase 'some bold steps' is rephrased as 'adventurous things', and 'single-mindedness' is altered to a figurative expression that says 'often charged ahead like carriage horses', which in fact equates the painters with beasts who are not responsible for the burden they carry. The last sentence in the quotation is, however, the most freely translated sentence among them. The phrase 'it is despicable to prevaricate further' is toned down. While the English text suggests the voice of a speaker who is finally speaking honestly, as in a kind of confession, the Japanese translation evokes the impression that the speaker is sceptical about and aloof from the action. In short, in this key passage Tobita's translation mitigates even the delicate and restrained attention to militaristic issues of the original in order to make the novel more acceptable to Japanese readers.

The discourse of militarism is not always altered in Tobita's translation. Ono's recollection of his amendments to the China Crisis poster demonstrates this clearly. In Ono's original China Crisis poster, the title 'Complacency' is later changed to the more rousing and hortatory 'Eyes to the Horizon' (Ishiguro 1986: 169). Similarly, the slogan on the earlier version of the poster declares 'No time for cowardly talking. Japan must go forward', but is later adapted to 'But the young are ready to fight for their dignity'. The Japanese translation not only keeps the sloganistic, patriotic tone of these lines, but also recreates the historical way of writing these slogans. Instead of using the more common Chinese ideographs and *hiragana* characters, a type of syllabary used for verbal hinges such as particles and conjunctions, the titles and slogans are translated in the language written by Chinese ideographs in conjunction with *katakana* characters. Before World War II, the official documents of the government were indeed published in Chinese ideographs and *katakana* characters, so this way of translating the military slogans is both historically accurate and even 'dangerous' to the Japanese readers because of its veracity. Indeed, the poster's problematic status is made clear even in the narrative: 'Eyes to the Horizon' is confiscated and does 'not remain in [his] possession' (Ishiguro 1986: 165).

Another reference to Japanese militarism that is translated in historically accurate language is the speech made by the Hirayama boy who is beaten up for 'singing one of those old military songs and chanting regressive slogans' (Ishiguro 1986: 59). The Hirayama boy sings: 'This village must provide its share of sacrifices for the Emperor. Some of you will lay down your lives! Some of you will return triumphant to a new dawn!' (Ishiguro 1986: 60). Rather than translating such militarist slogans and songs by using the same writing system as the contemporary narrative, Tobita reverts to an archaic form that creates a jar in the translation, reinforcing the discontinuity between Ono's own language and consciousness of the past and present. The effect gives emphasis to the fact that he *used* to utilize the language of the imperial government but that he now no longer uses that discourse. The distinction also makes it *seem* as if the politically sensitive problems of the past are resolved because the actual discourse and subject matter, which belong to the problematic period, have since become obsolete – an implication that is central to the ethical and political issues in play. Yet we need to remember that in Ishiguro's original this is not the case: it is a notable advantage available to the Japanese translator to be able to generate this effect.

Today Ishiguro's work is well-received in Japan, but this has really happened only subsequent to the publication of *The Remains of the Day*, and his move away from Japanese topics. His novels are now respectfully reviewed by most of the major literary magazines and daily newspapers at the moment of publication. Needless to say, this has retroactively affected the reception of *Ukiyo no Gaka*: a paperback edition was published in 1992, and the book has been reissued by Hayakawa Shobo, Ishiguro's current Japanese publisher, in 2007. A new generation of Japanese critics will, we are sure, examine further the tensions and challenges these texts so intriguingly invoke.

CHAPTER THREE

'Like the Gateway to Another World': Kazuo Ishiguro's Screenwriting

SEBASTIAN GROES AND PAUL-DANIEL VEYRET

Chapter Summary: Although Kazuo Ishiguro is first and foremost a novelist, television and film have had an important influence on his work, and he has much experience as a screenwriter. His screenwriting addresses many of the topics and themes that characterize his fiction but is often marked by a more overtly political stance. The early teleplay *The Gourmet* (1986) forms a fierce criticism of the corrosive effects of Thatcherism on the socio-cultural fabric of Britain. His screenplays *The Saddest Music in the World* (2003) and *The White Countess* (2005) offer ambivalent explorations of the possibility of creating a utopia where harmony between nations might be established, but must also necessarily collapse.

Kazuo Ishiguro has an important relationship to television and film, and any critical account of his work must consider the nature of this lifelong engagement with other modes of representation (the visual arts provide a further, if subsidiary, point of perspective for thinking about his work). There are several distinct elements to this relationship: the direct influence of specific films or cinematic genres on Ishiguro's writing, as evidenced in intertexts, allusions, and references; the adaptation of Ishiguro's work for the screen; and Ishiguro's own work in a variety of roles, for cinema and television. In this chapter we will concentrate primarily on the final category – his work directly for the screen – acknowledging that a full account of the influence of cinema on his writing, or of the issues involved in the adaptation of his fiction, is beyond the scope of a study of this size.

Ishiguro has frequently acknowledged the impact of cinema on his writing, remarking in the interview in this volume that

I had a 'Japanese phase' in my early twenties when I was hungry for everything about Japanese culture. I found that Japanese filmmakers, such as

[Akiro] Kurosawa and [Yasujiro] Ozu, had a profound effect on me, and they probably influenced me enormously as a writer. These movie makers were often called the 'humanist tradition' of film. (p. 116)

The film subgenre *Shomin-Geki*, a popular drama similar to soap opera, narrating the everyday lives and mishaps of office workers, or of school-children, wives, and husbands in a domestic environment, can be felt in particular in the early works (Lewis 2000: 69–72). Popular American cinema also has a consistent presence. The Hollywood icon Clint Eastwood, for instance, makes a brief appearance in *The Unconsoled* (1995), a cameo that has been highly instructive for accounts of the ingenious representational problems that Ishiguro's novels pose (Krider 1998: 148; Robinson 2006: 108; Wood 1995: 17–18). Richard Robinson, in his discussion of the novel in this volume, draws attention to still further, European cinematic intertexts (pp. 70–72).

Ishiguro has played a variety of roles, from writer to executive producer, in the world of film and television. He began writing for television in 1982 when Channel Four commissioned him to write two teleplays: *A Profile of Arthur J. Mason* (which won the Chicago Film Festival Award) and *The Gourmet*. They were broadcast in October 1984 and May 1986, respectively. In the late eighties, Ishiguro also started the screenplay for his first feature-length film *The Saddest Music in the World* (dir. Guy Maddin 2003). After publishing *When We Were Orphans* in 2000, he conceived and developed *The White Countess* (dir. James Ivory 2005), writing the screenplay with James Ivory – the director of the acclaimed Hollywood adaptation of *The Remains of the Day* (dir. James Ivory 1993). Ishiguro also served as jury member at the 1994 Cannes Film Festival, under Clint Eastwood, a jury that selected Quentin Tarantino's *Pulp Fiction* (dir. Quentin Tarantino 1994) for the *Palme D'Or*. He has most recently been executive producer for the adaptation of his 2005 novel *Never Let Me Go* (dir. Mark Romanek 2010), for which Alex Garland wrote the screenplay.

Even in such radically different media Ishiguro's writing addresses similar subject matter and ideas. His novels and screenwriting grapple with problems of memory and perception; the geographical and linguistic dislocation or alienation of the *émigré*; and the relationship between the crises of individuals and the life of the nation. However, in his work for television and film Ishiguro becomes more directly expressive of socio-political ideas, in comparison to the characteristically oblique and subtle tenor of his fiction. *The Gourmet*, as we argue in this chapter, is different from any other work by Ishiguro because it engages directly with the contemporary and can be read, or rather viewed, as a politicized, tragicomic gothic tale exposing the social and cultural catastrophe of Thatcherism. In the same way, *The Saddest Music in the World* and *The White Countess*, both set in times and places associated with economic downturn and military trauma, explore much more directly – and satirically – than the fiction the problems of utopian and idealistic thinking.

Anti-Thatcherite Goth-com: *The Gourmet*

In Chapter One Brian Shaffer suggested that *A Pale View of Hills* (1982) can be traced back to the short story 'A Strange and Sometimes Sadness' (1981), while 'Summer after the War' (1983) anticipates *An Artist of the Floating World* (1986). Similarly, Ishiguro's script *A Profile of Arthur J. Mason*, a mockumentary that represents a butler-turned-bestselling-novelist, acts as a preparatory study for *The Remains of the Day* (Lewis 2000: 76–77). However, *The Gourmet* can be seen as an independent and confident work of considerable merit, and *Granta*'s 1993 'Best Young British Novelists' issue opted for publication of this script rather than a short story 'owing to its author's narrative skills, because it reads so effectively on the page – like a short story or a novella' (Ishiguro 1993: 91).

The Gourmet is distinctive for its choice of protagonist. Rather than focusing on a passive or reserved main character, teleplay foregrounds a celebrated master of the arts, who reminds us of the successful painter Masuji Ono in *An Artist of the Floating World*, the gastronome Manley Kingston. After a global quest for undiscovered dishes and tastes, the story follows Kingston to London to fulfil his greatest desire: to eat 'something that was *not* of this earth' (Ishiguro 1993: 106): a ghost.

The narrative begins, in 1904, with a night scene in a London churchyard. Two men dressed in cloaks and hats are engaged in an obscure activity. They 'are carrying something heavy between them' and '[w]e hear whispering again, sinister, the words barely discernible' (Ishiguro 1993: 92). We are led to the crypt's vestry, 'a small bare room, which we see by the moonlight through a window. At the moment, we are interested only in the doorway which leads through to a back room. This doorway has no door – it is black and ominous, like the gateway to another world' (Ishiguro 1993: 92). What is happening soon becomes clear, but why and how remains vague: 'We have now come right up to the doorway, but there is utter blackness across the threshold. We then move down slowly, in time to see a thin line of blood run out from the blackness towards us along the vestry floor' (Ishiguro 1993: 92). Ishiguro assembles the archetypal gothic elements – night-time crypt, full moon, murder, a distinct supernatural dimension – though motives and significance remain obscure.

The narrative cuts to 1985. Manley arrives at Heathrow Airport, where he is collected by his driver, Carter – the name a nod to Angela Carter, whose own work reimagined the gothic tradition for the contemporary period. At a 'very expensive London house' (Ishiguro 1993: 94), Manley meets several of his admirers, explaining his intentions.

His host, Dr Grosvenor, tells him when and where to hunt for an edible spectre. Back at his own mansion Manley equips himself for his hunt: 'spread all over the bed are "tools" which look vaguely surgical, vaguely like more kitchenware' (Ishiguro 1993: 101). Manley's wife, Winnie, helps to attire him by 'fastening a small saucepan to Manley's belt' (Ishiguro 1993: 101). While Carter drives our culinary ghostbuster to the church we saw in the opening scenes, the audience is introduced to a Latin American gourmet, Rossi, who in a flashback entrusts to Manley further knowledge about how to catch and eat a ghost. During this scene they dine on meat 'not readily identifiable' (Ishiguro 1993: 105), suggesting that it is extremely rare, or perhaps human – prefiguring the climactic scenes of the teleplay.

Manley arrives at the church, which now provides supper and shelter for London's many vagrants, and locks himself in the vestry with a homeless traveller called David. When the ghost first makes its appearance, Manley fails to recognize it: 'He is middle-aged, small, with a friendly, cheeky face. There is absolutely nothing eerie about him' (Ishiguro 1993: 121). When Manley realizes that this is the ghost he has been waiting for, he catches it with the aid of some mysterious powder, a candle, and a butterfly net. He then cooks and eats some pieces of it. After leaving the church, he becomes sick and vomits. Although his mission is accomplished, Manley is thoroughly disappointed, concluding: 'Life gets so dreary once you've tasted its more obvious offerings' (Ishiguro 1993: 126).

The Gourmet connects in some ways with the gothic elements of the short story 'A Family Supper' (1983), in which the ghost of a forgotten mother embodies unresolved issues from the past, and with the Japanese novels, particularly *A Pale View of Hills*, in which Keiko's suicide haunts her mother, Etsuko. As in *A Profile of Arthur J. Mason*, *The Gourmet* also points forwards to *The Remains of the Day* (1989), in its representation of a star-struck butler, Watkins: 'Watkins, who should really be leading him [Manley] in, is delaying doing so to savour these few moments with a celebrity. He beams admiringly at Manley' (Ishiguro 1993: 95). We might also connect this early work to *Never Let Me Go* (2005), in which the harvesting of human organs forms a metaphor for the ways in which the comfort and wealth of middle classes is dependent upon the exploitation of the subaltern, working, or lower classes locally, nationally, and globally. In *The Gourmet* the original murder occurs because 'some human organs were needed for research purposes' (Ishiguro 1993: 120), the central theme of the later novel. In its criticism of celebrity culture, the teleplay anticipates *Nocturnes* (2009).

Yet *The Gourmet* is also strikingly different from Ishiguro's other writings. The directness of its representation of the contemporary political situation is wholly uncharacteristic of Ishiguro's work. The playful, satirical reworking of genres, conventions, topoï, and tropes is far more overtly characteristic of the postmodern moment than any of Ishiguro's other writing. The tale problematizes the relationship between the past and the present, exploiting ways in which different socio-cultural discourses serve to construct our understanding of the world. When David asks Manley whether he has ever eaten from a refuse bin, the homeless man means this literally but the lofty Manley interprets the question as a literary metaphor equating the gourmet with the artist. Manley's rapturous response transforms the idea into a metafictional image, a commentary on the processes of cultural production, and on *The Gourmet* itself: 'An interesting process takes place inside a refuse bin. A kind of stewing pot of randomness. The chance factor often produces recipes far beyond the capabilities of ordinary imaginations' (Ishiguro 1993: 111). *The Gourmet* takes a stock figure from highbrow Western culture, an embodiment of civilization, the gastronome, and situates him within a lowbrow, gothic context, and in the satire on Manley the piece also mocks the banality of metaphors associating contemporary urban society with the melting pot, that image of a classless, multicultural utopia.

By juxtaposing the London of 1904 to the metropolis 80 years later, Ishiguro delivers a telling commentary on the Britain of the Thatcher period. In this respect, the teleplay aligns itself with the postmodern London Gothic of Angela Carter, and that of the London writers Iain Sinclair and Peter Ackroyd (Todd 1996: 164–197; Luckhurst 2002: 527–546). These authors' interest in Gothic writing, their attention to the macabre and the dystopian, is in direct relation to the collapse of collective moral values in the wider political and social discourse of the time. The overtly nostalgic celebration of a romanticized Victorian Britain at the height of empire, which typified Thatcherite ideology, was challenged by these writers' dark evocations of the more problematic aspects of Victorian morality and heritage, their reminders of the violence and oppression that also characterize Britain's imperial history.

Richard Todd has argued that, in the late 1970s and 1980s, these writers 'realigned the city by reinventing it as a Gothic construct' (Todd 1996: 196) in which the contemporary city is haunted by its darker histories: 'the present is rarely present without being suffused, sometimes terrifyingly, sometimes comically, always arrestingly, with the past; place is haunted by voices and presences, some harmless, some baneful; and the realism of the action has become a realism of excess, of magic or of the dreaming world' (Todd 1996: 165). In the London fiction of Carter, Ackroyd, and Sinclair, the events of its imperial history come back to haunt the former centre of the British Empire. In *The Gourmet*, Manley, originally a Londoner and a product of imperial structures, now rejects his former home city: 'A city like this has little to offer someone like me' (Ishiguro 1993: 110). Ishiguro's focus on a London church as a site of mystic rites and crimes allows us to connect *The Gourmet* with such work as Peter Ackroyd's *Hawksmoor* (1985), which itself draws heavily on Sinclair's mystic prose-poem about the occult powers of London's churches and obelisks, *Lud Heat* (1975). Ackroyd's detective novel speculates about the ritual sacrifices of poor, defenceless children, and a child-like vagrant, at churches built by architect Nicholas Hawksmoor, while the city's past fuses with the present-day narrative to indict the corruption of Thatcher's Britain. Ishiguro's script similarly presents a member of a cultural elite who sacrifices innocent victims in support of a wider, inherently individualistic, and materialistic project.

The Gourmet also resonates with the imaginative and comic reworking of London in the fiction of Angela Carter and Salman Rushdie. The protagonist of *Nights at the Circus* (1984), the Cockney *aérialiste* Fevvers, presents us with a London 'the tourist rarely sees' (Carter 1984: 1), and Rushdie's apocalyptic vision of London in *The Satanic Verses* (1988) unveils a city of immigrants visible yet unseen. These works make room for the marginalized and powerless, for women and ethnic minorities, to come to the centre of the city, while formerly dominant groups, such as the white middle class, become marginalized. For Ishiguro, a community worker in Scotland in the mid-1970s, and a resettlement worker helping the homeless at the West London Cyrenians in 1979–1980, the satirical target is also this divided society. His script unpicks traditional class prejudices and oppositions, but also explores the ways a globalized new world order creates new divisions. Manley is introduced in clear class terms: 'Manley is in his fifties; large, formidable British upper-class presence. He wears a habitual expression of disdain and boredom, but there is also a maverick streak in his face – a hint of the decadent or criminal' (Ishiguro 1993: 93). He is sharply contrasted with archetypal representatives of the British underclass, such as the butler, the vagrant David, Manley's own wife, and his driver Carter, who 'has a London working-class accent' (Ishiguro 1993: 94). Such conventional oppositions are destroyed, however, during the scenes at the church. Whereas the vagrant from the early twentieth century is presented as 'an "old-fashioned" tramp, with a big raggy coat' (Ishiguro 1993: 121), the homeless men in Thatcher's London, are presented as follows:

> We are now moving along the queue of homeless men – about twenty in number. Some lean against the wall, some crouch, others sit on the pavement. There are only men here, because the church takes in only men. Otherwise a mixed crowd – multi-racial, all ages. Only a few of them are 'traditional' tramps; most are losing the battle to maintain a conveniently 'respectable' appearance. A significant number of teenagers. Their faces bored and weary. They look towards the passing Rolls without surprise and with little interest. (Ishiguro 1993: 107–108)

This marked difference emphasizes the 'classless' reality of poverty under Thatcher, poverty that affected a wide range of people, including the middle classes. Ishiguro's foregrounding of the ways in which

Thatcherism affected all citizens is in this way markedly different from Carter's emphasis on class, and Salman Rushdie's exposure of London's ignored ethnic minorities in *The Satanic Verses*.

The Gourmet poses questions about culture and art via the central metaphor of food and hunger. Ishiguro's foregrounding of these themes places *The Gourmet* in a long literary tradition, from William Blake and Charles Dickens to T. S. Eliot and even Franz Kafka, all of whom showed how the collusion between political and economic powers resulted in the commodification and consumption of the human body, leading to financial gain at a spiritual loss. Ishiguro's emphasis exposes this relentless, macabre consumption of the human body and spirit within the urban economy. Manley is the embodiment of ruthless greed and selfishness, of decadence and excess, which make him blind to the implications of his taboo-breaking behaviour. In the opening scene, a wooden plaque on the church gate reads: 'I was hungered and ye gave me meat / I was thirsty and ye gave me drink / I was a stranger and ye took me in (Matthew 25:35)' (Ishiguro 1993: 91). In the contemporary part of the narrative, this text is updated in modern diction (see below), pointing out the changing social context while ironizing the fact that religion as a spiritual and moral guide is replaced by the godless, amoral ideology of market forces and free market capitalism. Manley's quest cautions us against the dangers of an artistic desire and imaginative hunger divorced from moral value. He is blind to the social atrocities that take place around him, and to which he may, consciously or unconsciously, be contributing:

MANLEY:	I was hungry. I ate. Now I am sick.
HOMELESS MAN:	[*Shrugs.*] Right, right. See what you mean.
MANLEY:	You see what I mean? I very much doubt that. How could *you* ever understand the kind of hunger I suffer?
HOMELESS MAN:	Well. We all get hungry, don't we?
	Manley gives the homeless man another disparaging look.
MANLEY:	You have no idea what *real* hunger is. (Ishiguro 1993: 125)

Whereas Manley does not want to give shelter to his fellow citizens who are down and out, he does 'take in' the corpse of a ghost. If food is bound by culture, this culture of cannibals is a particularly ruthless and dehumanizing one, and the threat of spiritual regression to an animal consciousness and amoral behaviour is driven home in a comparison made by Dr Grosvenor:

In the primitive world, man was obliged to go out into an unknown wilderness and discover food. He was unbound then by prejudices about what did and did not comprise the edible. He tried anything he could get his hands on.

You, Mr Kingston, are one of the few in modern times worthy of our great pioneers in taste. The rest of us, even someone like myself, we're akin to the womenfolk who waited in the caves worrying about how to cook what the hunters brought back . . . (Ishiguro 1993: 100)

Although Grosvenor is attempting to flatter Manley by portraying him as the pinnacle of civilization, the irony is that his comparison unwittingly connects the culinary expert, and modern civilization, with primitive man and his barbarisms. The seriousness with which the gourmet and culinary representatives take themselves satirizes the culinary scene even further. Beneath the supposed sophistication of their palate and cultural discourse lies a barbaric insensitivity to the fate of their impoverished, starving fellow citizens, and London threatens to become a prehistoric swamp.

In this respect, Manley bears close resemblance to Ono in *An Artist of the Floating World* (1986), another artist who contributes to a political operation that inflicts suffering on innocent civilians. Yet whereas Ono is forced to re-evaluate his past, Manley does not learn from his punishment or acknowledge his wrongdoings. He is the unredeemable and unsympathetic embodiment of a selfish quest for gratification. Yet Manley's language, in his echo of the gospel, also suggests an alternative reading in which his hunger is a genuine lack at the centre of his being, the want of which warrants his attempts, in this case literally, to fill a spiritual void.

Inter-war Utopias: *The Saddest Music in the World* and *The White Countess*

The study of *The Saddest Music in the World* and *The White Countess* is particularly problematic because the original screenplays have not been published. The former was also rewritten by George Toles and director Guy Maddin, making Ishiguro's relation to the final script still more unclear. However, both films do have clear connections to Ishiguro's prose writing, specifically *The Unconsoled* and *When We Were Orphans*, and allow us to assess changes in artistic and thematic emphasis in the course of his career. *The Saddest Music in the World* takes place in 1933, during the depths of the Great Depression, in North America, and *The White Countess*, the material of which can be linked closely to *When We Were Orphans*, in 1930s Shanghai. This inter-war context provides, as it does in *An Artist of the Floating World* and *The Remains of the Day*, the opportunity for an investigation into the trauma inflicted upon individuals and the nation by war: *The Saddest Music in the World* is profoundly shaped by the legacy of World War I; *The White Countess* ends with the Japanese invasion of Shanghai.

The Saddest Music in the World presents us with a cunning if bizarre conceit that relates directly to the surreal tragicomedy of *The Unconsoled*, in which Ryder finds himself trapped in the strange territory of an unnamed European city. The story is set in Winnipeg (likely to be an intervention by Maddin, a Canadian who has set much of his work in his hometown). The town has, for the fourth year in a row, been chosen as 'the World Capital of Sorrow'. A brewery mogul, Baroness Lady Port-Huntley, organizes a competition whereby all countries in the world are invited to send musical representatives to compete for a prize of 25,000 'Depression Era Dollars' by performing the saddest music in the world – a soundtrack to the Depression. Her primary goal is the promotion of her own beer brand and the setting up of business in Canada (these are the years of Prohibition in the United States). The competition attracts contestants from all over the world, including the slick Chester Kent who has traded his Canadian roots for American citizenship; his brother, Roderick, who acts as the representative of Serbia; and their father, Fyodor (representing Canada), a doctor who fought in the 1914–1918 war.

The plotting of the story is improbable, and deliberately so: the narrative constructs a paradoxical logic whereby events associated with the war, in the public realm, are mirrored by those in the private lives of the protagonists. The Kent family's history is presented in a series of flashbacks: Fyodor is a former alcoholic and widower who, drunk, once caused a car crash involving his lover, Port-Huntley, and his son, Chester, who were at that time themselves engaged in an affair. Fyodor attempted to save the wounded Port-Huntley by amputating her leg. Unfortunately, he first amputated the good leg, thus leaving her – in a play on alcohol abuse and Port-Huntley's later business empire – legless. Following the accident, Chester leaves for the United States, blaming his father for the situation. Meanwhile, Roderick has left for Serbia, where he marries Narcissa. Tragically, their child dies. Driven mad (and into amnesia) with grief, Narcissa runs away to the United States where, improbably but inevitably, she falls into the arms of Chester. These intersecting love triangles come to a head in the contemporary narrative in the course of the competition.

An absurd logic, in which the division of peoples and nations is mirrored by the traumatic events within the family, is what drives *The Saddest Music in the World*. Although Port-Huntley's contest is at one level a commodification of national cultures, the very act of bringing them together in one place presents us with the possibility of a utopian ideal, of a space in which all cultures and nations co-exist in harmony through competition. On the one hand, Port-Huntley's contest forms a world war at the level of musical representation in which countries – Siam versus Mexico; Canada versus Africa; Spain versus America; Serbia versus Scotland – battle against one another. On the other hand, bringing these nations together demonstrates that they all share the universal language of music. The film thus suggests that we are all bound together by forms of art and the imagination.

The oddness of the story is reinforced by the film's form, and by Maddin's experimental, independent production. *The Saddest Music in the*

World is shot predominantly in black and white on video and 8 mm, then magnified, giving a distinctive, faded aesthetic that harks back, and pays homage, to the silent film era. It draws upon a wide range of cinematic influences, above all bearing the aesthetic stamp of German Expressionist film from the 1920s and 1930s. Elements of *The Saddest Music in the World* directly evoke *Das Kabinett des Doktor Caligari* ([*The Cabinet of Dr. Caligari*], 1920). A frame narrative provided by a fortune teller, the 'Blind Seer'; the use of flashbacks; and the figure of the doctor, can all be found in the earlier film. Cagliari's loyal associate, the somnambulist Cesare, returns in *The Saddest Music in the World* in the form of a character called 'Old Sleepwalker'. Still more strongly, Fritz Lang's futuristic dystopia *Metropolis* (1927) and *M – eine Stadt suchte einen Mörder* ([*M(Murderer Among Us)*], 1931) are evident influences. *M – eine Stadt suchte einen Mörder* narrates the story of the hunt for a child murderer in Berlin, a hunt that paralyzes everyday life, even among the criminal underworld. This disruption of normality defamiliarizes the world within the film, but also that of the viewer, a strategy also employed in *The Saddest Music in the World*. There are a number of overt references to the earlier film: the window within Port-Huntley's office, located above the bar where the music contest takes place, is shaped in the form of an 'M'; the investigation of responses to the death of a child are reproduced in Roderick and Narcissa's grief. The dystopian *Metropolis* resonates equally strongly within *The Saddest Music in the World*. *Metropolis* is set in a corporate city-state divided into two camps, the planners and the workers. *The Saddest Music in the World* also exposes the economic and social divisions of the modern city. Port-Huntley's office, a brightly lit, luxurious, and spacious room is juxtaposed with the dimly lit, cramped spaces beneath. Port-Huntley herself fulfils a double role: not only is she the unofficial mayor of poverty-stricken Winnipeg, but her prosthetic legs recall the robot-Maria who dominates *Metropolis*. While one hesitates to make too much of these parallels, given the uncertainties around the extent of Ishiguro's involvement in the project, it is nonetheless clear that the experimental form and particular intertexts of *The Saddest Music in the World* are consistent with his other writing from this period.

The White Countess is set in Shanghai during the mid-1930s, when the city enjoyed its heyday as a global trading centre, and was a dynamic hub of cultural and intellectual life. This cultural flourishing was partly due to the successive waves of immigration following World War I, the Russian Revolution, and the rise of Nazi Germany. The imaginative possibilities of such a location are, as we have remarked, already explored in *When We Were Orphans*, where one character tellingly remarks:

> it's quite natural for some of these gentlemen [. . .] to regard Europe as the centre of the present maelstrom. But you, Mr Banks. Of course, *you* know the truth. You know that the real heart of our present crisis lies further afield. [. . .] You know better than anyone the eye of the storm is to be found not in Europe at all, but in the Far East. In Shanghai, to be exact. (Ishiguro 2001: 137–38; emphasis in the original)

The setting permits a destabilizing of Western conventions and expectations, and offers a corrective to a Eurocentric vision of the world. Its unusual combination of social, cultural, political, and – at this time – military influences, its tense concentration of uneasy, potentially destructive, international forces and groupings, make the city a unique and fascinating location.

The main character, Todd Jackson, is a former U.S. diplomat who was once 'the last hope for the League of Nations', but after losing his wife and children in two separate incidents, has abandoned his career in order to open a bar. Jackson has lost his sight in a bomb attack. The blindness is also metaphorical: he is an idealist who gropes his way in the midst of ever-increasing chaos until the Japanese army eventually invades Shanghai. He wants to create 'the bar of his dreams', a space where a harmonious world might be formed in a Shanghai nightclub, and dedicates himself to the achievement of this goal, endlessly perfecting the details of his establishment in order to generate the perfect environment, seeking the appropriate employees and associates to realize his dream. Central to the plan is the White Russian refugee Sofia Alexeyevna Belinskya, the eponymous White Countess, who provides just the blend of seductive charm, tragic mystery, and icy poise to attract and stimulate the clientele. Todd has, as a result of his blindness but also by choice, retreated into the realm of the imagination, preferring the security of his imagination to the potentially painful and disappointing encounters of real life. He resists the reality of Sofia by refusing her invitation to touch her face – she thus remains a fantasy figure for him. Another key figure in the creation of the bar's success is Mr Matsuda, a Japanese gentleman with whom Todd strikes up a friendship. (The name Matsuda we already encountered in *An Artist of the Floating World*, where one of the artists contributing to Japan's war propaganda is given this name.) Matsuda's motives for helping Todd are unclear, but when Todd notes that the club's success is inhibited by what he, in a curious phrase, calls a lack of 'political tension', Matsuda arranges for groups from a variety of political and ideological backgrounds to come to the bar, enhancing still further both the nightly atmosphere in the bar, and its reputation. When the Japanese invade Shanghai, Todd accuses Matsuda, who is a senior figure in the Japanese administration, of having betrayed the utopian vision on which 'The White Countess' was founded, but Matsuda argues that Todd must 'construct another world with the real white countess, Sofia'. During the Japanese invasion, Todd, Sofia, and her daughter manage to flee together on a boat that might take them all to a new, joint future.

The White Countess addresses themes that, as we have seen, run through Ishiguro's whole *oeuvre*. The film explores the individual and collective damage that results from war, a topic common to nearly all the novels. It considers the ways in which the imagination – art, creativity – can provide at once the potential for renewal and a dangerous dislocation from reality. It is also preoccupied with the impact of class in the construction of identity: whereas the aristocratic family of Sofia is desperate to regain their former status, Sofia seeks liberation from the constraints of the upper classes. This liberation is captured in a *tour de force* sequence in which Katya, Sophia's daughter, is fascinated by a sideshow, a series of dark boxes into which an old Chinaman slides glass-painted photographs of local sights, one of which is Soochow, the magic Neverland where the young girl believes her broken family of exiles can be reunited and reconciled. As soon as she starts viewing the glass slides, her imagination takes control and the sepia views of the harbour metamorphose into colourful, animated images. During this short sequence, we have a *mise en abyme* of the director's – and screen-writer's – power of imagination bestowed on innocent Katya. The images show a form of expression freed from the constraints of docu-mentary reality and free to work with associations, metaphors, and symbols. In her mind's eye, the boat floats on the river, bearing a danc-ing couple, an echo of the opening shots of the film, as she also pictures herself hugging that couple. The sequence is echoed in the closing shots of the film as Jackson and Sophia finally escape. The child's vision serves to legitimate and place the optimism of the final scene.

This sequence recalls a passage in *When We Were Orphans*, when a *soirée* in the penthouse ballroom of the Shanghai Palace Hotel is disrupted by shelling between Japanese and Chinese forces over Shanghai's har-bour area. Stepping onto the balcony to look at the spectacle, Banks is handed a pair of opera glasses:

> I put the glasses to my eyes, but the focus was entirely wrong for me and I could see nothing. When I fiddled with the wheel I found myself gazing on to the canal, where I was faintly surprised to see various boats still going about their normal business right next to the fighting. I picked out one particular boat – a barge-like vessel with a lonely oarsman – that was so piled up with crates and bundles it seemed impossible for it to pass under the low canal bridge just beneath me. As I watched, the vessel approached the bridge rap-idly, and I was sure I would see at least a crate or two fall from the top of the pile into the water. For the next few seconds, I went on staring through the glasses at the boat, having quite forgotten the fighting. I noted with interest the boatman, who like me was utterly absorbed by the fate of his cargo and oblivious of the war not sixty yards to his right. Then the boat vanished under the bridge, and when I saw it glide gracefully out the other side, the precarious bundles still intact, I lowered the glasses with a sigh. (Ishiguro 2001: 160–61)

This passage contrasts ordinary life with violent conflict, suggesting something of the absurdity and oddness of war, but it simultaneously demonstrates how Ishiguro's protagonists so often retreat into a private realm rather than acknowledge the potentially dangerous events around them. However, whereas the Shanghai section in *When We Were Orphans* increasingly adopts a surrealist mode of representation reminiscent of *The Unconsoled*, *The White Countess* recalls such heritage films as *A Room with A View* (1986), *Howard's End* (1993), and *The Remains of the Day*. Consistent, as we have seen, with other films with which Ishiguro has been involved, the political context and message are much more explicit. What is intensely drawn in *The White Countess* is, on the one hand, the private, isolated world of the imagination – dramatized by Todd's blindness, and, on the other, the real world beyond the individual's consciousness. *The White Countess* is a film that simultaneously celebrates but also warns against the dangers of the artistic imagination. Todd views his bar as a world and work of art, but 'the heavy doors to keep the world out', as Mr Matsuda notes, will eventually be forced open to admit to the reality of war.

CHAPTER FOUR

History, Memory, and the Construction of Gender in *A Pale View of Hills*

JUSTINE BAILLIE AND SEAN MATTHEWS

Chapter Summary: The memory and representation of trauma is a recurrent theme in the work of Kazuo Ishiguro. His characters' more and less conscious struggles to tell their own stories demonstrate the central, dynamic relationship of narration and identity. In this chapter, a reading of *A Pale View of Hills* (1982), the narrator Etsuko's experiences in Nagasaki during the War, and subsequently in Britain, are examined in the light of recent feminist theory in order to illuminate the force and significance of this powerful novel.

The primary characteristic shared by the narrators of Kazuo Ishiguro's early novels is their unreliability. It is the nature and function of this unreliability that gives his work such distinctive, and powerful, contemporary resonance, and that has driven much of his critical reception. Etsuko, Ono, and Stevens, ordinary figures in extraordinary times and places, tell complex and ambiguous stories that reveal, in their haunting and curious incompleteness, the traumatized, fragmented sense of self of the narrators themselves. The troubled form and direction of these narratives reveal the difficulty of reconstructing an identity shattered by personal suffering in the midst of wider historical catastrophe. Typically, the events of their original trauma, which are at once personal and general, remain absent or occluded from the account, beyond description or precise recall. Universal themes of love and loss are so interwoven with historical events that any distinction between private and public trauma is collapsed, the narrators struggle against processes of misremembering, forgetting, and repression, to construct for themselves a story that draws together either the fragmented elements of their own identity, or a coherent account of the traumatic historical events. These stories have been read as subtle and delicate evocations of universal human concerns, an interpretation given sanction by Ishiguro himself in his interview in this collection. Cynthia Wong (2000), for instance, writes that protagonists in Ishiguro's novels are engaged in a 'quest for consolation' that is 'universal' (Wong 2000: 5). Despite these universal questions, however, Ishiguro's narrators are nonetheless situated at precise points of imperial crisis and collapse, whether in post-war Japan or in the country houses of Britain, and it is significant how the problems of their narratives can be brought into clearer focus through analysis of the ways in which the stories they tell involve the construction of historically specific identities. Professional, national, and, as we argue in this chapter, above all *gender* identities are destroyed not only by the unspeakable catastrophic event, but also by the processes and institutions of nationhood, government, and ideology that determine, and then mediate, such events.

It is in this sense that we might think of Ishiguro's work as postmodern. Jean-François Lyotard (1988) argued that the irrationality of the Holocaust demonstrated the error of the belief in the grand narrative of human progress, of the orderly and rational amelioration of human existence, which was at the foundation of the Enlightenment. For Lyotard, representation or understanding of such an event, of the complexity of the modern world, was impossible in 'the accepted idioms' (Lyotard 1988: 162) of narrative history and philosophy. The best one might manage, he suggested, would be a narrative that 'invents allusions to the conceivable which cannot be presented' (Lyotard 1992: 81). In a world where Truth and Reality are always contingent, history itself enjoys no privileged status, but is a narrative always open to question and interpretation. As Motoyuki Shibata and Motoko Sugano make clear in Chapter Two of this volume, Ishiguro presents, he has said, a 'personal, imaginary Japan' (Oe and Ishiguro 1991: 110), not the conventional 'historical text' (Krider 1998: 150). Always very much connected to history and the world, Ishiguro's work is an example of what Linda Hutcheon (1989) calls 'historiographic metafiction', interrupting the discourse of history to reveal the ideological essence of all its representations (Hutcheon 1989: 47–61).

Feminist literary criticism has drawn upon this postmodern aesthetic in exploring the ways in which gender representation is constructed through language, through stories, through discourse. In such constructions women most often remain absent or misrepresented and so, as with history in Ishiguro's novels, gender often assumes significance by its absence, or by the irruption of problems associated with its experience and articulation. Ishiguro's former teacher, the novelist Angela Carter, argued in her essay on sexuality, *The Sadeian Woman* (1979), that 'flesh comes to us out of history; so does the repression and taboo that governs our experience of flesh [...] Sexuality, in short, is never expressed in a vacuum' (Carter 1979: 11). Feminist theorist Judith Butler, concerned with wider issues of gender and the way in which it is culturally produced and performed, echoes Carter's point when she writes in *Gender Trouble* (1990):

Gender is not always constituted coherently or consistently in different historical contexts, and [. . .] gender intersects with racial, class, ethnic, sexual, and regional modalities of discursively constituted identities. As a result, it becomes impossible to separate out 'gender' from the political and cultural intersections in which it is invariably produced and maintained. (Butler 1990: 3)

It is within such a framework that we will consider how unspoken or indescribable trauma intersects with the construction of historically specific gendered identities in *A Pale View of Hills*.

'You Must Keep Your Mind on Happy Things'

A Pale View of Hills explores the formation of narrator Etsuko's troubled maternal identity in Japan, in the difficult period of post-war reconstruction, a time when 'the world had a feeling of change about it' (Ishiguro 1983: 11). From the perspective of England in the 1970s, following the suicide of her first daughter, Keiko, Etsuko looks back on her life in Nagasaki in the years following the dropping of the first atomic bomb. Contrary to Salman Rushdie's (1991) casual suggestion that the novel 'was set in post-war Nagasaki but never mentioned the Bomb' (Rushdie 1991: 246), the story is saturated with references to it. On the third page itself we are told that Etsuko's apartment block is built on the site of a small village destroyed by the Bomb (Ishiguro 1983: 11); Mrs Fujiwara lost a husband and four sons in the blast (Ishiguro 1983: 111); Etsuko and her father-in-law Ogata-san visit the Nagasaki Peace Park, with its 'massive white statue in memory of those killed by the atomic bomb' (Ishiguro 1983: 137). The war, similarly, is strongly present in the text, most obviously in the condemnation, by the young teacher Shigeo Matsuda (tacitly supported by Jiro, Etsuko's husband), of the complicity of Ogata-san and his generation in the evils of Japanese imperialism (Ishiguro 1983: 29–32; 35; 60; 66; 126; 144–48), but also in references to the continuing presence of the American occupation forces (Ishiguro 1983: 11), and to the political wrangles of the re-emergent Japanese political class (Ishiguro 1983: 99). Everyone in Etsuko's story is in some way touched by the tragedy of the war and the Bomb, a fact that she neither avoids nor conceals; it is indeed the ground and foundation of the text. The significance of the novel, rather, is in the way Etsuko's narrative demonstrates quite what it might mean, in the matter of an individual life, to have been caught up in such an event and how, specifically, her own identity – as a woman and as a mother – has been complicated and confused, but these issues are not so much explicitly discussed as directly demonstrated in the form of her narration. Etsuko only momentarily alludes to the defining event of her life, which is never directly explained. Far more than even the fall of the Bomb, it is 'those last days in Nagasaki' (Ishiguro 1983: 90), during which she made the decision to leave her Japanese husband and flee to England with her foreign lover and her child, around which her story circles.

We are given oblique hints, in Etsuko's narration, in the 'several letters' and 'two or three small photographs' kept secretly in her marital home (Ishiguro 1983: 71); in a conversation in the course of which Mrs Fujiwara recalls Etsuko's 'heartbroken' state before Ogata-san offered her shelter (Ishiguro 1983: 76–77), and in Ogata-san's own recollection of Etsuko's frantic condition when she first came to his home in those 'terrible days' (Ishiguro 1983: 57–58), of a whole way of life, and of a lover (perhaps also her own family [Ishiguro 1983: 23]), lost when the Bomb fell. This is all we learn of Etsuko's earlier life, however, the life 'before', and her narrative concentrates instead on the efforts of rebuilding and reconstruction that are apparent everywhere around her, in the very form and fabric of the city, just as much as in her own life. Characters reaffirm relentlessly the need for optimism and forward-looking energy: 'You must keep your mind on happy things now. Your child. And the future,' urges Mrs Fujiwara (Ishiguro 1983: 24); 'I'm going to be optimistic from now on' (Ishiguro 1983: 112), says Etsuko, not altogether convincingly. We learn of her marriage to Ogata-san's son, Jiro, but also of its disappointments, of his patriarchy and arrogance. We know that seven years later she took the momentous decision to take Keiko and leave Japan, with the unnamed lover, a journalist, who is the father of her second child, Niki (Ishiguro 1983: 90–92). But the greater part of the narrative concerns the summer during which she was pregnant with Keiko. She remembers the changing world of newly built apartment blocks, the development of new corporate practices, the advent of democracy, and the ambivalent vogue for 'America', which represented all that was new and challenging – or threatening and disruptive – in the nation's future.

The narrative makes clear the pressures of the historical moment in which Etsuko is caught, torn between her residual attachment to traditional values and responsibilities, as exemplified by Ogata-san, by the Nakagawa area of the city, by Mrs Fujiwara, and the pull of radical, new, and shocking ideas of independence and self-determination, as embodied in the figure of Sachiko, with her ideas of escape, alongside her lover Frank, to America. Etsuko does not recount her dilemma in such explicit terms. Her narrative suggests, as we shall see, that Sachiko and Mariko are perhaps only projections of her own experiences and hopes, since certainly the narrative of her own departure from Japan blends with theirs in her accounts of a disturbing incident involving Mariko/Keiko and a rope (Ishiguro 1983: 83, 174), and of the trip to Inasa (Ishiguro 1983: 103–125, 182), but her broken identity is instead indirectly expressed in hesitancies, uncertainties, and contradictions, in the evident pain and struggle of remembering and forgetting. The trauma of her time in Nagasaki becomes present after the fact, but in reconstructed or displaced form, not as the direct experience of the event itself. She herself warns the reader that it 'is possible that my memory of these events will have grown hazy with time, that things did not happen in quite the way they come back to me today' (Ishiguro 1983: 41), a warning she reiterates near the end of the novel: 'Memory, I realize, can be an unreliable thing; often it is heavily coloured by the circumstances in which one remembers, and no doubt this applies to certain of the recollections I have gathered here' (Ishiguro 1983: 156). Trauma itself is always at once present and absent: the traumatic past is always present, but never in its original form.

The contradictions in Etsuko's narrative are most apparent in her ambivalence towards motherhood. Etsuko admits that during her pregnancy 'small things were capable of arousing in me every kind of misgiving about motherhood' (Ishiguro 1983: 17), and her narrative is remarkable for its inability directly to acknowledge negative feelings about pregnancy and motherhood. She insists repeatedly on her happiness and excitement about the coming birth, 'Unhappy? But I'm not unhappy in the least' (Ishiguro 1983: 77), even as her narrative overflows with malign, disturbing references to maternity: the series of child murders in Nagasaki (Ishiguro 1983: 100); a mother's drowning of her own baby witnessed by Sachiko and Mariko (Ishiguro 1983: 43; 74), followed later by the woman's own suicide (Ishiguro 1983: 74); the drowning of the kittens, with its uncanny resonances and echoes of that scene of infanticide (Ishiguro 1983: 166–68); and above all the recurrent motifs of Mariko's fear of Etsuko (Ishiguro 1983: 17; 83; 173), and Etsuko's own unease about the alarming 'thin' women who stalk her narrative (Ishiguro 1983: 74; 92; 125; 157). Etsuko's memories of her encounters with Mariko fuse with, and somehow displace, her own life as a mother, and in particular her relationship with Keiko. The troubled Mariko functions as a premonition, a foretelling of the psychological trauma of Etsuko's own daughter's suicide later in England. The identity of the young girl found hanging, which Etsuko both half-remembers and dreams, never becomes clear but is somehow at once both Mariko *and* Keiko, and someone else entirely (Ishiguro 1983: 47; 55; 95–96; 100). Sachiko and Mariko serve as a mirror, even as scapegoats, onto which Etsuko projects, or through which she explores, her own anxieties about her identity and actions as a woman and as a mother, and ultimately as the agent who breaks utterly with her past and with her conventional role in society. When Niki reports that her friend is writing a poem about Etsuko's experience, Etsuko refuses even to concede the matter is worth consideration, since 'such things are long in the past now and I have no wish to ponder them yet again. My motives for leaving Japan were justifiable' (Ishiguro 1983: 91). These motives, though implicit in her narrative, are indeed never discussed, with the result that it is through Etsuko's relation to Sachiko that we read a debate about her rejection of Japan, duty, and motherhood. Sachiko, if she existed at all, is a form of alter-ego, embodying in Etsuko's memory one half of her own divided life and identity.

Etsuko's identity is divided between her desire for fulfilment and independence as a woman, and her responsibilities, socially defined within a conservative and patriarchal environment, as a wife and mother. She is literally divided, in narrative terms, as Sachiko assumes the role of her spectral double: 'I remember with some distinctness that eerie spell which seemed to bind the two of us' (Ishiguro 1983: 41). The French feminist critic Julia Kristeva, in her essay 'Women's Time' (1979), refers to the 'radical ordeal' of the splitting of the subject that is pregnancy and motherhood (Kristeva 1986b: 206). In an earlier essay, 'Stabat Mater' (1977), she writes that a 'mother is a continuous separation, a division of the very flesh. And consequently a division of language – and it has always been so' (Kristeva 1986a: 178). In motherhood, she argues:

> My body is no longer mine, it doubles up, suffers, bleeds, catches cold, puts its teeth in, slobbers, coughs, is covered with pimples, and it laughs. And yet, when its own joy, my child's, returns, its smile washes only my eyes. But the pain, its pain – it comes from inside, never remains apart, other, it inflames me at once, without a second's respite. As if that was what I had given birth to and, not willing to part from me, insisted on coming back, dwelled in me permanently. One does not give birth in pain, one gives birth to pain: [. . .] a mother is always branded by pain. (Kristeva 1986a: 167)

Kristeva's concern with the psychological dimensions of motherhood resonates profoundly with Etsuko's maternal experience. Her daughter Keiko, and Keiko's suicide, inhabit Etsuko as the pain that cannot be dispelled. In Kristeva's terms, Keiko takes possession of her mother as the pain that never leaves, but a pain that also accrues the attributes of the still deeper pain of her whole history.

Kristeva's analysis is open to the charge of placing the maternal body before culture and its social construction, and therefore recreating a universalized and naturalistic version of motherhood from her own, very personal, experience. In her critique of Kristeva, Butler claims that: 'Her [Kristeva's] naturalistic descriptions of the maternal body effectively reify motherhood and preclude an analysis of its cultural construction and variability' (Butler 1990: 80). The risk of this 'writing the body', which is at the heart of efforts to generate a language and form for women's experience that is not already held within the conventions and determinations of tradition and patriarchy, is that women's identities are removed from history and rendered essential and unchanging. Both maternity and, as we shall see, masculinity are rather subject to variation according to the specific historical contexts within which they are shaped; they are not inherent or given. It is this tension that *A Pale View of Hills* so effectively represents. Etsuko is forced to consider this in a conversation with Niki. She finds it hard to believe that Niki's unmarried nineteen-year-old friend can plan and welcome a pregnancy, maintaining that 'people always pretend to be delighted [. . .] I'm sure nobody ever receives the news of a baby like these people do in these films' (Ishiguro 1983: 49). Etsuko is aware of ideological constructions of motherhood, but does not acknowledge that notions of maternity have changed still further since her own post-war experiences.

In 'Women's Time', Kristeva makes a distinction between maternal time – an experience of time relating to the cyclical and reproductive repetitions of biology and motherhood – and the time of history, which is linked to linear time, and the linearity of language as a sequence of words. Kristeva attempts to reconcile these notions of time in her formulation of a feminism that encompasses both, allowing the maternal body to exist in the linear historical moment, but find expression through a poetic form of language that subverts linearity and allows for the recovery of the maternal body. In Kristeva's schema, poetic language disrupts the dominant linguistic patterns inherent in patriarchal societies, but as Butler points out this relies upon a rather simplistic idea of patriarchy. First, it assumes a homogeneous, unitary, and stable paternal law and, second, if poetic language is taken to exist in relation to this law, its subversive function nonetheless remains secondary to it; it is only ever a transgression against, and within, the dominant mode. Moreover, it is a temporary and unsustainable condition as the subject must inevitably return to ordinary language in order to avoid the radical psychological disruption that the perpetual use of such a poetic language would ultimately engender (Butler 1990: 80–91). Butler thus identifies in Kristeva's position precisely the tension that characterizes Etsuko's experience. Despite Etsuko's displacement of her anxieties through the re-telling of the story of Sachiko and Mariko, she is unable to exist in a stable present *and* recover her maternal self. Her inability wholly to occupy linear time is revealed in the continual and contradictory eruptions of her repressed memories of motherhood and of Keiko's childhood.

Keiko's possession of her mother is ultimately a detrimental form of what, in psychological terms, we think of as 'repetition'. Niki has to some degree come to terms with this, in her separation and distance from Keiko, and she herself becomes the embodiment of a possible future. In the process of creating her own version of her mother's past she both praises the achievement of flight, and assimilates Etsuko's story into the public frame of her friend's poem about her mother as a feminist role model – it is significant that it is through *poetic* language that the story might be told (Ishiguro 1983: 89; 177). Niki also wants to return to London and construct her own identity beyond the field of her mother's memories and choices. There is no equivocation in her comment to Etsuko that she 'can't think of anything I'd like less' than having children. 'It's nothing to do with how young or old I am. I just don't feel like having a lot of kids screaming around me' (Ishiguro 1983: 48).

The gothic mode of *A Pale View of Hills*, evident in its spectral and nightmarish imagery, the recurrent motifs of fear and uncertainty, and the pervading sense of horror and dread, conveys the difficulty for Etsuko of finding any immediate recovery through her maternal role or the promises of personal and national regeneration with which it is associated. Etsuko is at best sceptical of Mrs Fujiwara's optimism about motherhood and the future – 'You must keep your mind on happy things now. Your child. And the future' (Ishiguro 1983: 24) – and finds little consolation in the hopes and aspirations of the older generation exemplified by Etsuko's father-in-law, Ogata-San, with his ambitions towards learning cookery and music (Ishiguro 1983: 33; 58). This generation's relation to the future has its foundation in the privileging of family duty and a traditional conception of national identity and values that the younger characters – Jiro, Shigeo Matsuda – reject. This chimes again with Kristeva's argument; she explains that 'the Second World War, though fought in the name of national values [. . .] brought an end to the nation as reality' (Kristeva 1986b: 188). Ironically, however, she also suggests the end of unity in nationhood leads to the construction of a 'new social ensemble superior to the nation':

> [W]ithin which the nation, far from losing its own traits, rediscovers and accentuates them in a strange temporality, in a kind of 'future perfect', where the most deeply repressed past gives a distinctive character to a logical and sociological distribution of the most modern type. (Kristeva 1986b: 188–89)

The unproblematic desire shared by Ogata-San and Mrs Fujiwara for regeneration figuratively and literally embodied in maternal reproduction is a symptom of their inability to acknowledge the changing circumstances of the new Japan, and places an intolerable strain on Etsuko, as she is expected to bear children in the name of an archaic nationalism now disguised as progress. Like the young pregnant woman whom Mrs Fujiwara sees weekly at the cemetery, Etsuko, the reader suspects, 'finds it hard to forget' the devastation of the Bomb, and hard to accept the contradictions of the new dispensation. Without the space to mourn and remember she cannot agree with Mrs Fujiwara's opinion that 'It's a shame, a pregnant girl and her husband spending their Sundays thinking about the dead [. . .] They should be thinking about the future' (Ishiguro 1983: 25).

The discord struck by Ogata-San's 'hideous' attempt to play her violin, an attempt symptomatic of his efforts to move on, is ironically pivotal in Etsuko's recovery of memories lost in trauma. 'Was I like a mad person?' (Ishiguro 1983: 57) she asks her father-in-law when reminded of how she herself played the violin during the aftermath of the Bomb. In her exchange with Ogata-San the discordant notes played by the older man symbolically return her to history, to contemplation of the immediate effects of the Bomb: 'They must have thought I was a mad girl' (Ishiguro 1983: 57–58). Her realization that she has repressed memories of her former traumatized self suggests we can consider her narrative as an attempt to rationalize a past that has never been truly confronted. Such eruptions belie the calm and reflective tone that characterizes her narrative, betraying the state of mind that renders the surface narrative of her story so unreliable. Without the consolation to be found in music, a happy marriage, and a fulfilling maternal experience, Etsuko's story – her whole identity – is distorted by projection, repression, and mis-remembering. Despite the understanding shown by Ogata-San, and his assurance that during her visit to his household immediately after the Bomb she was 'very shocked, which was only to be expected. We were all shocked, those of us who were left. Now, Etsuko, let's forget these things' (Ishiguro 1983: 58), Etsuko has not left the past behind, but rather we find in her story a pattern of repetition and confusion, as evidenced in the recurrence of the different scenes involving the child and the rope. It is impossible for her to function in the maternal regenerative role allotted to her by her elders, her husband Jiro, and the new Japanese state. Nor can the abandoned symbols of traditional Japanese culture, chess and musical creativity, be easily re-established in post-war Nagasaki. Etsuko's violin remains un-played, up on a high shelf (Ishiguro 1983: 57) and her first husband Jiro sweeps away the chess board in his eagerness to entertain his colleagues (Ishiguro 1983: 61), a gesture at once signifying his rejection of tradition and his embrace of the future. As patriarchal and social patterns shift, Etsuko finds herself faced with the worst of both worlds as Japanese masculinity now conflates with aspirations for corporate promotion and a business sensibility that all too easily permeate the home and distort family relations.

In the post-war society, even in a fledgling democracy with new ideologies, Etsuko ultimately rejects her proscribed maternal role, choosing an exile from loyalty, duty, and assimilation that echoes that of Sachiko, and in which the fate of the hanging child, of Keiko, and perhaps even of Mariko become one. The Bomb, ironically, exposes Etsuko to new opportunities, to the ambiguous challenge of new forms of individualism and fulfilment, and this guilty fact may be at the heart of her ambivalence towards maternity. The choice becomes for Etsuko one of creative selfhood, or maternal, and by extension, national, duty. Ogata-San expresses regret for the development of democracy and what he regards as the passing of traditional Japanese values:

> Discipline, loyalty, such things held Japan together once. That may sound fanciful, but it's true. People were bound by a sense of duty. Towards one's family, towards superiors, towards the country. But now instead there's all this talk of democracy. You hear it whenever people want to be selfish, whenever they want to forget obligations. (Ishiguro 1983: 65)

The consequence of Etsuko's rejection of these duties, we realize by the end of the novel, is in the troubled selfhood so evident in her narrative voice.

CHAPTER FIVE

Artifice and Absorption: The Modesty of *The Remains of the Day*

DAVID JAMES

Chapter Summary: Kazuo Ishiguro's fiction is remarkable at once for its technical and formal accomplishment and its lack of artistic extravagance: his writing is characterized by an aesthetic integrity, a kind of stylistic modesty. His narrators are at once rhetorically idiosyncratic, yet at the same time reserved and understated. The representation of the butler Stevens in *The Remains of the Day* (1989) is a fine example of how Ishiguro's writerly control is ultimately the mark of creative innovation. Alternate phases of distance and immersion characterize the reader's experience of memory in this novel. Ishiguro compels us to coordinate the pleasure of being absorbed in the story with awareness of the artifice that *is* this story's style, drawing attention to alternative forms of engaging critically and affectively with the register of Stevens's perpetual retrospection.

Why should we care about Stevens? What is it about the *way* Stevens is presented that compels us to take an interest in him? These questions are perhaps as obvious as they are unanswerable, but they are central to novels like *The Remains of the Day* (1989), novels that unfold entirely in the first-person, where our capacity to sustain relationships, sympathetic or otherwise, with confessional or reminiscing narrators is put to the test. We might assume such questions about believability and sympathy are implicitly answered by everything we do as readers. We rarely worry about our ability to suspend disbelief, to engage with fictional prose fully aware of, yet undeterred by, that artifice inherent in the representation of a narrator's thoughts. First-person narratives require us to be agile in warding off incredulity. They encourage us to know how, and why, we are becoming absorbed in the memories, self-examinations, and diversions of a fictional mind, but not so self-conscious, so aware of the fictionality of what we read, as to jeopardize the sympathy we develop towards the protagonist and his or her plight.

This chapter examines the way *The Remains of the Day* places heavy demands on the reader, requiring us to navigate between, and ultimately synchronize, various *degrees* of engagement with Stevens's narration, to the extent that we are at once made aware of Ishiguro's skilfully wrought presentation of perception and inner thought while also appreciating how far these formal accomplishments rest upon the novel's modest refusal of showmanship and stylistic display. This modesty is a formal component, as my closing remarks will suggest, that has much to tell us about Ishiguro's complication of genre in this novel, as the narrative modulates between wholesale tragedy and domestic repartee, between the affecting inevitability of personal outcomes for Stevens and his comic persistence in pursuing self-improvement by learning the art of witty conversation.

Formally polished, yet deeply moving, *The Remains of the Day* epitomizes Ishiguro's recurrent challenge to the reader: it compels us to reconcile our enthrallment in events as they progress and our appreciation of the style that conveys Stevens's reactions to those events. In effect, to become absorbed in what happens within the world of this novel is also to be made of aware of *how* our absorption can coalesce with, though without being compromised by, a heightened awareness of Ishiguro's craft. For his rhetorical skills are not only evidenced by the verbal distinctiveness of Stevens's narratorial idiosyncrasy, but also by the kind of dual behaviour that he cultivates in his readers – consumed as we can often be with Stevens's perception of everyday situations yet simultaneously alert to the aesthetic workmanship that lies behind the way things are perceived. It is not that Ishiguro simply wants us to pay attention to how fiction can meditate upon its own construction; he takes the more ambitious step of inviting us to recognize how our aesthetic experience of reading *The Remains of the Day* is enhanced precisely *because* of our consciousness of form, our sense of the imaginative agility that underlies the creation of a character like Stevens.

One should not, therefore, confuse this kind of technical facility with that textual self-consciousness typically associated with post-war metafiction. Ishiguro has firmly distinguished his work from such formal self-reflexivity, insisting, 'I'm only interested in literary experiment insofar as it serves a purpose of exploring certain themes with an emotional dimension. I always try to disguise those elements of my writing that I feel perhaps are experimental' (Mason 1989: 346). Ishiguro's practical sense of what formal innovation should entail is all the more significant in light of the candid medium of testimony that makes *The Remains of the Day* so compelling. In this novel, self-conscious experimentalism takes second place to Ishiguro's fastidious maintenance of Stevens's narrative voice. The result is indeed artful, originally so, yet thoroughly self-effacing as well. It is best characterized as a mode of authorial *modesty*.

The significance of modesty to Ishiguro is best indicated by his comments about musicianship. Learning the guitar, he was struck by the need to be highly absorbed in technique without being demonstrative. 'After a while you begin to sort out the people who can play beautiful music from the people who can play very fast', he remarked, 'asking yourself the whole time, are you playing this lick just to impress other people who can't play, or are you playing it because there is an emotional effect that you want?' (Krider 1998: 148). Refusing the attractions of artistic showmanship, Ishiguro's writerly commitment to a self-effacing craft is above all in evidence in the creation of his rhetorically idiosyncratic narrators. Epitomizing this sense of integrity in a practitioner mindful of the dangers of exhibitionism, the style of *The Remains of the Day* exhibits Ishiguro's control over any 'new technical accomplishment' (Krider 1998: 148). It is precisely the novel's poise that makes it so innovative, reflecting Ishiguro's belief that technique is something one should experiment with only when 'it's really what's required' (Krider 1998: 149). Such moderation – or modesty – is an attitude that Ishiguro has promoted in various interviews, often in response to quite different questions.

It is this rule of stylistic reserve that underpins the register of *The Remains of the Day*, a restraint reciprocated by Stevens himself, especially when he equivocates over the order and arrangement of his discussion:

> But I feel I should return just a moment to the matter of my father; for it strikes me I may have given the impression earlier that I treated him rather bluntly over his declining abilities. The fact is, there was little choice but to approach the matter as I did – as I am sure you will agree once I have explained the full context of those days. (Ishiguro 1989: 69–70)

The qualifying 'But' that begins this paragraph draws attention to Stevens's own sense of the contrivance of narrative. His words are purposefully arranged rather than spontaneous, more strategically organized than we might expect from a story composed from involuntary memories. Yet Stevens's retrospection is all the more intriguing for what it reveals about the demands Ishiguro placed upon himself in writing this novel, especially when choreographing this narrative voice. For one, Stevens is emblematic of Ishiguro's admission that 'I can focus what is important and what isn't important for me, as a writer, if I choose a narrator or protagonist who is, on the surface at least, very different from me' (Bigsby 2008: 22). These 'surface' differences have become, as Ishiguro would doubtless accept, a deeper 'part of my style' (Bigsby 2008: 23), because the digressive and often self-deluding manner of his characters conditions his decisions about mode and diction. Such is Ishiguro's level of commitment to the surrender of formal display in order to do justice to the particularities of individual experience, mindful that 'the narrator you choose has a very significant impact on the texture of the narrative' (Bigsby 2008: 23).

This is not merely to imply that Ishiguro's work reinforces a familiar notion of the bond between style and theme in fiction, but rather to suggest that his writing draws attention to the way that rhetorical features play a still more active role than we might expect. The narrative mode of *The Remains of the Day* alternates between working with, and working against, the insecurities Stevens strives to conceal. By its idiom of reserve, the novel paradoxically alerts us to all that lies beneath: the verbal convolutions that allow Stevens to elide his emotional instabilities also inhibit him from addressing us as confidants. He forestalls candour and confession with the rhetoric for which *The Remains of the Day* is so renowned. This potential dislocation of form from content is crucial for understanding the dramatic potential of Ishiguro's first-person technique. It has a dual effect detected by Salman Rushdie (1992): 'Just below the understatement of the novel's surface is a turbulence as immense as it is slow' (Rushdie 1992: 244). Rushdie's comments concern what happens dramatically, rather than the exact linguistic properties underpinning its execution, but his distinction could be applied to our reading experience. Ishiguro invites us to balance our sense of the way Stevens would prefer to tell his past and the force with which memories return unexpectedly to alter his priorities as a narrator.

By perpetuating our sense of being periodically captivated by and detached from events, Ishiguro exemplifies some of the most recent ideas about aesthetic response offered by commentators on literary emotion. It is useful to bear this in mind when considering Stevens's way of allowing his present car journey to engender 'surprising new perspectives on topics one imagined one had long ago thought through thoroughly' (Ishiguro 1989: 117). Memories, for Stevens, are more manageable when objectified as 'topics', repackaged and protected from being recalled as potentially more traumatic instances of self-doubt or regret. In effect, Stevens warms to his theme precisely when 'speaking in broad generalizations' (Ishiguro 1989: 116), choosing self-erasing forms of articulation that promise a certain degree of emotional protection, insofar as his brightly intoned truisms forestall his descent into periods of graver contemplation. By alerting us to these tonal dynamics – and, in turn, to the way Stevens's aphorisms and generalities reveal the pivotal role that diction alone plays in Ishiguro's approach to characterization – *The Remains of the Day* exemplifies Jenefer Robinson's suggestion that various elements contribute to our sense of the importance of a novel's form, with the implication that form itself has the capacity to shape meaning. Robinson remarks that we should think of form 'not so much as an object of our aesthetic admiration in its own right, but as a means of guiding and managing our emotional experience of a work' (Robinson 2005: 196). She goes on to argue that '[f]ormal devices direct the sequence of appraisals and reappraisals that we engage in as we read', monitoring our contact with a text's dramatic content 'in such a way that we are enabled to *cope* with what we encounter emotionally in a literary work'. But the idea that form allows us to cope with, and even appease, our responses to what we are shown in a novel does not answer the question of how we become so intrigued by Ishiguro's markedly different narrators in the first place. It is not that his formal methods 'help us to focus attention on positive aspects of the content', as Robinson would have it, much less 'to divert our attention from painful aspects' (Robinson 2005: 207). Rather, Ishiguro wants to involve us in the *process* of coping, a process for which he solicits our sympathetic attention at the level of technique.

If anything, the form of *The Remains of the Day* 'help[s] us to focus attention' precisely on that which is difficult and potentially traumatic, rather than diverting us towards less disconcerting aspects of Stevens's life and work. This intensification of our attention becomes especially apparent when Stevens changes pitch, angling in from the world of domestic affairs to his own inner world of truisms about professional perfectionism. In these instances, Ishiguro allocates considerable space to tracking Stevens's inward shift, conducting as he often does a debate with himself. This interior debate turns into a probing justification of his own dissection of dignity in abstract terms:

> Indeed, the more one considers it, the more obvious it seems: association with a *truly* distinguished household *is* a prerequisite of 'greatness'. A 'great' butler can only be, surely, one who can point to his years of service and say that he has applied his talents to serving a great gentleman – and through the latter, to serving humanity. (Ishiguro 1989: 117; emphasis in the original)

We are privy here to a more tightly argued process of assertion and qualification. In this debate as to what constitutes 'greatness', Stevens struggles to retain the prototype of a '"great" butler' as his object of analysis. The pathos of the situation is that Stevens ends up rehearsing a discussion of esteem for which he refuses to become the ideal case-study. Only by disseminating professional roles in terms of abstract virtues can he reward himself by association: praising the archetypal 'talents' of experienced butlers down the years in order to gesture indirectly to his own contribution to that heritage. This kind of oblique self-praise, born out of self-scrutiny, is rather different to Stevens's manner of rehearsing his proud allegiance to the 'aspiration of all those of us with professional ambition' (Ishiguro 1989: 115). As he pivots between talking to his imagined audience and scrutinizing his service to the tradition that his employment under Darlington preserves, one can observe how the reader's sympathy is mediated not only by what Stevens says and does, but also by incremental variations in the measured expressions with which he distances himself from the more 'unsettling experience' of remembrance (Ishiguro 1989: 113). The pathos of this detachment is confirmed by Stevens's tendency to avoid the concrete instantiation of what dignity might involve in workaday life, in favour of more abstract claims or recycled maxims. Indeed, the importance of his service is supposedly confirmed by an assumption masquerading as the assertion of fact that 'debates are conducted, and crucial decisions arrived at, in the privacy and calm of the great houses of this country' (Ishiguro 1989: 115).

Our immersion in Stevens's story, therefore, can be interrupted by our awareness of the stylistic modulations that Ishiguro uses to represent thought and recollection, modulations that are focalized in a partial rather than objective manner. The narrative is told from a perspective that can never be as impartial as Stevens himself might prefer it to be. Impartiality, the narrative quality Stevens most desires to cultivate, is the primary source of exasperation and resentment for Miss Kenton, a source too of potential frustration or discomfort for Ishiguro's readers. Her anger at his emotional detachment is amplified in the episode when the Jewish maids Ruth and Sarah are dismissed. The aftermath of this episode is explored through dialogue, rather than through Stevens's calm retrospection; in a sense, the episode deviates from the novel's modal norm, freed from the loquacious yet self-admonishing tenor of Stevens's recollections as he travels, in the novel's present time, through rural Wiltshire and Dorset. We're plunged into the discursive edginess of that fraught exchange, where Kenton asks whether Stevens can appreciate 'how much it would have meant to me if you had thought to share your feelings last year?' (Ishiguro 1989: 153). As an effect of this exchange, readers are placed directly into a scene where Kenton's frustration is provoked by the very manner of disengagement that Stevens prefers to maintain in addressing us:

> 'I suffered so much over Ruth and Sarah leaving us. And I suffered all the more because I believed I was alone.'
>
> 'Really Miss Kenton . . .' I picked up the tray on which I had gathered together the used crockery. 'Naturally, one disapproved of the dismissals. One would have thought that quite self-evident.'
>
> She did not say anything, and as I was leaving I glanced back towards her. She was again gazing out at the view, but it had by this point grown so dark inside the summerhouse, all I could see of her was her profile outlined against a pale and empty background. I excused myself and proceeded to make my exit.
>
> Now that I have recalled this episode of the dismissing of the Jewish employees, I am reminded of what could, I suppose, be called a curious corollary to that whole affair: namely, the arrival of the housemaid called Lisa. (Ishiguro 1989: 154)

The dialogue not only demonstrates the tone of their dispute but also the effect of its coming to a close, in that the paragraph break between that heated episode and Stevens's resuming narration changes the chord again back into the settled tonic key of Stevens's retrospective elucidations. The abstractions ('curious corollary') return, breaking off Stevens's direct and candid response to Kenton's admission that she had 'suffered'. We *do* glimpse a response of that kind before the section break in the passage. The pathetic fallacy of the encroaching gloom offers an aptly impressionistic backdrop for the moment when Stevens, quite uncharacteristically, sums up the mutual resignation that ends their scene in a tableau comprising Kenton's 'profile' as she withdraws into silence, while Stevens himself retreats ascetically back into the world of domestic routine. After this striking, portentous image, the resumption of Stevens's functional commentary – in which such a forthright dispute is an 'episode' merely – serves to place event, memory, and reader once more at a distance. The typography reinforces that remoteness, the new section of prose visually announcing the return to Stevens's dependable scheme for objectifying the past by opting for the facts surrounding events over his disruptive feelings towards their consequences.

What this episode exemplifies is the way in which Ishiguro pulls our attention in two directions, challenging our expectations as readers. In Stevens he has created a character whose narration shifts between unquestioning belief in the credibility of the domestic history he recalls, and a more self-conscious sense of his role as a participant in past events and the turning-points they emblematize. Presenting us with this kind of narrator, Ishiguro presupposes that his reader will move between levels of credulity – assuming, in other words, that we can be entirely absorbed in the experience of following Stevens's recollections while also remaining alert to the fictional and fabricated nature of what we are being told. This is the dual reaction that Ishiguro invites across the novel, as our immersion is punctuated with moments of incredulity, just as Stevens oscillates between reporting, even recreating, the past and probing with hindsight the extent to which he might have acted otherwise. Where our imaginative engagement is concerned, this cycle of enchantment and detachment makes reading feel more like a process of constant *surfacing*, of re-emerging from the immediacy and intensity of events. Put simply, those phrases in *The Remains of the Day* in which I find myself most compelled will often give way to their opposite: to episodes, as given earlier, that redirect my attention to the very stylistic devices that most cultivate my interest in Stevens's troubled self-examination. Ishiguro alerts me to the fact that, even if I lose myself in events, I can simultaneously remain aware of *how*, formally, those events are being organized and conveyed. In this way, the narrative ensures that the pleasure of becoming absorbed in Ishiguro's style is balanced with awareness of the artifice *of* that style, highlighting the alternative ways of engaging critically and emotionally with the register of retrospection that Ishiguro so tightly controls, and whose controlled omissions and digressions are themselves the very stuff of tragedy. Aspects of self-control thus become a stylistic feature while revealing to us a habitual state of mind – the self-command that twists into self-constraint, the guardedness that Stevens cannot prevent his professional self from habitually retaining, carrying over to, and enfolding his private self at the close of day.

It may be true to say therefore that *The Remains of the Day* epitomizes two related sides of Ishiguro as a novelist: the modest chronicler of psychological confinement, intrigued by the sympathetic portrayal of perseverance and duty along with the emotional underdevelopment and supplication these values perpetuate; and the inconspicuous stylist who confines himself to the first-person mode, only to alert us to the imaginative possibilities of notating human perception at work. Indeed Stevens's retrospection often becomes all the more compelling when it shifts into *argumentation* (as we saw after his exchange with Miss Kenton), demanding a questioning of the veracity of the scenes that he recounts from his past, and solely from his perspective. In such instances, Stevens's sudden switch to the here-and-now usually entails an anxiously repeated assessment of personal responsibility. Because these mini-psychodramas entail a turn from past to present, Ishiguro swaps the syntax of remembrance (an idiom characterized by the straightforward past tense of Stevens's recollections) for a syntax attuned to the rhythms of immediate self-inspection (marked in the following passage by the defensive present-tense self-acquittals, couched in 'more humble standard', such as 'it is not for me', 'let me be clear', and the circumlocutory 'if I go so far as to suggest'). This change at the level of the sentence allows *The Remains of the Day* to shift key again, where its well-paced documentary on the history of a household diminishes into a more tortuous mode of subjective self-qualification:

> Of course, it is not for me to suggest that I am worthy of ever being placed alongside the likes of the 'great' butlers of our generation, such as Mr Marshall or Mr Lane – though it should be said there are those who, perhaps out of misguided generosity, tend to do this. Let me be clear that when I say the conference of 1923, and that night in particular, constituted a turning point in my professional development, I am speaking very much in terms of my own more humble standards. Even so, if you consider the pressures contingent on me that night, you may not think I delude myself unduly if I go so far as to suggest that I did perhaps display, in the face of everything, at least in some modest degree a 'dignity' worthy of someone like Mr Marshall – or come to that, my father. Indeed, why should I deny it? (Ishiguro 1989: 110)

Stevens's final question is rhetorical. It is deeply tragic as well, however, insinuating as it does that Stevens could not have answered in any other way. This query seems genuine and wholly required; it sounds like a gesture of appeal. But at the same time, Stevens poses it to himself, to the values he has inherited. The purpose of the question is not to seek an answer, but to reassure Stevens who, in isolation, tries to gauge his achievement, while feeling heretical for doing so – standing up to the arbiters of 'dignity' before applying that august noun to himself.

Moments of pause like these reveal how Stevens's mannerisms secrete deeper implications about a life devoted to professional confinement. Hesitancy, for instance, is a more than a verbal tic. It is freighted with history, betraying a speaker who has become a victim of his own rhetorical propriety, almost too cautious to associate his own work as a butler with a word that he considers to be loaded with honour. Complementing the fact that for Stevens it seems impertinent to award himself the mark of 'dignity', Ishiguro also has him contravene certain rules of address that have prevailed to this point in the novel. A second-person ('you') mode intrudes, not so much consolidating our sympathy as co-opting us as jury members open to being persuaded – so long as 'you' join Stevens to 'consider the pressures' upon him in service. This modulation to the second-person achieves the effect of implicating the reader in a stringent, sincere, and personal debate about 'greatness', while at the same time confronting us with the apparent arbitrariness of making such a prescription at all. Again, this change in register is revealing of the connection between characterization and narrative discourse. It is an instance of a narrator who has all but relinquished his own customary style, disowning what linguists call the *iconicity* of his own voice: the traits by which we identify a character's lexical habits and predispositions. Forgoing his hallmark temperance and propriety, Stevens directs questions to us and to his own 'humble standards', questions whose resolute tone discloses the very insecurities he seeks to appease when 'speaking' in this practised rhetoric of modesty.

Equally unostentatious is Ishiguro's structural use throughout of associative memories, as they impact on the arc of the novel's narrative. Stevens's road trip into the provinces, occupying the 'present-day', corresponds with that other journey – from reminiscence to self-examination and finally to regret – that he cannot prevent himself from embarking upon. 'Day One – Evening, Salisbury' invokes that metaphor of the voyage that Ishiguro has exploited throughout his fiction, where quests become structural tropes, turning his narratives into journeys punctuated by sudden recollections:

> It is hard to explain my feelings once I did finally set off. For the first twenty minutes or so of motoring, I cannot say I was seized by excitement or antici-pation at all. This was due, no doubt, to the fact that though I motored fur-ther and further from the house, I continued to find myself in surroundings with which I had at least a passing acquaintance. Now I had always sup-posed I had travelled very little, restricted as I am by my responsibilities in the house, but of course, over time, one does make various excursions for one professional reason or another, and it would seem I have become much more acquainted with those neighbouring districts than I had realized. For as I say, as I motored on in the sunshine towards the Berkshire border, I con-tinued to be surprised by the familiarity of the country around me. (Ishiguro 1989: 23)

The grammar of the opening sentence encapsulates the challenges Stevens faces in finding a language adequate for describing his recent experiences of displacement. It is as though the voyaging into what might seem to be benign rural landscape has entailed a voyage away from customary modes of articulating himself. Instead, he begins his reflections with a clause that immediately draws our attention to its awkwardness, revealing how much more comfortable he would be documenting from decades rather than days ago. The tortuous twist in tense from present-perfect to the anterior thought of 'feelings once' he 'set off' embodies syntactically the difficulty he has in dealing with more immediate emotions with any precision.

Stevens's increasing yet uncharacteristic use of elaborate analogies to describe what he feels draws our eye again to the episode's language over its background landscape. From his swelling ornamentations we can infer his gradual estrangement from this new countryside:

> But then eventually the surroundings grew unrecognizable and I knew I had gone beyond all previous boundaries. I have heard people describe the moment, when setting sail in a ship, when one finally loses sight of the land. I imagine the experience of unease mixed with exhilaration often described in connection with this moment is very similar to what I felt in the Ford as the surroundings grew strange to me. (Ishiguro 1989: 23–24)

Stevens growing 'unease' is almost childlike insofar as he is immediately and intuitively fearful of stepping into unfamiliar landscapes that mark his distance from home. It is a measure of Ishiguro's achievement, in orchestrating vision and voice, that he so consistently delineates the world through Stevens's compulsive circumspection. Just as Ishiguro described his guitar playing, so we too can become absorbed in his narrators' immediate expressions while remaining aware of the devices that create their immediacy. In performing the guitar, as we saw, Ishiguro drew a distinction between pure demonstrativeness, at one extreme, and complete immersion in the sounds he was creating, at the other. As a guitarist he discovered the rewards of dedication over pyrotechnic display, knowing that a piece demands from its performer a combined form of concentration: a sense of immersion in the medium alongside the scrupulous employment of practised techniques. It is precisely this kind of concentration that Ishiguro's fiction requires readers to sustain.

Fiction written in the first-person mode highlights this dialogue between surface and depth, between our credulous absorption and the narrator's unreliability, between verbal effects and their formal construction. Yet across his *oeuvre*, Ishiguro has favoured first-person narration not simply as an arena for showing off his craft, so much as a vehicle for concealing his authorial self. It is a mode that has allowed him to be 'less inhibited, more intimate', with each new novel enabling him to 'hide behind a narrator who is very different from me' (Bigsby 2008: 22). Yet this difference, this distancing between character and creator, scarcely counteracts the compassion with which Ishiguro elucidates Stevens's own inhibitions. Nowhere are these more explicit than in everyday conversations, or rather in Stevens's subsequent reflections upon his own capabilities as a conversant. This is where Ishiguro's interest in artifice descends from a purely compositional level, as it were, and enters the world of narrative action, where verbal 'bantering' becomes a topic of concern for Stevens. First, he ponders the risks of exploiting quips and mocking colloquial phrases without forgoing all sincerity. Yet he soon starts to consider, with mild paranoia, his own conversational agility and effectiveness. Such instances of self-scrutiny are touchingly ironic, precisely because they are formulated and presented like moments of higher intuition. Tragicomic statements, they also retain what Ishiguro has called the 'murkiness of someone trying to wade through their memories, trying to manipulate memories' (Mason 1989: 337). Conflicts between rhetorical stunts and conversational sincerity, between Stevens's appearance of control and his disruptive confessions, become part and parcel of that 'texture of memory' as Ishiguro describes it (Mason 1989: 337). These conflicts and instabilities also reveal Stevens's underlying vulnerability. His reluctance to abandon discursive proprieties, even deliberately in the case of convivial banter, is altogether ingrained – integrally part of his physiological make-up, like a failsafe on his speech that cannot be voluntarily unlocked:

> It is quite possible, then, that my employer fully expects me to respond to his bantering in a like manner, and considers my failure to do so a form or negligence. That is, as I say, a matter which has given me much concern. But I must say this business of bantering is not a duty I feel I can ever discharge with enthusiasm. It is all very well, in these changing times, to adapt one's work to take in duties not traditionally within one's realm; but bantering is of another dimension altogether. For one thing, how would one know for sure that at any given moment a response of the bantering sort is truly what is expected? One need hardly dwell on the catastrophic possibility of uttering a bantering remark only to discover it wholly inappropriate. (Ishiguro 1989: 16)

Colloquialisms and witticisms are devices, equivalent to a 'duty'. 'Bantering' is held at arm's length, a 'manner' contrived rather than owned. To banter in the presence of Farraday is to risk exposure and embarrassment, demanding quick-fire interlocutions too artificial to be enjoyed, while making Stevens conscious of assuming verbal idioms that he knows he cannot expertly use. Ishiguro's ironic implication here is that 'bantering' is actually less of an artifice than the professional 'dignity' Stevens holds in such high esteem.

This is not to suggest that Ishiguro is simply exposing constrictive links between propriety and awkwardness for their own sake. For in that case we would have to entertain the ethically unsettling notion that *The Remains of the Day* amounts to satire of its own vulnerable protagonist.

Instead, Ishiguro does something compassionate with the trope of bantering. The duplicitous nature of bantering, as Stevens regards it, is eventually resolved in the novel's closing paragraphs. The subject returns but in a less worrisome guise, as Stevens shifts into an unprecedented idiom of enthused speculation, looking forward to contributing to bantering as 'the key to human warmth' (Ishiguro 1989: 245). His resistance towards what is 'hardly an unreasonable duty' now subsides, disabling that tendency earlier in the novel for pondering his lack of comic eloquence. By way of this shift in tone, Ishiguro offers a touching reprise: reintroducing the topic of bantering as a sometime cause of concern, now of hopeful 'renewed effort'. Bantering has motivated Stevens's self-scrutiny throughout the novel; so its positive return at the close is even more affecting for the way it suspends his emotional stoicism, sparking an admission that turns into a declaration of intent: 'I have of course already devoted much time to developing my bantering skills, but it is possible I have never previously approached the task with the commitment I might have done' (Ishiguro 1989: 245). Alone here yet alive to the prospect of new discursive exchanges, Stevens handles his inadequacies with a certain ease that in itself seems to appease his memory of being such a conversational 'disappointment'. That we find this sense of resolve and determination touching is a measure of the affective relationship we have built up with the novel's tonal and thematic keynotes by this stage. In this sense, Ishiguro adds emotional content to narrative design, using the structure of a repeated motif (that of bantering and its associated anxieties) to elicit sympathy from the reader, as Stevens's thoughts open wide to a solution for what has hitherto led only to introspection, insecurity, even bafflement. While we may be alert to this structural sense of repetition, it does not detract from our feeling of what has changed in Stevens. Hence, we can be fully aware of Ishiguro's craft – insofar as he contrives the thematic return of bantering on the closing page – without diminishing the pathos of Stevens coming to reconsider it now as an activity with which he can potentially engage. In effect, Ishiguro solicits a memory of Stevens's earlier discomfort towards bantering so as to intensify the poignancy of its recapitulation. In the final paragraph of a novel so consumed in retrospections, then, we are left with an image of a character looking forward, switching tenses, stepping into the future-perfect to envision himself cultivating the kind of ironic sensibility from which he appeared so alienated.

By the example he sets in *The Remains of the Day*, it might be tempting – were it not for the subsequent challenge of *The Unconsoled* (1995) – to think of Ishiguro as a writer who remains cautious of overt experimentalism in an effort to have it both ways: to write original fiction without being so artful as to alienate his readership. Yet there are precedents offered by earlier post-war writers who might not immediately be associated with Ishiguro, but who negotiated as he continues to do that choice between telling absorbing stories and extending the possibilities of aesthetic form. In a 1967 essay on the 'Dilemma of the Contemporary Novelist', the novelist and critic Angus Wilson worried about novelists 'no longer having any real communication' with their audience (Wilson 1983: 245). Wilson warned of the modern novel becoming 'over-smooth', lulling its readers into complacency and passive appreciation. As a remedy, he envisaged new benefits to

> [A]llowing the author to speak again, suddenly pulling up the reader who, used to the technique by which he is included in the mind of the narrator, will be reminded in curious and odd ways that this is a novel with the author's voice coming in, being funny at the moment when the reader expects him to be serious, and being deeply serious at the moment when he expects him to be funny. (Wilson 1983: 245)

It would seem that Wilson is pointing out the benefits of writing in the third-person, where the implied author has more room for manoeuvre as a commentator. Ishiguro continues to work 'behind a narrator' who recalls experiences so distinctly his own, rather than 'allowing the author to speak again' intrusively, as Wilson might recommend. Nevertheless, there are affinities between Wilson's hopes for a reader who is observant of writers who adopt various authorial personae, amusing and tragic, and Ishiguro's way of bringing us to the surface of his prose when we least expect it – compelling us to appreciate his narrative artistry without impinging upon our fascination with his narrator's psychology. For like Wilson, Ishiguro knows that in fiction '[t]here are all sorts of games one can play [. . .] to wake people up' (Wilson 1983: 245), knowing too that there are limits to self-conscious experimentation. For evidence of the extent to which Ishiguro achieves this balance in *The Remains of the Day*, we need look no further than Stevens himself, a character who speaks for his creator when admitting 'a reluctance to change too much of the old ways', yet who equally shows us 'that there is no virtue at all in clinging as some do to tradition merely for its own sake' (Ishiguro 1989: 7).

CHAPTER SIX

'To Give a Name, Is That Still to Give?': Footballers and Film Actors in *The Unconsoled*

RICHARD ROBINSON

Chapter Summary: *The Unconsoled* (1995) draws many of the names for minor figures from footballers who have played in the World Cup finals and from characters in Josef von Sternberg's film, *Der Blaue Engel* (1930). This chapter examines this naming practice as one example of the way the novel buries rather than flaunts secret codes and arcane knowledge. These name-signs are not quite arbitrary but neither do they solve the riddles of this enigmatic text: they invite both under- and over-interpretation. What is the value and significance of such names? By attending to *The Unconsoled*'s cryptonyms, the reader shares still more closely in the experience of disorientation so typical of Ishiguran narrators.

The Unconsoled (1995) accommodates over a hundred different proper nouns. Beyond the nuclei of the main characters and the supporting cast, many of these names are those of walk-on characters or episodic settings, or of even more peripheral figures and places mentioned fleetingly in dialogue: 'the Jürgen Flemming prize' (Ishiguro 1995: 74); 'The Werdenberger Woods are very pleasant' (Ishiguro 1995: 184). This pyramidal nomenclature seems to replicate the orthodox apparatus of the realist novel. The psychological conflicts of the protagonists, and the interior world of Ryder himself, are propped up or fleshed out by the illusion of particularity these names seem to confer.

However, the Central European city that forms the setting of the novel itself, and the country to which it belongs, are conspicuously *unnamed*. Ishiguro himself has said that 'you could set that thing [i.e., *The Unconsoled*] anywhere' (Krider 1998: 151). This broader anonymity has attracted the critical charge that the novel lacks cultural, social, and historical 'determinants' (Chaudhuri 1995: 30). *The Unconsoled* provides names for its fictional milieu, but leaves blank the specificities of a recognizable historical environment.

This chapter focuses on how this discrepancy is further complicated by the covert naming practices of the novel. Names, it emerges, have been borrowed from a series of sources that can neither be fully established nor ignored. I will first concentrate on two intertextual 'supplies', World Cup footballers and the film *Der Blaue Engel* (1930), before discussing the implications of this naming procedure in relation to realism and postmodernism. Finally, I will ask what broader questions of textual interpretation – regarding the intentions of the author, the paranoia or freedom of the reader, and what Jacques Derrida called the 'safeness' of the name – are thrown open by *The Unconsoled*.

World Cup Footballers

A remarkable number of names in *The Unconsoled* derive from European (mainly West German) footballers who have appeared in finals of the World Cup. Some names are common enough, but others are not; the disproportionate number leaves beyond doubt our perception of authorial design.

The World Cup final of 1954, between West Germany and Hungary, unearths Helmut Rahn ('And that dog attacked Mrs Rahn only earlier this year'; Ishiguro 1995: 143); Werner Liebrich ('There was for instance the unfortunate case of Mr Liebrich'; Ishiguro 1995: 100); Hans Schaefer ('with him is Mr Schaefer' [Ishiguro 1995: 100]) and Alfred 'Aki' Schmidt ('Mr Schmidt keeps coming in every so often'; Ishiguro 1995: 251). That is not the last we shall hear of the final dubbed the 'Battle of Berne'.

To the English reader, the best-known of all finals, England versus West Germany in 1966, is well-represented. Hans Tilkowski, Germany's goalkeeper, beaten four – or was it three? – times ('I had Mrs Tilkowski as my piano teacher'; Ishiguro 1995: 71); goal scorers Helmut Haller ('Of course, Mr Haller'; Ishiguro 1995: 142); and Wolfgang Weber ('One of the gentlemen, I think it was Mr Weber, was escorting her out'; Ishiguro 1995: 161); and the captain, Uwe Seeler ('our local company, Seeler Brothers'; Ishiguro 1995: 379).

Other West German footballers from the 1970s onwards possibly include Manfred ('Manny') Kaltz ('Ah, old Mr Kaltz'; Ishiguro 1995: 432); Klaus Fischer ('and Mr Fischer'; Ishiguro 1995: 234); Bernd Schuster, blond-haired, maverick libero who fell out with the German football federation and was not taken to the finals ('According to Mrs Schuster'; Ishiguro 1995: 501); Wolfgang Dremmler ('But Mr Dremmler here'; Ishiguro 1995: 106); and Jürgen Kohler ('Mr Kohler the chemist'; Ishiguro 1995: 101).

Of non-West German footballers of the 1970s, the most prominent are Alan Mullery, scorer for England against Germany in Mexico 1970 (the modernist composer Mullery, author of challenging works such as *Asbestos and Fibre* (Ishiguro 1995: 328) and *Ventilations* (Ishiguro 1995: 346); Wlodzimierz Lubanski of Poland (Dr Lubanski is the seditious former friend of Christoff; Ishiguro 1995: 193ff.); Johann ('Hans') Krankl, prob-ably Austria's most famous footballer ('Mr Krankl's coffee house'; Ishig-uro 1995: 29); and perhaps Jan Jongbloed, Holland's goalkeeper ('Hans Jongboed!'; Ishiguro 1995: 105). Edmundo ('even that Edmundo'; Ishig-uro 1995: 251); and Angelo Peruzzi ('I need to go somewhere bigger, study under someone like Lubetkin or Peruzzi'; Ishiguro 1995: 520) were 1990s World Cup footballers.

The reader may be alerted to these sources because the World Cup forms an explicit though minor theme in the novel. First of all, on the plane journey to the city, Ryder remembers a man asking him 'some lit-tle quiz question' about World Cup footballers (Ishiguro 1995: 15). Ryder himself tries to recall the names of the 1970s Dutch players in a match between Holland and West Germany but fails to remember two names, which are on 'the rim of his recall': he fails fully to 'unlock' his memory, claiming he is put off by the plashing of the fountain (Ishiguro 1995: 24).

We later discover what the trivia question put by the man on the plane was: who were the three pairs of brothers who had played together in World Cup finals (Ishiguro 1995: 161–162)? The memory has now become strangely distant: 'But then ever since, on occasions such as this when I found myself with a rare few minutes to myself, I would find the man's question coming back to me' (Ishiguro 1995: 162) – that 'ever since' suggesting the question was not in fact put to Ryder the day before. This is a minor example of how Ryder's memory distends or compresses time in the novel, so that, for example, a rusty family car from childhood – a fragment of Proustian 'lost time' – rises to the sur-face of the present (Ishiguro 1995: 260–262).

Ryder remembers the Charlton brothers for England and the Van der Kerkhoffs for Holland. If Ishiguro were playing a fully Nabokovian game, the third pair of brothers would perhaps not exist. But the text's codenames, which have thrown up the Berne final against the 'marvel-lous Magyars', give us the answer. It was in this game that the famous West German captain Fritz Walter appeared together with his less well-known brother, Ottmar. The answer is in the text, but at a subconscious rather than conscious level.

The 'total football' Dutch side of the 1970s seems to obsess Ryder. There is a precise description of the second goal – a stupendous 40-yard shot scored by Adrianus ('Arie') Haan for the Netherlands against a 'curiously transfixed' Italian defence. Although he has earlier recalled his name (Ishiguro 1995: 24), and describes the goal in some detail, he cannot name Haan. TV footage reveals how accurately Ishiguro – through Ryder – describes rather than invents this football memory.

Whenever Ryder is immersed in World Cup trivia, he fails to recover a complete memory. As a boy Ryder played with toy soldiers as his par-ents argued furiously downstairs; Boris enacts ludicrous comebacks on a faintly archaic-sounding Subbuteo table (also reminiscent of 1970s foot-ball) and hankers after his Number Nine. The destructive perfectionism of the concert pianist, we realize, is not unconnected to his Panini-sticker completism: manifestations of the obsessive-compulsive type. The solipsism and displacement activity of a child from a troubled home are continuous with the pathology of the adult. That Ryder dwells on football, like Boris, reminds us that the child is father to the man.

The *Unconsoled* and *Der Blaue Engel*

Names are not *exclusively* drawn from World Cup footballers. There is, for example, another subset taken from the film *Der Blaue Engel*. It is as though half the cast and crew of that film appear in disguise in *The Unconsoled*: director Josef von Sternberg ('Sternberg Garden'; Ishiguro 1995: 146); Erwin Jannings, the male lead ('Horst Jannings, the city's most senior actor'; Ishiguro 1995: 381); Karl Vollmöller, a playwright and screenwriter ('Mr Vollmöller, a very fine composer'; Ishiguro 1995: 98); Wilhelm Diegelmann, in the cast and also an actor in Lubitsch films ('Professor Diegelmann's children'; Ishiguro 1995: 71); Robert Liebmann, co-writer ('Liebmann Park'; Ishiguro 1995: 101); Eduard von Winterstein, actor (the often mentioned mayor, Mr von Winterstein; Ishiguro 1995: 60); and Friedrich Holländer, who composed the music ('I agree with Mr Holländer'; Ishiguro 1995: 143).

Der Blaue Engel, based upon Heinrich Mann's pre-war novel *Professor Unrat*, was released in 1930, towards the end of the golden era of Weimar and German Expressionist cinema. The film is well-known for bringing international attention to Marlene Dietrich, and the song known in English as 'Falling in Love Again (Can't Help It)'. A buttoned-up, strict schoolteacher, Professor Rath (played by Emil Jannings), learns his pupils have been attending a disreputable nightclub. Determined to confront the source of this immorality, Rath visits the *Blaue Engel* and is immediately enchanted by the singer Lola Lola (played by Dietrich). He proposes to her and joins her troupe, but is subsequently degraded and humiliated. The climax of the film involves Jannings performing a routine back at the *Blaue Engel* in front of an expectant home-town audience, in which he imitates the crowing of a cock. Driven mad, he continues his crowing off-stage and tries to strangle the unfaithful Lola; he crawls back to his old schoolroom to die.

An intertextual interpretation of the film and *The Unconsoled* may be constructed as follows. Both plots include the combination of artistic performance and anxiety about public humiliation. Siegfried Kracauer (1947) emphasizes the cruelty of the petit bourgeois audience in *Der Blaue Engel*, 'the masses [who] are irresistibly attracted by the spectacle of torture and humiliation' (Kracauer 1947: 217). Rath performs his schoolmasterly role in front of an unsympathetic classroom of boys; eventually, a baying audience sees eggs cracked over his head while his crowing grows ever wilder.

Ryder, the artist, perceives the awaiting audience as a painfully dependent organism capable of rapture or contempt. The perfectionist imagines the disaster of critical opprobrium being heaped upon him, only to be relieved and then nonchalant when everything works out well, as it always seems to. Those who have to put up with this cycle, like Sophie, recognize the pattern all too clearly:

> From all over the world you phone to say the same thing [. . .] They're going to turn on me, they're going to find me out. And what happens? A few hours later you call again, and you're very calm and self-satisfied. I ask you how it went and you sound mildly surprised I should even bring it up. (Ishiguro 1995: 444)

The occupational obsessiveness of the long-serving porter (Gustav), the hotel manager-cum-artistic director (Hoffman), the aspirant or internationally acclaimed concert pianist (Stephan, Ryder), and indeed of the author promoting a new book, must finally be tested and proved in the public's gaze. It is no coincidence that, in one of the funniest set-pieces of the novel, Ishiguro puts Ryder through the prospect of a question-and-answer session (Ishiguro 1995: 381–382) – seemingly absurd for a pianist on stage though now *de rigueur* for the writer.

Although the inhabitants of the Central European city are often creepily deferential to Ryder, the spectacle of public humiliation is near the surface. In the classic expression of dream anxiety, Ryder does expose himself in public, though luckily without dire consequences (Ishiguro 1995: 143). The citizens can be withering about whomever is out of favour, be that Christoff or Brodsky, and the audience's antagonism reaches nightmarish depths: during the local poet's recital drunken sections of the audience play cards while hectoring him as a cuckold (Ishiguro 1995: 484–85). Stephan's first performance (of a difficult modernist piece) takes place without the audience even noticing: the auditorium lights are not dimmed and they take him to be a sound technician (Ishiguro 1995: 478). Brodsky's humiliation, complete with sawn off wooden leg, collapsing ironing-boards, and febrile conducting, is perhaps closest to Professor Rath's chicken-and-egg routine at the *Blaue Engel*. Ryder himself, of course, strides on to the stage at breakfast time, before a completely empty auditorium in which all chairs have been stacked away; he does not even have the chance to fail (Ishiguro 1995: 519). These are the irrational imaginings of artistic inadequacy – of the performance being met with scorn or indifference, or of it simply being a non-performance – that the unconscious produces.

Professor Rath goes mad and dies. While the novel stops short of this, Ryder nonetheless breaks down, sobbing in front of Miss Stratmann because of the non-appearance of his parents, and then suffering the final rupture from his partly unacknowledged family, Sophie and Boris. The community has reached an equilibrium of its own accord, despite the personal disasters of Brodsky and Hoffman and the death of Gustav; Ryder, the saviour, is even deprived the consolation of consoling others. He circles the city on the tram in a kind of contentment, but like Rath's schoolroom, the carriage in which the rider revolves is a temporary shelter from an outside world that has defeated him.

The aesthetics of the film, while not as outrightly Expressionist as those of F. W. Murnau and G. W. Pabst, for example, are still associable with Weimar Expressionism. Kracauer writes that the 'inner life manifests itself in various elements and conglomerations of external life', and of Sternberg as a 'master of the art of rendering *milieus* so that they amplified imperceptible emotions' (Kracauer 1947: 7; 216). In the film 'narrow interiors are endowed with a power of expression' (Kracauer 1947: 217), and psychological dispositions are manifested in film – space that, in Erwin Panofsky's words, 'itself moves, changing, turning, dissolving and recrystallizing' (Kracauer 1947: 6). Sternberg's film may be seen as a work of Central European modernism. The physics of Ishiguro's novel – with its own narrow interiors, its 'whole milieu a scene of loosened instincts' (Kracauer 1947: 217) – seem to borrow not only from Kafka but also from the space-time of Expressionist films of this sort. Anxiety is turned inside out: psychic fissures are made visible as wounds, stroked in public.

Generally, Kracauer's thesis is that the Weimar films repress a psychological portrait of pre-Nazi Germany, and can eventually be shown to represent and stigmatize a 'secret history' first (Kracauer 1947: 11) involving the mentality of an immature German people. This idea is aligned with the repression and pathological civic insecurity of the citizens in *The Unconsoled*, who have their own 'secret history', gnomically memorialized by the controversial Sattler monument. Kracauer shows that though the film's Expressionist mode may exclude historical and political explicitness, it should not be thought of as ahistorical. The same could be said – in terms of its own cultural and aesthetic grounding – of Ishiguro's novel.

This lack of direct determinants acts as a necessary blankness that encourages allusive enrichment from indirect sources. Dostoevsky, Beckett, Thomas Mann, and of course Kafka, among others, have been identified as literary antecedents. But Ishiguro is a screenwriter and something of a *cinéaste* (see Chapter Two); critics have often noted how his novels suggest the language of film, and Ishiguro himself, referring to Clint Eastwood's unexpected appearance in *The Unconsoled*'s version of *2001: A Space Odyssey* (1968), has spoken of seeing movies in dreams that are 'sort of versions of the real films, but [which] have different actors in them' (Krider 1998: 148).

Thus, the idea of a film as an intertext is not far-fetched. What is more, the practice of half-alluding to films through actors' names may not be new to the author. Ishiguro has acknowledged the influence of the Japanese post-war filmmakers Ozu and Naruse on his novels (Mason and Ishiguro 1989: 336); and Matthew Mead remarked to me that the names of the two sisters in *An Artist of the Floating World* derive from the three Noriko characters, played by Setsuko Hara, in Ozu's Noriko Trilogy: *Late Spring* (1949); *Early Summer* (1951); and *Tokyo Story* (1953).

Names and the Novel

How do the naming procedures of *The Unconsoled* relate to those of the realist and postmodernist novel? The realist novel often aims for – though never seems to quite manage – a certain neutrality or ordinariness in its labelling. Verisimilitude, with its ambition of using real-seeming names, is modified by the acknowledgement, even enjoyment, of how characters can be made allusive, symbolic, or allegorical.

Take, for example, Henry Fielding's *Tom Jones* (1749). A character called Squire Allworthy is, not surprisingly, a good man, but he is also naïve, misjudging Tom and prey to less virtuous characters. So that 'all worthiness' is more than tinged with irony, as if saying that a character cannot match a single moral quality outside of fiction. The sturdy but unremarkable pair of monosyllables 'Tom Jones' is a direct counterpoint to the *notional* goodness of Allworthy. Tom is supposedly 'real' because he has his faults; Tom must have his faults because he is 'real'.

Of course, Tom is no more real than Allworthy: the signifier 'Tom Jones', like 'Allworthy', has a signified. The difference is that it is concealed: Tom has a plausible and concrete 'whatness' designed to make us forget he is fictional. In Graham Greene's novels, even names like Mr Brown or Mr Wilson have a fictional aura – they somehow import, by their sheer common-or-garden status, a certain English drabness into Greene's tropical climes. These are manifestations of Roland Barthes's (1989) 'reality effect'. In realism, the given name may often disguise itself as a marker of a character's (often moral) role; it may suppress the idea of name-as-sign, producing the paradoxical idea that the name is semantically anonymous. But often an opposite tendency emerges. Thinking of Dickens as a model of classic mid-nineteenth-century realism is evidently problematic, and his use of caricatured names like M'Choakumchild merely confirms this. Even for George Eliot, there are nomenclatural dilemmas intrinsic to the realist ambition of mapping 'Middlemarch' – an inconspicuous, representatively middling type of place.

The archetypal postmodern novel flaunts the idea of name-as-sign. In his reading of Paul Auster's *New York City* (1987) trilogy, David Lodge (1992) points to how the names and naming procedures of these novels are aimed to emphasize the arbitrariness of the sign and the 'fall of language' from its pre-linguistic, Edenic state in which '[a] thing and its name were interchangeable' (Lodge 1992: 39). In *City of Glass* (1985), the detective Stillman deconstructs the name 'Quinn' – rhyming it with twin and sin, and ironically moving on to the 'quintessence of quiddity' it evidently lacks; in *Ghosts* (1986), character names such as Blue, White, and Brown – we may note that two of these names could be taken as realist surnames – nevertheless introduce a 'manifestly arbitrary naming system'. Lodge (1992) writes of how Auster's narratives 'end with the death or despair of the detective-figure, faced with an insoluble mystery, lost in a labyrinth of names' (Lodge 1992: 40).

Where does this leave *The Unconsoled*? It seems to share some sense of postmodernist arbitrariness but without the characteristic postmodern relish for the poststructuralist omni-directionality of the signifier. *The Unconsoled* is more covert about its fabulism. Marlene Dietrich, star of *Der Blaue Engel*, is *not* secreted in the novel; Johan Cruyff and Franz Beckenbauer, the two most famous names among European footballers of the 1970s, are also conspicuous by their absence. Ryder does *not* get lost down Beckenbauerstrasse, is *not* accosted by a certain Marlene Cruyff, as he would in a flamboyantly postmodernist text. Such compound names, because of their cultural ubiquity, would be too near the surface of consciousness. Postmodernist defamiliarization and provisionality, such as that of Auster, would be too easily available.

Rather, there needs to be something peripheral and clandestine about the names of *The Unconsoled*. Valentine Cunningham complained that with the writing of this novel Ishiguro had joined the anti-Forsterian 'Oh-Dear-Me-No-the-Novel-Doesn't-Tell-a-Story lot, the cheese-paring Kafka-Borges-Calvino-Handke tendency' (quoted in Lewis 2000: 125). He thus unfavourably aligned *The Unconsoled* with a radical poetics of postmodernism, but, as we have seen, in secreting rather than flaunting the borrowed names Ishiguro does not go 'as far over', so to speak, as more obviously self-reflexive texts.

As part of this hedged postmodernism, we may refer to Ishiguro's remark that Eastwood's appearance in *2001: A Space Odyssey* was 'a mistake' on his part (Krider 1998: 148). The Eastwood mistake – of course, deliberate – is from Ishiguro's point of view 'the one place in the book you can actually point to where there is a difference between the book and reality in life' (Krider 1998: 148). Ishiguro goes on to add that he 'would have preferred it if people couldn't have put their finger on what was going on' (Krider 1998: 148).

This seems to be an expression of regret at giving the reader a kind of foothold into an unambiguously anti-realist fictional world. The Eastwood moment is given an objective material substance as flat 'wrong', and confirms the negative ontology of what Brian McHale (1987) sees as the postmodernist other- or anti-world. Eastwood in space – a joke as well as a deliberate mistake – breaks the author-reader contract of *The Unconsoled*: that it must hover around the border between the oneiric-fantastical and the plausibly and concretely 'real', and not allow one mode to predominate. Thus eight or nine things that do not happen in real life (or that happen in dreams) punctuate passages that begin to fall into mimetically real scenes. The novel should never be quite too dreamlike, never quite too lifelike.

The Unconsoled's play with names fits the already established idea that it inhabits a midway point between the ontologies of stable realism and those of postmodernism. But this is no compromised mediation. The disquieting experience of reading this long novel – of being alternately drawn into empathy and then alienated from such credulity – deliberately combines the worst rather than the best of realist and postmodernist worlds. They are disorientatingly fused together in a designedly *un*happy medium.

Model Reading and 'Overstanding'

What general theoretical questions of interpretation – and of the relationship between author, text, and reader – does Ishiguro's curious naming practice throw up? Although we may feel there is a secret significance in World Cup statistics or interwar German films, we cannot blithely discount the possibility that the author, needing to get names from somewhere, surrenders to chance by sticking a pin in an index. This compositional idiosyncrasy may be purely aleatory. At what point does the conscious patterning of names give way to randomness? It seems absurd to argue that someone called Schmidt is connected to a West German footballer in 1958, but it is equally absurd to overlook that there are characters – Seeler, Tilkowski, Weber, and Haller – whose names correspond to the team of the 1966 World Cup final. I would now like to relate this critical question to a debate in *Interpretation and Overinterpretation* (1992) between, among others, Umberto Eco and Jonathan Culler, and in particular their comments on secret meanings, interpretative paranoia, under- and 'overstanding'.

Eco, taking a position against the unlimited semiosis of post-structuralism, argues for a model reader who interprets economically. Can coincidences in the text be explained without resort to some sort of conspiracy theory, without a sense of the author deeply embedding clues and puzzles that only the intrepid detective-reader can bring to light? If they can be explained by a shorter route, argues Eco, then that is the better interpretation. He equates Hermeticism with this readerly paranoia, which sees a direct meaning nowhere and a secret everywhere. This 'excess of wonder' in the reader involves looking for 'signatures' – that is, clues that reveal occult relationships (Collini 1992: 50).

A Hermeticist reader of *The Unconsoled* would emphasize the wonder and importance of uncovering the 'signatures' of the World Cup players and *Der Blaue Engel* cast. This would be a key to cracking the code of the narrative. There would be no doubt about the importance of the intertext – and parallel readings between Weimar cinema and the aesthetics of the novel could proceed confidently. It would not be in this reader's interests to think of these nominal signifiers as randomly chosen.

Judged purely on this exchange in this volume, Culler is less averse to the idea of textual secrecy, of asking questions the text does not encourage us to ask about it. Culler approves Wayne C. Booth's concept of 'overstanding' (as against understanding) – the pursuit of 'questions that the text does not pose to its model reader' (Collini 1992: 114). This avoids a complacent critical consensus, and sheds new light on old texts. He summarizes Barthes' definition of 'overinterpretation' as a 'method that compels people to puzzle over not just those elements which might seem to resist the totalization of meaning but also *those about which there might initially seem to be nothing to say'*. Such a method 'has a better chance of producing discoveries [. . .] than one which seeks only to answer those questions that a text asks its model reader' (Collini 1992: 122; my emphasis). Culler argues that fear of overinterpretation may repress just this 'excess of wonder' that gives us an exciting awareness of our role in finding or joining in the play of meaning (Collini 1992: 122–23).

This approach would regard the identification of the shadowy sources of *The Unconsoled* as a 'discovery'. There initially seems to be nothing much to say about proper nouns in novels – or if there is, it is as a prelude to the business of 'deep' interpretation of the content. Finding there is something to say about a seemingly unimportant stratum of the text brings on a quiet 'state of wonder'. These names may be clues to a non-existent mystery, but they cannot be dismissed as red herrings.

Eco himself recognizes that there may be an unintended attaching of values to the name. He named a character in *Foucault's Pendulum* (1988) Casaubon, after Isaac Casaubon, who demonstrated that the *Corpus Hermeticum* was a forgery. He had forgotten that Casaubon was the name of a character in *Middlemarch* (serialised form in 1871–72, one volume 1874), and inserted a scrap of dialogue into the novel, in which Casaubon denies knowing the Eliot character, in order supposedly to 'eliminate' the reference to George Eliot. Are we as readers thus overinterpreting by linking Eliot's Mr Casaubon, who was writing *A Key to all Mythologies*, to Eco's book about the kabbalah, forgeries, and secret meanings?

Though there was no authorial intention, a meaning is *in the text*. Eco admits to having read Eliot's novel decades before – who is to say it was not residing at a deep level of his unconscious? This transmigration from the unconscious to the page reveals that between 'the unattainable intention of the author and the arguable intention of the reader there is the transparent intention of the text' (Collini 1992: 78); 'the text qua text still represents a comfortable presence' (Collini 1992: 88). The border between an author's conscious intentions and his or her unconscious motivations is porous and finally unknowable, as is the border between a reader's securely economical if uninspired interpretations and his or her exciting, though possibly tenuous, overinterpretations. But the notion of an intention in the text helps us to negotiate these borders more confidently.

Would the model author of *The Unconsoled* want the model reader to be completely indifferent to our antennae picking up on 'Kazan' (film director Elia), 'Walser' (Swiss writer Robert), 'Lubetkin' (modernist architect Berthold), for example? Is it the act of the properly 'overstanding' model reader to trawl the film and football archive, or is it rather the paranoia of the Hermeticist? We may feel unable to answer this question, but we should not let the real author answer it either. The main point to be made is that the act of interpretation has been anticipated – deliberately designed – to prompt certain responses in the reader. The urge to seek connections co-exists with an awareness of our inability to prove them. We might wonder if we have been 'set-up'. We are, quite appropriately, bemused by this hermeneutic displacement, banished from final meaning.

Safe, the Name?

The Unconsoled blurs the borders between a waking life we can account for, and the latent life of our unacknowledged compulsions. As Garry Adelman (2001) has written, there is in the novel 'a double level of consciousness: that of the external world as seen by the subjective, or solipsistic dream narrator, and that of the narrator's core personality as portrayed, that is, cast and performed, by the other characters' (Adelman 2001: 168–169). The football and film names are indeed such a cast of *performers*. Adelman's conception of the novel's structure would suggest that its names are not distributed randomly but are determined by an inner self – that Ryder displaces identities through some obscure logic of the unconscious. Thus, Germany's hapless goalkeeper *becomes*, in the dream state, a revered female piano teacher; their captain, a renowned carriage-maker. An actor from *Der Blaue Engel* can turn up as the city's mayor.

This Freudian model of Ryder's mind implicates the proper name, as *The Psychopathology of Everyday Life* (1901) makes quite clear. Freud (1982) had to invent names for his casebook analysands. He realized that he had not accidentally called his patient Dora, for example: the only Dora he knew, his sister's nursemaid, had to forfeit her real name Rosa while working in the house (there was another Rosa there); both 'Doras', then, were affected by their employment in someone else's house (Freud 1982: 302). The name is not inertly at one with the person: it is a floating signifier in the unconscious. Freud explains that he kept forgetting to buy blotting paper (which he would write down as *Löschpapier* but crucially ask for as *Fliesspapier*) because of anxieties over his friendship with Wilhelm Fliess (Freud 1982: 212).

The sourcing of names in Ishiguro's novel thus suggests ways of reading Ryder, of bringing the depths of his unconscious memories to the surface. The novel begins to read as a Freudian casebook, a mimetic objectification of the 'messy' unconscious. But we are not psychoanalysts, decoding Ryder's dream-work, converting manifest into latent content. The Expressionist, inside-out subjectivity of *The Unconsoled* should not assume too great an ontological solidity.

We are made aware that Ishiguro has also teasingly set up a treasure hunt in which the reader's own role, in recovering ghostly oneiric meanings or in over-determining meaning, is emphasized. Deep psychological truths, we are alarmed to concede, may have their origin in an act of authorial contingency – an afternoon's flipping through film directories or World Cup archives. In many of his notebook entries Henry James wrote long lists of names that he had come across in that day's newspapers; he would even scour Ordnance Survey maps to provide character names (Edel and Powers 1987). Working in his Parisian apartment, Joyce would have an Armenian dictionary to hand, or a gazetteer listing the world's rivers; and these words and names – starting life as depthless signifiers – would enrich the semiosis of *Finnegans Wake* (Joyce 1939; see also Škrabánek 2002).

How meaningful could such names be? The name *seems* to guarantee a certain safeness, *seems* to be different from less reliable parts of the language. Jacques Derrida writes about the punning meanings of '*Sauf le nom*', asking to what extent we should except (*sauf*) the name from other words which are not safe (*sauf*). The name expresses a lack, a need to re-name with the *surnom* (not a surname but an added nickname: William cannot be just William but William *the Conqueror*). To Derrida (1995), there is a kind of nullity and referential inadequacy to the name that can prompt him to ask, 'To give a name, is that still to give? Is that to give something?' (Derrida 1995: 84). The name neither belongs to those who give it nor to those who receive it. To Derrida, the name is unsurprisingly as supplementary as the rest of language – 'sur-naming' is the excess of re-naming after the lack.

At the same time, the proper name retains a singularity or untranslatability as 'pseudonym, or cryptonym' (Derrida 1995: xiv). The naming of *The Unconsoled* includes this inauthenticity of the pseudonym and this secrecy of the cryptonym. Ishiguro gives secret names, but he may be giving nothing. The 'core' of Ryder is peopled by an ersatz cast of lay figures. Though Ishiguro's first-person narrators – once we have broken through their armature – seem to offer us the full subjectivity of an inner life, they too reveal themselves to be made up a string of signifiers that lie flat upon the page.

Most importantly, attempting to decrypt Ryder, and those who inhabit his dream-world, is a readerly experience that ends up as part of the Ishiguran 'content'. We know how Ishiguro's earlier narrators, with their own processes of self-delusion and occlusion, misread the past, both personally and historically. Ryder is another of those who over- and under-interpret, but his interpretative deficiencies imply an acknowledgement of our own. We collude in, and are secret sharers of, Ryder's disorientation, and perform the same allegories of misreading.

CHAPTER SEVEN

When We Were Orphans: Narration and Detection in the Case of Christopher Banks

HÉLÈNE MACHINAL

Chapter Summary: Readers of *When We Were Orphans* (2000) are immersed in a world redolent of the tales of Sherlock Holmes and the classic detective stories. Our generic and formal expectations, however, are gradually shown to be in tension with the course of historical events – the fall of Shanghai – in which the narrator, Christopher Banks, is caught up. This chapter explores how Kazuo Ishiguro's strategy of having the world of the book distorted, adopting the logic of the narrator exposes the ideological implications of the whole genre of the turn-of-the-century detective story.

The narrator of *When We Were Orphans* (2000) is a familiar figure to readers acquainted with Kazuo Ishiguro's work. A first-person narrator engaged in a complex process of retrospection, Christopher Banks demonstrates a combination of conviction, uncertainty, and unreliability as he seeks to understand his world, himself, and his past. We are again faced with a diligent professional examining of his relation to world-historical events; the fate of his parents; the nature of his closest personal relationships; and, ultimately, the ethics of his chosen role. The most obvious, immediate connection one makes is with *The Remains of the Day* (1989), in which the elderly butler looks back on the heyday of his professional career and reflects on what he has, and has not, achieved. That narrative explores Stevens's role in the great events of history with which the country house has been connected, but also in personal relationships, with his father, with the housekeeper Miss Kenton, and with Lord Darlington, which have defined his life.

Despite such similarities, and the evident thematic continuities with the first-person narrators of his early novels, in many important ways *When We Were Orphans* marks a dramatic change in Ishiguro's fiction, a change at least as radical and dynamic, if less overt, as the one signalled by the immediately preceding novel, *The Unconsoled* (1995). The ethics of personal responsibility, and the relation of the individual to broad historical currents and processes, certainly remain the central concerns of this writing, but there are significant formal, generic, and stylistic innovations in *When We Were Orphans* that embody a further stage in the evolution of this variegated and powerful *oeuvre*. Ishiguro commented at the time of publication on the nature of this shift:

> I didn't want to write a realistic book with a crazy narrator. I wanted to actually have the world of the book distorted, adopting the logic of the narrator. In painting you often see that [. . .] where everything is distorted to reflect the emotion of the artist who is looking at the world. [. . .] The whole world portrayed in that book starts to tilt and bend in an attempt to orchestrate an alternative kind of logic. (Richards 2000)

In this chapter I will examine, in particular, the way Ishiguro achieves this goal, 'to actually have the world of the book distorted, adopting the logic of the narrator', by exploiting the reader's generic and formal expectations – of classic detective fiction, of contemporary first-person narrative, and of Ishiguro's own typology of unreliable narrators. *When We Were Orphans* is a powerful examination of the conventional figure and function of the detective, and a text that exposes and ruptures the deeper ideological implications of the genre itself.

Narration and Detective Fiction: 'But Surely He's Rather Too Short To Be a Sherlock'

When We Were Orphans directly invokes the narratological traditions and expectations of classic detective fiction, and above all the familiar figure of Sherlock Holmes. In the opening section allusions to the canonical texts of Arthur Conan Doyle are legion; indeed Banks begins to write, according to the date on the opening page (24 July 1930), shortly after Conan Doyle's death (7 July 1930). Address, *décor*, and geography of Banks's lodgings, 14b Bedford Gardens, closely recall 221b Baker Street and the nineteenth-century London of Sherlock Holmes:

> The rent was not high, but my landlady had furnished the place in a tasteful manner that evoked an unhurried Victorian past; the drawing room which received plenty of sun throughout the first half of the day, contained an ageing sofa as well as two snug arm-chairs, an antique sideboard and an oak bookcase filled with crumbling encyclopedias – all of which I was convinced would win the approval of any visitor. (Ishiguro 2001: 3)

Banks is visited here by an old acquaintance Osbourne, with whom he engages in a discussion ('the activities of the workers' unions, [. . .]

a long and enjoyable debate on German philosophy' [Ishiguro 2001: 4]), which ostentatiously evokes Holmes's intellectual *brio*, and, although Banks is reticent about declaring his own ambitions, the two young men then contemplate the city presented as the future stage of their exploits. In the course of the novel we learn only incidentally of his cases, which is another Holmesian trait: the numerous undocumented investigations to which the great detective and Dr Watson allude in the course of *other* inquiries are a familiar, teasing motif in Conan Doyle's tales. Banks's rhetoric and methods, such as the magnifying glass (Ishiguro 2001: 9; 31; 254), the confidence in theoretical reasoning and science as the means to combat criminals (Ishiguro 2001: 7; 16; 32), and above all the famous Holmesian self-assurance (Ishiguro 2001: 21; 137–38) are precisely derived from those of his famous forbear. Economically and effectively, Ishiguro establishes this recognizable terrain by setting up the generic expectation that our rational and dispassionate detective will solve whatever mystery is laid before him. In endowing Banks with something of the aura and esteem of Sherlock Holmes, he establishes his narrator's credentials as, by profession and temperament, trustworthy and humane. Banks *is* apparently a renowned and successful detective, even allowing for any elements of exaggeration in his self-presentation (Ishiguro 2001: 36; 67; 161).

The reader's inclination to trust this particular first-person narrator, and to cherish some anticipation as to the course of the narrative, is further reinforced by Banks's manner and attitude. He is given to thoughtful reflection about his own past, and his voice differs according to the distance – and, as he repeatedly remarks, the hindsight (Ishiguro 2001: 58; 163; 240) – he has acquired. He is repeatedly and quite disarmingly frank concerning his uncertainty about his recollections (Ishiguro 2001: 25; 42; 67; 85; 113; 189). In the opening sections of the novel, written from the vantage of 1930 and 1931, the narrator recalls his early years in London, back in 1923, and this older, self-deprecating, narrative voice emphasizes his more mature and measured understanding of that period through expressions such as 'How curious to recall a time' (Ishiguro 2001: 18), and 'It is again typical of my smugness of those days' (Ishiguro 2001: 20). The reader is perhaps more ready to trust a first-person narrator who seems able so rationally and objectively to evaluate his own reliability both in the past, and in his recollection of that past.

When Banks recalls his departure as a child from Shanghai, he scrupulously tries to reassess his memories, taking into account the vision of the child he was at the time (Ishiguro 2001: 68). As befits the meticulous detective, he appears profoundly conscious of the way memory selects and modifies facts and situations according to the pressures of the affect, context, and intention involved in the process of recollection:

> [T]here is little chance Jennifer will fail to remember very clearly our last encounter there. But she is an intelligent girl, and whatever her immediate

emotions, she may well understand all that I will say to her. She may even
grasp, more quickly than did her nanny last night, that when she is older –
when this case has become a triumphant memory – she will truly be glad
I rose to the challenge of my Responsibilities (Ishiguro 2001: 149).

Despite such reassuring evidence of narratorial scruple, however, readerly suspicion is nevertheless awakened as a result of a number of gaps
and inconsistencies that point towards discrepancies between the detective's self-image and the vision others have of him, be it in the present
or in the past. Certainly many characters refer to Banks's impressive
record and reputation as a detective (Ishiguro 2001: 32; 137; 159), and he
appears to have resolved many cases. However, even in the opening
chapters of the novel, first Osbourne, and then Colonel Chamberlain,
offer accounts of Banks's childhood that irritate our narrator, who rejects
their versions as erroneous (Ishiguro 2001: 5; 27). Banks's self-image is
much more positive: 'It has always been a puzzle to me that Osbourne
should have said such a thing of me that morning, since my own memory is that I blended perfectly into English school life' (Ishiguro 2001: 7).
These moments begin to weaken the credibility of the narrative voice,
although – as with Stevens – their primary function is to indicate something of Banks's vanity or self-conceit – note that in the description of
his lodgings reproduced earlier, he records his conviction that the rooms
'would win the approval of any visitor', a remark that reveals both
vanity and the desire for the approval and validation of an audience.

Once the detective is in Shanghai, however, Anthony Morgan recalls
the schoolboy Banks as a 'miserable loner' (Ishiguro 2001: 183), a memory again at odds with the narrator's vision of himself. Banks's explanation of Morgan's 'self-delusion' is one that the reader might readily
suspect is more apt an account of the narrator's own disposition:

> But his assertion that I had likewise been a 'miserable loner', one with whom
> he might have made a matching pair, was such an astounding one, it took me
> a little while to realize it was simply a piece of self-delusion on Morgan's
> part – in all likelihood something he had invented years ago to make more
> palatable memories of an unhappy period. (Ishiguro 2001: 183–84)

Our sense of Banks's psychology and motivation runs increasingly
counter to the generic expectations embedded in the first two parts of
the novel. Banks is represented as something of a type, but then his own
childhood, and his own commitments and desires, introduce personal
and specific elements to the story that jar with the model of the great,
impersonal, and disinterested detective. Sherlock Holmes's character
and temperament is for the most part presented as intrinsic to his unique
ratiocinative qualities, and his behaviour is seen always to be in the
service or peculiar logic of his inquiry. Banks's personality has little evident or focussed relation to his work or his mission, nor do they seem to

fit him necessarily for a career in detective work. Little is ever revealed of Holmes's motivations, but our narrator explains that his ambition to be a detective derives directly from his experiences as a child. Banks reports, for instance, that his 'research into the background of those years I spent in Shanghai' was preparation for 'the day I began in earnest my investigations into the whole affair concerning my parents [. . .] It remains my intention to embark on such an investigation in the none-too-distant future' (Ishiguro 2001: 113). His personal 'case' is thus presented as the origin of his desire to become a detective, an aspiration that is clear in his childhood games with Akira and is readily observed by his fellow schoolboys (Ishiguro 2001: 7; 15). Oddly, the emphasis on the personal case throws into relief a tendency in Banks towards prevarication and delay, which we find to be one of his defining characteristics. In this he differs greatly from Holmes, whose famous indolence is cast off the instant a case presents itself. It is *twenty years* after the events in Shanghai, and quite some time after discovering her location, that Banks finally visits Hong Kong to see his mother, and even then it is the 'third day' of his trip before he goes to visit her (Ishiguro 2001: 300). The narrative circles back upon the traumatic events preceding his departure from Shanghai following his parents' disappearance (Ishiguro 2001: 23–29; 101–103). In sharp contrast, we learn nothing of the motivations or inner life of Sherlock Holmes, and he is never the focus, object, or beneficiary of his own investigations. Moreover, only five of the Conan Doyle stories – all of them minor, late pieces – are narrated by Holmes himself. It is as we make these distinctions between our narrator and the character upon which he so clearly models himself that we begin to realize that the very form of *When We Were Orphans* is, as it were, a clue to the work's meaning and significance.

In classic detective fiction, form and convention preclude any direct access to the detective's thoughts, his hunches or intimations of a solution to the mystery. First-person narrative might spoil the suspense of a tale that depends for its success not only upon the ultimate revelation of 'who did it' but also the exhibition at that point of the exceptional intellectual skills of the detective. Access to the deductive processes of the sleuth in real time, sharing his suspicions, hunches, and manoeuvres as they happen, would dissolve the force of the *finale*. In Sherlock Holmes stories the narrative voice is generally that of Dr Watson. The focalizer, the primary consciousness in the story (in these cases, the narrator), is close to the detective but acts as a foil, preserving the pleasure of reading until the last moments of revelation and closure. The detective's behaviour is often enigmatic or mysterious, and the resolution of the tale depends upon his (and it is almost invariably 'his') explanation of the process of detection or deduction. In Ishiguro's novel, despite the surfeit of signifiers associating Banks with the classic genre, the detective is himself the narrator – a narrative structure that introduces an introspective dimension characteristic of a later, primarily North American variation of the detective genre, 'hard-boiled' fiction – the work of Raymond Chandler or Dashiell Hammett. This shift from a narrator who can never quite grasp the reasoning process of the great detective, to a detective-narrator whose subjectivity, whose *emotion*, often over-whelms the scientific and rational aspects of the detective function reveals at the level of the form itself a tension at the heart of this novel. This disjunction within *When We Were Orphans* enacts a criticism of the Cartesian rationalism at the heart of the Enlightenment tradition (and the detective fiction genre) by its insertion of a modern, twentieth-century subject whose limited self-knowledge and 'fictionality' disrupts the conventional line of the narrative with ever more problematic subjectivity and partiality.

Classic or traditional detective novels typically work to re-establish a collective social order that has been threatened by a criminal or other subversive agent. In his celebrated essay on detective fiction, W. H. Auden (1948) argued: 'The job of the detective is to restore the state of grace in which the aesthetic and the ethical are one [. . .] [He is] a genius from outside who removes guilt by giving knowledge of guilt. (The detective story subscribes, in fact, to the Socratic daydream: "Sin is Ignorance")' (Auden 1948: 409; 411). In *When We Were Orphans*, Banks certainly gives repeated, even hyperbolic, emphasis to this collective social mission, to his *impersonal* role in combating evil and saving the world: 'Don't you see how very urgent things have got? The growing turmoil all over the world? I have to go!' (Ishiguro 2000: 146). More problematically, how-ever, as we shall see, this mission is increasingly bound up with, and ultimately overwhelmed by, his *personal* quest to save his parents. In the closing pages, he reflects without apparent irony on this conflation of the two objectives, 'all my trying to find her, trying to save the world from ruin' (Ishiguro 2001: 306). The disparity between these two goals is something that Banks never acknowledges – 'everything is distorted to reflect the emotion of the artist who is looking at the world' (Richards 2000).

The mounting tension between Banks's private quest (the search for his mother) and his avowedly public objectives ('to slay the serpent' [Ishiguro 2000: 145]) becomes more and more explicit, and is reproduced at the level of the formal stresses that progressively come to mark the text. It is here that the novel most directly begins to probe the ethical and political significance of the detective genre. Banks's narrative has all the *décor* of the celebrated detective story, but in fact very little of the substance or internal logic. His celebrated cases, the detail of his work, which conventionally provide the central determination, the thematic purpose, of the genre, remain stubbornly incidental to his story. As the novel unfolds, our expectations, and the preconceptions that underpin them, are more and more radically challenged, and eventually wholly disappointed. Indeed, it becomes clear that Banks's role as a detective is, precisely, a *performance*, the adoption of an identity derived from a fictional source. Just as in his description of his lodgings he commented on the potential approval of a visitor, attention to the form of his narrative reveals a consistent preoccupation with how he is being perceived, a preoccupation that borders on a requirement that he *is* perceived – that he become a celebrity, a figure on the public stage. This tendency is evident from his earliest recollections: Banks notes, when faced with the directors of the company following his mother's disappearance, 'my impression was that all the adults shrank back until they were lining the walls like spectators' (Ishiguro 2001: 25). *Acting* the parts of the great detectives is the staple of his childhood games with Akira, which he calls 'our dramas' (Ishiguro 2001: 110), particularly following his father's departure.

This trait becomes increasingly pronounced in the Shanghai sections of the novel:

> I had become aware by this point of ever more people pressing in on all sides, eager not just to glimpse me in the flesh, but to overhear something of our conversation [. . .] I got the idea that it was not just the immediate group around the balcony, but the entire ballroom that had fallen into silence and was awaiting my response. (Ishiguro 2001: 158; 161)

The role of a detective is a public role, but the very theatricality of Banks's enjoyment of the position is instructive, associating him with *fiction* and *drama*, with *spectacle*, rather than with the detail or mechanics of sleuthing. When he prepares to elope with Sarah Hemmings, his thoughts in the course of their first kiss also turn immediately to his imaginary audience: 'She carefully put down her cigarette holder and stood up. Then we were kissing – just like, I suppose, a couple on the cinema screen' (Ishiguro 2001: 222). As the search for his parents reaches its climax in the Chinese quarter, the suggestion that they might be held prisoner in a house opposite the residence of the blind actor Yeh Chen implies Banks's own status and abilities are perhaps an illusion, that his own insight and vision is restricted, and his role a mere performance.

For the fourth, fifth, and sixth sections of the novel, in which Banks recounts the climax of his quest, the scene shifts to Shanghai, in the weeks before its surrender to the Japanese on 9 November 1937. A detective novel that takes place in Shanghai instead of one of the great centres of Western civilization, London, is in itself unusual. Even though exoticism appears in Golden Age detective novels it is conventionally contained within the safe boundaries of England's green and pleasant land – where it is also, of course, so much more exposed. When he arrives in the city he is feted by the residents of the International Settlement, and much reference is made to his, and their, 'case' (Ishiguro 2001: 156; 159; 161). Again, there is a remarkable absence of detail about the nature of his inquiries or his objectives, which stands in contrast to the fastidious precision of Banks's retrospective dating of his writing and serves to underscore his surprising, wilful ignorance of the events unfolding around him. Rather, there is only the repeated reiteration – and it is not wholly clear how far this is Banks's perception or that of his interlocutors – that the 'case' somehow, and even that obscurely, concerns at once the plight of his parents and the fate of civilization. The connection between the recovery of his parents and drawing the world back from the brink of conflict is insistently articulated, but the nature of the linkage is never explained. To return to Ishiguro's comments, it is an element of the way 'the whole world portrayed in that book starts to tilt and bend in an attempt to orchestrate an alternative kind of logic'. Ironically, following an accelerating sequence of demonstrations and revelations of Banks's misjudgement and misapprehension of the state of affairs (Ishiguro 2001: 156; 185; 200), his personal case – the search for his parents, which has effectively become his sole concern – founders on the exposure of his mistaken conviction of their continuing incarceration in the city (Ishiguro 2001: 272–73), and then on the refutation of Banks's deductions by the infamous informer, the Yellow Snake, his Uncle Peter (Ishiguro 2001: 284–94). This radical disruption of the conventions of the genre, which is exacerbated by Banks's plans to leave Shanghai with Sarah and abandon the case (Ishiguro 2001: 216), demands that the reader, too, must reassess the assumptions and inferences of the preceding narrative.

Our anticipation of, in Auden's terms, the restoration of the state of grace has been frustrated because the conditions that allow for such fine predictability and neat closure have altogether unravelled. Uncle Peter makes clear that Banks's whole persona – the materially comfortable life in London, the social status, education, and luxury upon which his career has been built – derives from his mother's extraordinary sacrifice. Banks is formed by the very corruption and criminality he ostensibly opposes. The opium trade, which is both symptom and cause of the region's troubles, and represents both the exemplification and the corruption of the logic of the imperialist project, is also the primary determinant of Banks's position – and, by extension, of detective fiction. 'But now do you see how the world really is?' asks Uncle Peter:

> You see what made possible your comfortable life in England? How you were able to become a celebrated detective? A detective! What good is that to anyone? Stolen jewels, aristocrats murdered for their inheritance. Do you suppose that's all there is to contend with? Your mother, she wanted you to live in your enchanted world for ever. But it's impossible. In the end it has to shatter. (Ishiguro 2001: 294)

In a moment that places *When We Were Orphans* more properly in the mode of classic Greek tragedy, the frame and narrative logic of the detective genre, and of the 'enchanted world', is broken apart. The tragic form is itself at the same time implicated not in some universal, ahistorical 'human condition', but in the chaotic events that have marked our time, most specifically the violent climax of the Age of Empire. It is in this moment that the structural contradiction within the novel, between Banks's slavish and self-conscious adoption and performance of the role of detective, in accordance with the conventions and expectations of the fictional genre, and the inexorable movement of the historical narrative towards the known events of war and the death throes of colonialism, that Ishiguro's achievement becomes clear. Banks is confronted with a revelation of the truth of his condition and status which precisely parallels the *anagnorisis* (realization or discovery) and *peripeteia* (change in fortune) of Oedipus. Oedipus's uncovering of his true identity and origins – that he is not an orphan, or is an orphan no longer – entails the ruin of his sense of identity and self-conception, with catastrophic results for both himself and the state. The grounds of Banks's status are exposed – when he was an orphan he was, in fact, more than ever, the beneficiary of his mother's continuing care and sacrifice. Finding the truth about the case results in the opposite of closure and resolution. He is forced to reconsider his sense of self, and the reader must also reassess the significance of his tale. Being, and being seen to be, a detective, which is the substance of Banks's identity and self-presentation (along with his orphan state), was predicated on a necessary ignorance of the true sources not only of his wealth but of the wider social and political structure in which he moves. The effect of the narrative is to demonstrate that the very genre of 'detective fiction', as exemplified in its 'high' or 'golden age', is in a far more uneasy relation to the 'evil', the 'other', its stories (and its protagonists) control, and order, than its conventions suggest. Once the origin and identity of the detective is at stake, and once the historical and international contexts so specifically excluded from these tales is readmitted, it becomes impossible to sustain either the logic or the comforts of the genre.

As the scene with Uncle Philip unfolds and Banks confronts these realizations, he comments: 'As I leant towards him into the glare of the lamp, an odd feeling came over me that behind my back the darkness had grown and grown, so that now a vast black space had opened up there' (Ishiguro 2001: 290). The metaphor is particularly appropriate. The two men, in the glare of the lamp, are playing out a scene, but for the first time Banks thinks not of an admiring audience, but of a gaping void. The annihilation of the fictional parameters of his self-conception leaves only a great, dark emptiness, the threatening space of nothingness. The irony of the scene rests on the paradoxical results of his quest, of his search for his parents and an end to his orphanhood. His achievement of these goals generates a still more radical unsettling of his place in the world. Classic detective fiction of the early twentieth century effected the expulsion of otherness and the unknown, the control of disruptive forces. It stigmatized the threats to individual and collective security (as located in the class fraction – commonly an elite class fraction – to whom a private detective might offer his services) by circumscribing them as criminal deviancy rather than revolt or resistance, giving the illusion of controlling and indeed eradicating deviant and transgressive behaviours. As these forces irrupt in *When We Were Orphans*, the fragility of Banks's world comes to represent the vulnerability of the whole genre, or the *myth* of detective fiction.

The Myth of the Great Detective

It is by thinking about *When We Were Orphans* in terms of collective and social mythical ordering that we can assess more clearly the intriguing equation the novel makes between detection and fiction. Christopher Banks is a character who constructs himself as, and in accordance with, a work of fiction, conceiving his life's work within the logic of that fictional role. Banks is an actor who 'wrongly' interprets the reality around him in terms of a specific, conventional dramatic fiction in which he plays a central role. The collision of the uncomfortable external reality of Shanghai, of conflict, war, and chaos, exposes the fragility of both Banks's fabricated identity and the consoling but self-deceiving ideological structures inherent in the detective genre itself. *When We Were Orphans* explores historical shifts in social and political structures in the 1930s through an analogy between social power and the generic rules of representation.

To illustrate how this works we might consider an image that Christopher Banks twice invokes to define his role in society. The first appearance of this motif is during his recollection of a conversation with Akira:

> Then he sat up and pointed to one of the slatted sun-blinds at the moment hanging partially down over a window. We children, he said, were like the twine that kept the slats held together. A Japanese monk had once told him this. We often failed to realise it, but it was we children who bound not only a family, but the whole world together. If we did not do our part, the slats would fall and scatter over the floor. (Ishiguro 2001: 73)

When the image next appears, the *detective* becomes this agent of coherence, 'those of us whose duty it is to combat evil, we are . . . how might I put it? We're like the twine that holds together the slats of a wooden blind. Should we fail to hold strong, then everything will scatter' (Ishiguro 2001: 135). The simile is, in one way, a positive illustration of the cohesive role of the detective in society. The twine is the fundamental link, the necessary element to achieve coherence, to make the wooden blind hold. However, if the wooden blind stands for society in this image, we can wonder why society as a coherent whole is assimilated to a *blind*, which prevents vision and obscures reality, which shades or darkens our view, which keeps out the light. Such an image gives further emphasis to the novel's point that there can be no unmediated understanding of the 'real', that our consciousness is determined by rules of representation that are in large measure collective.

The image of the twine and the blind is pregnant with meaning, meaning that is still further complicated by a later textual echo. In the nightmare scene in the Chinese quarter, Banks releases a Japanese soldier whom he convinces himself is Akira: 'I went about cutting his bonds. I had imagined Akira had said "string" because of his limited English, but I now saw he was indeed tied with old twine that yielded easily under the blade' (Ishiguro 2001: 252). The twine is a complex signifier: the bonds that hold society together, our social structures and conventions, may as effectively restrain or bind us as enable us to survive.

It is in this context that we might return to the comparison between *When We Were Orphans* and *The Remains of the Day*. These stories share the common structure of journey or quest, a voyage that is as symbolic as it is real. In the course of the journey we explore the form and the central characteristics of, in Raymond Williams's term, the 'knowable community' of the novel (Williams 1984: 16). The journey permits an examination of the dominant social myths of Western societies between the wars, evoking a range of ontological, social, political, and ideological facets of that society that the literary genres of detective fiction and the emblematic social role of the butler did so much to distil and codify. The functions of both detective and butler are thus, to take our cue from Roland Barthes, 'mythic', in that they act as signifiers that serve to reinforce the social cohesion of the nation, the reference points of a shared identity (Barthes 2000: 137–38).

A contrast between these two novels emerges if we compare their differing representations of the social myths of modernity. Stevens and Banks are both unable to grasp the political complexity of Britain's position in the 1930s. Their social roles impose a restricted perspective of reality, which contributes to a process of mystification of contemporary history. *When We Were Orphans*, however, enacts the process of rupturing the literary genre and form through which the myth of the detective has been established – of cutting the narrative twine that holds the fictional slats in place – whereas *The Remains of the Day* is formally consistent, the challenges to Stevens's self-conception are external, and are represented within the logic of his reflections. In part, this is a function of the resource that the detective genre affords Ishiguro, there is little extensive formal or generic resource relating to butlers. (P. G. Wodehouse's Jeeves is the only significant model.) Banks and Stevens are both confronted by the realization of the limits of their worldview, but in Banks's case the whole generic – or mythic – mode of detective fiction unravels. The propensity of myth to transform historical and contingent reality into a natural and eternal state of things applies to both Banks and Stevens, and to the British social order they embody, with their assurance of certain certainties and language of the dominant order of the world.

The obsolescence of the myth of Britain as an imperialist power is exposed not only in the light of the historical emergence of the new colonial powers such as Japan, but – still more tellingly – through the collapse of the narrator's confident organization of his world. Just as much as Banks, the reader is confronted with the artificiality of the fictive frames that have defined but also paralyzed our vision of historical reality in the twentieth century.

CHAPTER EIGHT

Controlling Time: *Never Let Me Go*

MARK CURRIE

Chapter Summary: This chapter explores the various ways in which the formal structures of Kazuo Ishiguro's *Never Let Me Go* (2005) determine the novel's dark, even despairing, moral tone. The work's temporal organization establishes a pattern of remembered anticipation and unsought, even unwanted, freedom. The temporal doubleness caused by the primary narrative mode of recollection shapes all levels of the novel's discourse, from setting to voice, yet Ishiguro also captures the remembered anticipation of a hopeful, if retrospectively ironic, future that prevents the novel's narrator, Kathy H., from fully realizing the horror of the clones' condition.

Unwanted Freedom

As a request for everlasting captivity, Ishiguro's title *Never Let Me Go* (2005) provokes a question about why we might not only accept but actually beseech our own confinement. The importance of this question stands out in relief against the triviality of the idiom that expresses it. Ishiguro's novel invents and names itself after a pop song, which belongs to a recognizable category of pop songs, or to a field of imagery, in which the paradox of unwanted freedom is simply the upshot of a conventional comparison of love and confinement. It is the other side of Englebert Humperdinck's coin: not love we don't want as captivity, but love as captivity that we want.

The distance between this serious question and its trivial idiom is traversed in many ways by the novel, perhaps most obviously by the staging of its refrain, 'Baby, Baby, never let me go', as a hermeneutic puzzle. The song's dead metaphor is brought back to life first by Kathy H.'s literalization of 'baby':

What was so special about this song? Well, the thing was, I didn't used to listen properly to the words; I just waited for that bit that went: 'Baby, Baby, never let me go . . .' And what I'd imagined was a woman who'd been told she couldn't have babies, who'd really, really wanted them all her life. Then there's a sort of miracle and she has a baby, and she holds this baby very close to her and walks around singing: 'Baby, never let me go . . .' partly because she's so happy, but also because she's so afraid something will happen, that the baby will get ill or be taken away from her. Even at the time, I realised this couldn't be right, that this interpretation didn't fit with the rest of the lyrics. But that wasn't an issue with me. The song was about what I said, and I used to listen to it again and again, on my own, whenever I got the chance. (Ishiguro 2005: 64)

By severing the lyric from its context and making the baby literal, Kathy is able to elaborate a deliberately erroneous, knowingly personal interpretation of an otherwise bland refrain. The hermeneutic puzzle that this presents turns partly on the invisibility of this interpretation to an observer, so that when Madame observes Kathy dancing to the song with a pillow, none of this is apparent. As we discover at the end of the novel, Madame's interpretation of this scene, and of the song's lyric, departs from the blandness of the lyric in a different direction: 'I saw a little girl, her eyes tightly closed, holding to her breast the old, kind world, one that she knew in her heart could not remain, and she was holding it and pleading, never to let her go' (Ishiguro 2005: 167). Some of the contradiction, or the paradox of unwanted freedom, is revealed in both of these interpretations, since in each case the captor is imaged as the captive. The first interpretation seems to be an image of a mother held in voluntary captivity, but in danger of being cast off, by her baby. In the second interpretation, a child is in danger of being cast off by the old, kind world that she holds to her breast as if it were her baby. The relations between literal and metaphorical meaning in this hermeneutic puzzle are far from straightforward. In Kathy's own mind, the pillow stands in for a baby, so that the pillow is a metaphor for the baby, which is a literalization of the baby metaphor in the song. In Madame's interpretation of the event there is a kind of double metaphor, whereby the pillow stands for a baby, which in turn stands for a kind old world to which the child clings, so that the baby is a mother and the mother is a baby, and the baby is still a literalization of the baby metaphor of the song. It is partly the reader's invitation into this prism, with its convergence and mutual reflection of literal and metaphorical meanings, by which the novel develops its most portentous questions about unwanted freedom, where the interpretation of the song acts as an emblem for the novel's central metaphor and its interpretation.

The resemblance between *Never Let Me Go* and the writings of Franz Kafka does not end with the echo of Josef K.'s name in Kathy H. The literalization of a metaphor, so vividly illustrated in this central hermeneutic puzzle, is a mode of operation that has also often been used to characterize Kafka's work. It describes not only a process of turning a concrete situation into a metaphor, but also of metaphors turned into concrete situations, as if the purpose of a narrative were to concretize linguistic idiom such as 'life is a trial', 'faceless officialdom', or 'they're all the same'. The comparison can be pushed further if we think of Kafka's parable of the doorkeeper, that allegory of unwanted freedom that torments Josef K. at the end of *The Trial* (1925), or the more general predicament of Kafka's narratives, in which characters accept the unacceptable, treat the grotesque as if it were normal, or confer a kind of homeliness on the most offensive of social injustices. Kafka and Proust are in fact two of the writers who are actually named in the narrative of *Never Let Me Go* [along with Thomas Hardy, Edna O'Brien, and Margaret Drabble (Ishiguro 2005: 97); *War and Peace* (1865-69; Ishiguro 2005: 121); and *Daniel Deronda* (1876; Ishiguro 2005: 120); *The Odyssey*; and *A Thousand and One Nights* (Ishiguro 2005: 233)] and in this pairing we find the conjunction of two species of paradox that organize the novel's themes. On one hand there is a set of contradictions around questions of freedom and captivity, and on the other, a set of temporal structures in which these issues are embedded. If Kafka's relevance is primarily to the paradox of unwanted freedom, Proust's name can be attached to the family of temporal paradoxes that dominate the narrative voice, such as the recollection of forgetting, or perhaps more prominent still, the recollection of anticipation. It is in this conjunction of unwanted freedom and remembered anticipation that the novel's most sinister observations unfold.

Remembered Forgetfulness

Tense, which is the clearest marker of the relation between narrative time and the time of narrated events, is in play in any narrative. This relation is deployed for particular purposes by particular novels, none more so than *Never Let Me Go*. In *Never Let Me Go*, time has a particular atmosphere, a kind of doubleness, that shapes all levels of the discourse, from setting to narrative voice. A very general example of this doubleness might be a characteristic that *Never Let Me Go* shares with the Harry Potter novels. The novel is narrated from the late 1990s in England, so that most of its events take place in the last thirty years of the twentieth century, but one of the principal characteristics of the novel is a kind of timelessness, achieved in part by the scarcity of historical locators and specific temporal references. There is the occasional car, and a significant cassette tape, but otherwise the temporal atmosphere pulls away from any identifiable location in the historical present in both directions. There is, on one hand, a sense of the future, which inheres in the novel's interest in cloning; and on the other hand a sense of the past, in the form of a kind of public school memoir, or a recollection of a childhood apparently isolated from the forces of history.

This odd historical present, with its atmosphere of the past and the future, provides a broad setting for a more precise double structure in the narrative voice, which derives from the relation between narrated time and the time of the narration. Particularly in the early sections of the novel, Kathy, our narrator, is never quite sure of the accuracy of her own narration, as a result of the significant gap between narrated time and the time of narration. The distance of events in time, however, is not the only source of her unreliability: alongside protestations of temporal distance – 'This was all a long time ago so I might have some of it wrong' (Ishiguro 2005: 12) – there are indications of interference in the memory from acts of recollection and narration that mediate between a narrated event and the time of its narration. Just as one often remembers a photograph in place of an event, or the story that one has told of an event rather than the event itself, Kathy consistently indicates that the most distant events in her narration have been remembered before, and possibly told before, to the point of obscuring the events themselves. Her characteristic phrases, such as 'That was when . . .' and 'There was the time when . . .', suggest a kind of foreknowledge of the events to be narrated, or a community of addressees for whom these events, or the stories of them are already known. Everything has been told before, and there has often been a collective agreement on a particular version of events.

This constant mediation of events by some act of recall later offers a basic tense structure for the analysis of the narrative voice, a structure of reference that might be called the *proleptic past perfect*. The past perfect is a tense that refers to an event that is previous to another event in the past. In other words, there are three time locations involved: the narrated event, the time of its narration, and a time zone in the middle, and this middle location may be constituted by events that are posterior to the events being narrated, including acts of recollection that are posterior to the events being narrated and yet anterior to the time locus of our narrator. This mediating time locus is interesting because it can function both as recollection (in relation to the narrator) and as anticipation (in relation to the narrated), and even as both, as the recollection of anticipation.

A simple example of the structure of the proleptic past perfect would be a sentence of this kind: 'Ruth and I often found ourselves remembering these things a few years ago, when I was caring for her down at the centre in Dover' (Ishiguro 2005: 15). The 'these things' of this sentence refers to events at Hailsham, Kathy and Ruth's school, and these constitute the primary sequence of the narration at this point. But there is also a recollection here of an act of recollection later, between Ruth and Kathy, which takes place a few years before the time of the narration, and this mediating position gives to the past perfect the power also to be proleptic, in this case by referring forwards to a time when Ruth is in a recovery centre in Dover, a snippet, or evocation of future time in the narration that arouses the expectations of an as yet unexplained occurrence.

A more complex example of this structure can be found in the recollection of a recollection that is not agreed upon:

> We'd been in the middle of what we later came to call the 'tokens controversy'. Tommy and I discussed the tokens controversy a few years ago, and we couldn't agree when it had happened. I said we'd been ten at the time; he thought it was later, but in the end came round to agreeing with me. I'm pretty sure I got it right: we were in Junior 4 – a while after that incident with Madame, but still three years before our talk by the pond. (Ishiguro 2005: 35)

In this example of the proleptic past perfect, the middle event is again an act of recollection, but there is a disagreement about the timeline of the events being recollected. There is also perhaps a more collective 'we', which may refer to a more general community of recollectors who have, since then, named the episode as the 'tokens controversy'. And again, this mediating location in time operates partly as the recollection of recollection, but also as prolepsis, in the excursion it offers into a future event cryptically referred to here as 'our talk by the pond'. It is worth noting also that in an example such as this, the cryptic flashforward seems to be based in an assumption that the reader shares in the knowledge of future events, or belongs to the community of recollectors concerned, so that prolepsis is an unwitting effect produced in the gap between the assumed and the real reader.

Memory failure is a familiar source of unreliability in the first-person narrative voice, and Kathy's constant references to previous difficulties of recollection can be thought of as a subspecies of this kind of unreliability. If unreliability is sometimes marked by protestations of memory failure, this subspecies will also include accounts of prior difficulties and disagreements in remembering:

> This was a long time ago so I might have got some of it wrong; but my memory of it is that my approaching Tommy that afternoon was part of a phase I was going through around that time – something to do with compulsively setting myself challenges – and I'd more or less forgotten all about it when Tommy stopped me a few days later. (Ishiguro 2005: 12)

The proleptic past perfect is accompanied here by protestations about the difficulty of remembering, but in this example we are presented not only with a recollection of a recollection, but also with a recollection of an act of forgetting. This idea, this apparent paradox, or remembered forgetting, is a recurring feature of Kathy's retrospection. Perhaps the most interesting thing about remembered forgetting is that it requires a subsequent act of remembering in order for forgetting to come into view. In this example Kathy had more or less forgotten all about the events she is narrating until she was reminded later by Tommy. If memory and forgetting coincide, on the other hand, a more difficult logical problem arises, as Saint Augustine describes in Book X of *Confessions* (397–98):

> I can mention forgetfulness and recognize what the word means, but how can I recognize the thing itself unless I remember it? I am not speaking of the sound of the word but of the thing which it signifies. If I had forgotten the thing itself, I should be utterly unable to recognize what the sound implied. When I remember memory, my memory is present to itself by its own power; but when I remember forgetfulness, two things are present, memory, by which I remember it, and forgetfulness, which is what I remember. Yet what is forgetfulness but absence of memory? When it is present, I cannot remember. Then how can it be present in such a way that I can remember it? If it is true that what we remember we retain in our memory, and if it is also true that unless we remembered forgetfulness, we could not possibly recognize the meaning of the word when we heard it, then it is true that forgetfulness is retained in the memory. It follows that the very thing which by its presence causes us to forget must be present if we are to remember it. Are we to understand from this that, when we remember it, it is not itself present in the memory, but is only there by means if its image? For if forgetfulness were itself present, would not its effect be to make us forget, not to remember? (Augustine 1961: 222)

Augustine gets very vexed about this kind of *aporia*, and it often looks as if there is a simple answer to the problem that so troubles him. It looks here, for example, as if there is confusion between forgetting as the manner and as the object of a recollection. It seems unproblematic, in one sense, to remember forgetting. And yet, if I can remember forgetting an appointment yesterday, am I really remembering what it was like to forget? Forgetting that appointment yesterday was after all very much like not having an appointment at all, so that to remember it as forgetting would be to remember nothing. It only becomes forgetting when it is transformed by a subsequent remembering of the appointment, so that the idea of remembering forgetting is only unproblematic when it is accepted that this is the nature of memory itself: not to make present again the former present, but to transform the former present with the temporal distance of retrospect. Remembering is never real, in the sense of making present again the former present of the past. In the act of remembering, we transform the former present, and this is particularly clear in the memory of forgetting, which is identified as forgetting only by becoming what it was not. This is exactly what the structure of the proleptic past perfect enables, since its triple structure of the time of an utterance, the time to which it refers, and a time between, can accommodate an event, the act of forgetting it, and a subsequent act of remembering that it has been forgotten. It is only when the spacing of these time locations is removed, when memory and forgetting coincide, that they collapse into contradiction.

Recollected Anticipation

There is a family resemblance between the idea of a recollection of for-getfulness and the temporal structure that dominates Kathy's narrative, the recollection of anticipation. It is one thing to remember the failure of memory, but something subtly different to remember what the future used to be like, or how one used to envisage it. Kathy's narrative is full of such recollections:

> After that morning I became convinced something else – perhaps something awful – lay around the corner to do with Miss Lucy, and I kept my eyes and ears open for it. But the days passed and I heard nothing. What I didn't know at the time was that something pretty significant *had* happened only a few days after I'd seen her in Room 22 – something between Miss Lucy and Tommy that had left him upset and disorientated. (Ishiguro 2005: 84; emphasis in the original)

The family resemblance between remembered forgetting and this kind of remembered anticipation is that the object of the recollection in both cases is an absence of knowledge, and that the recollection of not know-ing is impossible except in relation to a subsequent state of knowing. This is most clearly represented in this example by the temporality of 'what I did not know at the time', which contains a movement from ignorance to knowledge. On top of that there is something more com-plexly proleptic at work here as Kathy remembers becoming convinced that something awful lay around the corner, but the future that she remembers envisaging in this moment of dread is significantly less dreadful than the one that is going to come about, so that the very idea of dread develops an irony produced in the chasm between Kathy's remembered anticipations, and the anticipations made by a reader of the more extreme horrors that lie in wait. Many of the novel's remem-bered anticipations work in this way, as ironic failures to anticipate the *really* awful thing around the corner.

To recall what one did not know at the time is to recall in the light of a later event, or an outcome, or to view the past in the mode that is sometimes referred to as teleological retrospect. The mode of teleologi-cal retrospect (and I'm not convinced there can be any other kind of retrospect) is to explain past events in the light of later events, and there-fore to confer on those events a significance that they did not possess at the time of their occurrence. For Kathy, this kind of revision of the significance of events is a feature of many of her sentences:

> As I've said it wasn't until a long time afterwards – long after I'd left the cottages – that I realised just how significant our little encounter in the churchyard had been. I was upset at the time, yes. But I didn't believe it to be anything so different from other tiffs we'd had. It never occurred to me

that our lives, until then so closely interwoven, could unravel and separate over a thing like that. (Ishiguro 2005: 180)

There is anticipation embedded in this recollection, of the unravelling of lives, but whereas in previous examples the prolepsis has been part of a recollection of anticipation, in this case the memory simply functions in a double structure, as both a memory and an anticipation. The novel, then, constantly projects backwards to remember what Kathy did and did not know about the future, and if it is difficult to remember what one did know, it is much more difficult to remember what one did not:

> So why had we stayed silent that day? I suppose it was because even at that age – we were nine or ten – we knew just enough to make us wary of that whole territory. It's hard now to remember just how much we knew by then. We certainly knew – though not in any deep sense – that we were different from our guardians, and also from normal people outside; we perhaps even knew that a long way down the line there were donations waiting for us. But we didn't really know what that meant. (Ishiguro 2005: 63)

Though there are many moments in which Kathy considers openly in this way what she did and did not know of the future in the past, more commonly, questions of what Kathy knew operate as a distancing device between character and reader, as a gap begins to open between her own remembered false anticipations and our own increasingly accurate ones. The narrative also deploys a temporal strategy that brings together our two temporal paradoxes of remembered forgetting and recollected anticipation in which hope is seen to depend upon an act of forgetting:

> Maybe once Hailsham was behind us, it was possible, just for that half year or so, before all the talk of becoming carers, before the driving lessons, all those other things, it was possible to forget for whole stretches of time who we really were; to forget what the guardians had told us; to forget Miss Lucy's outburst that rainy afternoon at the pavilion, as well as all those theories we'd developed amongst ourselves over the years. It couldn't last of course, but like I say, just for those few months, we somehow managed to live in this cosy state of suspension in which we could ponder our lives without the usual boundaries. Looking back now, it feels like we spent ages in that steamed up kitchen after breakfast, or huddled around half-dead fires in the small hours, lost in conversation about our plans for the future. (Ishiguro 2005: 130)

The act of recollection in such delusional moments is a recollection of two absences: the absence of memory in forgetting, and the absence of knowledge of the future in hopeful anticipation.

It is not only at the level of the tense structures of the narrative voice that such false hopes are developed. Memories of false hope, and the false idea of a dream future, also run through the novel at a more obviously thematic level. One example is the theory of 'possibles', a word used by the Hailsham students to refer to those people in the outside world from whom they may have been genetically copied. With an ironic echo, perhaps, of Jean-Paul Sartre's account of the future as the realm of pure possibility and therefore freedom, the idea of the 'possible' for the students is a living vision of the future:

> Then there were those questions about why we wanted to track down our models at all. One big idea behind finding your model was that when you did, you'd glimpse your future. Now I don't mean anyone really thought that if your model turned out to be, say, a guy working at a railway station, that's what you'd end up doing too. We all realised it wasn't that simple. Nevertheless, we all of us, to varying degrees, believed that when you saw the person you were copied from, you'd get some insight into who you were deep down, and maybe too, you'd see something of what life held in store. (Ishiguro 2005: 127)

Something of the technique of literalization or concretization can be seen at work here, where the notion of possibility is incarnated and available to vision. As both a model and a future, the 'possible' is the reification of an ideal. Ruth, for example, has a dream of working in a glass-fronted office in her ideal future, and when the students go to Norfolk in search of her possible, a strange confusion is created between her genetic source and a more general reification of her hopes. The episode also gives rise to an opportunity for a reified double time structure of the kind that we have been observing in tense structures: as the location of Ruth's possible, Norfolk functions as a protention of the future, but it also functions in the novel as a place of retention: a place, the students believe, in which everything that has been lost in the past will reappear in the future. To this double structure belongs the rediscovery of Kathy's cassette tape, and its injunction for the future – never let me go.

I argued at the end of the last section that the proleptic past perfect allowed for a kind of spacing between remembering and forgetting, and that this spacing produced temporal distance between contradictory elements that, if they were to coincide, would collapse into contradiction. The same argument can be made for the temporality of the remembered false anticipation, or for the self-deceit involved in the hope of an ideal future. If we think about confession generally, the temporal gap between the narrator and the narrated is often a moral gap, a distance in time that allows the narrator a moral distance on what a sinner he used to be. The problem in confessional structures like this is that, as the narrative progresses, the time gap between the narrator and the narrated diminishes, and with it, the moral distance between the narrator and the narrated threatens to disappear. We depend, in confession, on being able to trust the narrator about what an untrustworthy person he used to be, and cannot allow the untrustworthiness to spill over into, or coincide with, the time of narration. It is no surprise that, in texts like Augustine's *Confessions* and Proust's *In Search of Lost Time* (1913–22), at the moment of coincidence, when the story being told catches up with the time of its telling, the narratives erupt into philosophical discussions of the nature of time. An alternative possibility, perhaps, is to allow the reliable time locus of the narrator to become contaminated with the deceits and delusions of the narrated. The question we must ask in *Never Let Me Go* in this regard is this: at what point do these false anticipations transform into reliable ones? At what point does falsity transform itself into truth? Though there is clearly a slow process of realization, of coming to knowledge, in the novel's forward movement, we also regularly see Kathy in the novel's 'now', in the time of narration, still falsely anticipating the future. At the beginning of the novel, she tells us: 'I won't be a carer any more come the end of the year, and though I've got a lot out of it, I have to admit I'll welcome the chance to rest – to stop and think and remember' (Ishiguro 2005: 34). It certainly looks here as if the false anticipations continue untransformed. For Kathy, to stop being a 'carer' means to start her 'donations', or in a less euphemistic language, to die a premature death. The very persistence of this euphemistic language supports the supposition that the truth of what happens for Kathy at the end of the year is not being honestly apprehended, and that the horror of realization is averted in cheerful optimism. Likewise, at the end of the novel, by which time the reader has developed a full understanding of this horror, we see Kathy extending the delusion in her anticipatory remarks: 'by the end of the year I won't be driving around like this any more' (Ishiguro 2005: 262). It is towards the collapsing of the gap, the conflation of narrated time and the time of narration, or the contamination of an honest recollection with the delusions that have been recounted that the memory of anticipation points.

Privileged Deprivation

The paradox of unwanted freedom and the temporal paradoxes of remembered forgetting and the recollection of anticipation can be brought together by a third paradox that presides over the novel – the paradox of privileged deprivation. This idea, of a sense of privilege around the condition of atrocity in which Kathy and the others find themselves, is one of the most striking features of the novel. It offers an answer to the question: to what end is the temporal structure deployed in *Never Let Me Go*? But it also serves as an answer to some of the more basic responses to Kathy's passivity, and to the mystery of her unwanted freedom. Why doesn't Kathy run away? Why, after she is freed from Hailsham, doesn't she save herself?

One way of answering such questions is with reference to a theory of social control that relates particularly well to the total institution – that is, the kind of institution that doesn't let you go home in the evening, like a prison, or the army, or perhaps most relevantly, a boarding school – known as 'relative deprivation'. In its most abstract form, the theory of relative deprivation can be understood in the following way:

> A is relatively deprived of X when (i) he does not have X, (ii) he sees some other person or persons, which may include himself at some previous or expected time, as having X, (whether or not this is or will be in fact the case), (iii) he wants X, and (iv) he sees it as feasible that he should have X. Possession of X may, of course, mean avoidance of or exemption from Y. (Runciman cited in Wakeford 1969: 69)

The key feature of this concept of social control is that a person who enters a total institution must be systematically deprived of individual freedom, personal space, and opportunities for self-expression relative to other individuals in the institution. The privilege of others must therefore be made visible and possibly offered as an enticement to an individual, as an expectation for the future. This initial deprivation must be relieved slowly over time, often as a consequence of seniority itself (that the mere serving of time will ensure some relief from deprivation), but also as a reward for conformity to the institution's rules and values. In this way, relative deprivation creates an entirely internal economy of privilege and deprivation, where comparisons are not relative to the general population or standards in the outside world. As a socialization process, the function of relative deprivation is observed in effects on behaviour and values that survive the experience of the total institution itself, and that persist in life afterwards. Such effects might include a generalized legitimation of social inequality, or a feeling of privilege in relation to conditions perceived by others as deprived.

The control of time is central for relative deprivation in a number of ways. If we take a boarding school, for example, it is in the rigid control of daily routines that deprivation is most directly controlled, with each day and each week being divided into time zones of varying degrees of constraint: periods of work and play, of being in and out of houses, of being silent and being allowed to speak, with frequent assemblies for roll calls and inspections. Over longer time periods the rigorous constraints of daily time will be slowly relieved, so that initial levels of relative deprivation yield to greater degrees of freedom, of free periods in the day, and of the freedom to move in privileged ways around the school. A written code of rules will normally enforce a wide range of prohibitions, on personal possessions, on geographical movement, on the use of public and personal transport, on social contact with the outside world, on listening to music, on what you can wear, and on who you can talk to. School rules will normally encode a highly visible relief from prohibition, or a system of privileges that entails the removal of basic constraints on freedom. In *Never Let Me Go*, Hailsham is exactly this kind of total institution: an elaborate system of prohibitions and privileges, of constraints upon and opportunities for personal expression. At times, Hailsham exerts an entirely plausible control over daily time, as, for example, in the very limited opportunity it presents to its students for private conversations. Such interactions have to take place in lunch queues, by the pond, in whispered moments, and always with great difficulty. At other times, Hailsham represents a subtle exaggeration of boarding school practices, and a kind of comic literalization of recognizable aspects of the total institution. One of the crucial features of the public boarding school, for example, is that students are separated from their parents, and that parental functions are replaced by institutional figures such as matrons and housemasters. In *Never Let Me Go*, the separation from parents is exaggerated into the literal parentlessness of a community of clones. Similarly, a typical prohibition like a rule against smoking, a rule that removes the freedom to damage one's own body, is given an exaggerated importance at Hailsham because, for a community of clones being grown for their body parts, smoking amounts, in a literal way, to the corruption of somebody else's organs.

The most important effect of relative deprivation as a socialization process, in which notions of time and of control are most closely forged together, lies in the ability of the total institution to control behaviour in the future, after the constraints of the institution have been removed. In *Never Let Me Go*, this post-institutional world is represented by 'the Cottages', a kind of transitional institution clearly imaged as a university:

> If someone mentions the cottages today, I think of easy-going days, drifting in and out or each other's rooms, the languid way the afternoon would fold into evening then into night. I think of my pile of old paperbacks, their pages gone wobbly, like they'd once belonged to the sea. I think about how I read them, lying on my front in the grass on warm afternoons, my hair, which I was growing long then – always falling across my vision. I think about the mornings waking up in my room at the top of the Black Barn to the voices of students outside in the field, arguing about Kafka or Picasso. (Ishiguro 2005: 109)

In this spoof of college nostalgia, there is momentary freedom from the control of time, in which the future is not thought about, and the past forgotten. And yet, in this realm of apparent freedom, a mysterious post-institutional force limits the way that this freedom is apprehended and used. Kathy continues to be controlled by the routines to which she has become accustomed at Hailsham in this new realm of freedom, and continues to expect a future that we know, by now, is not the one that lies in wait for her. She has been designated as a carer, rather than as a donor, in the Cottages, so that she thinks she is privileged when in fact she is doomed. This internal difference between carer and donor not only prevents comprehension of her true situation, but seems to act as a continuing prohibition on interaction with others in the world not governed by such distinctions. To this project – the internal system of comparisons of relative deprivation – we might also attribute the closed community of the novel's characters, the absence of outsiders, and the closed circle between the narrator and her addressees: Kathy continually addresses her narrative to other graduates of total institutions on the model, 'I don't know how it was where you were, but [. . .]' (Ishiguro 2005: 13). And this highly introverted focus is also an explanation of the novel's extensive lexicon of euphemisms: a vocabulary known only to inmates, which names as 'guardians', 'training', 'students', 'carers', 'donations', 'deferrals', and 'completion' a brutal reality more properly named as captors, socialization, clones, prefects, enforced organ donations, false hope, and death.

It is for the maintenance of this gap, this chasm between two realities, one a closed institution, the other a brutal domain of inequality and social injustice, that the temporal structures of remembered forgetting and recollected anticipation are deployed. The time structure of the novel functions as a control of distance, keeping the reader yoked to Kathy, close enough to the truth to experience the process of relative deprivation with her, and yet not so close as to prevent judgement of her, or to be able to see the truth of what is coming to her in the future. The proleptic past perfect, with its oscillation between a half-forgotten past and a falsely anticipated future, is therefore a mechanism for the management of the relationship between knowing and not knowing, and more specifically between knowing and not knowing what the future holds. The temporality that it creates – the slow acquisition of a privileged deprivation, the diminishing gap between delusion and truth – acts as an explanation for why we sometimes accept the unacceptable, or why we sometimes not only accept but actually beseech our own confinement: because relative deprivation causes us to misapprehend social injustice as privilege. In *Never Let Me Go*, we can never satisfactorily separate the anticipation of retrospection from the recollection of anticipation, or prolepsis from analepsis, as if something of the asymmetry of time has been removed by the novel. More specifically, the proleptic past perfect casts us into an uncertain middle, or a location in time that is uncertain about what did happen and what will happen, and the complex tense structures that cast us backwards and forwards make the distinction between the anticipation of recollection and the recollection of anticipation difficult to uphold. A final paradox might then be offered as a point of convergence for this issue about the temporality of narrative and this theme of accepting social injustice: the paradox of a future that already exists, that is the open future of the novel, of any novel, a future that lies in wait for us to reach it, and from which there is no possibility of freedom.

On First Reading *Never Let Me Go*

JOHN MULLAN

The first-time reader of Kazuo Ishiguro's *Never Let Me Go* (2005) is tempted into a false start by the information given at the opening: 'England, late 1990s'. Published in 2005, the novel might seem to be · announcing a scrutiny of the way we now live. Most of Ishiguro's novels have had settings remote from contemporary Britain. Here the novelist seems to be edging towards the present. It is a necessary illusion as the opening announcement does not, as it turns out, root us in a contemporary reality. Instead it is calculated to have a defamiliarizing effect. While this novel measures carefully the passing of time, its chronology, we soon realize, is removed from any historical reality that we can recognize.

The announcement is itself unsettling, the one place where the author speaks, and Ishiguro does so in order deftly to remove his story from the genre to which it would perhaps most readily be assigned. The prefatory announcement tells us that the novel cannot quite be science fiction. Nor, by those bare, emphatic details of place and time, can it be its more literary offshoot: dystopian fiction. *Never Let Me Go* is written at a tangent to this genre, recently favoured by many literary novelists. It does not imagine a future world at all, nor does it bother about the grounds for the unsettling reality it posits. Ishiguro's lack of interest in the science of his fictional world is overt and is encoded within the narrative. The 'students' talk to each other about their 'possibles theory', the idea that for each of them there must be a person from which he or she has been 'copied', but there is no talk of genetic material or of the technological processes involved. When the word 'clone' does eventually get used by Ruth, it is in a spasm of anger and self-disgust (Ishiguro 2005: 164). The itch to identify a 'possible' is abstracted from any scientific enquiry, any idea about who has created them and how. Kathy tells us of the uninformed and awkward conversations she and her fellow students have had about possible 'possibles': 'Some students thought you should be looking for a person twenty to thirty years older than yourself – the sort of age a normal parent would be. But others claimed this was sentimental' (Ishiguro 2005: 137).

If this were either a work of science-fiction novel or a dystopian fable, the central character would rebel, but here there is never any question of that. The haunting fatalism of Ishiguro's narrator has puzzled or frustrated readers who nonetheless admire the novel. When I spoke to Ishiguro about *Never Let Me Go* at the Guardian Book Club, it was a puzzle over which several members of the audience worried. What means of control was 'the State' (absent from the novel but inferred by many readers) exerting? How might it be resisted? Why could the cloned humans not hide? Above all, why, as they reach adolescence and then adulthood, do the 'students' not rebel? 'Let's suppose that there is a reason', answered the novelist. It could be whatever reason any reader wanted. The point had to be that the narrator's failure to imagine a way out, her failure even to resent her destiny, was axiomatic. Ishiguro's fictional experiment begins with her acceptance of her lot, and therefore with his evasion of generic expectations.

So deep have these expectations been rooted that the students' failure to be explicitly appalled by their fate is sometimes felt as an offence against realism. 'Surely they would . . .' begins the usual objection. Yet the cleverest, saddest constraint of the novel is the limit it places upon its characters' imaginings. When she looks back on her life, Kathy H. finds herself trying to resist smugness rather than protesting. She thinks herself, knows herself, privileged. 'I'm a Hailsham student – which is enough by itself sometimes to get people's backs up' (Ishiguro 2005: 3). She has been lucky and is ready to see the luck of others like herself. 'I wouldn't mind at all if that's where I ended up,' says Kathy of the 'recovery centre' where her friend Ruth lies in bed after her first 'donation' (Ishiguro 2005: 17). She appreciates the good fortune of her friend being in a well-appointed building with good views from the window, but apparently says and thinks nothing against what is being done to her.

Kathy H. remembers how, when they were 'students' at Hailsham, one of their 'guardians', Miss Lucy, appeared angry about their fate, and she describes herself and her friend Tommy as curious, but uncomprehending. Even in retrospect, our narrator does not see why this 'guardian' had to leave the school. The first-time reader may infer Miss Lucy's discontent, and her resistance but Kathy H. recalls only her odd behaviour. It is Miss Lucy who dispels the book's ostensible mystery, telling the students – and us – what they are and what is their destiny. Less than a third of the way through the novel, she makes explicit what they have 'been told and not told' (Ishiguro 2005: 79), what we have known but not been certain of:

> Your lives are set out for you. You'll become adults, then before you're old, before you're even middle-aged, you'll start to donate your vital organs. That's what each of you was created to do [. . .]. You were brought into this world for a purpose, and your futures, all of them, have been decided. (Ishiguro 2005: 80)

The sense of what is fated is so ingrained that Kathy and Ruth later disagree about what knowledge they owe to this outburst.

'I think that was all she said [. . .] she claimed Miss Lucy had told us a lot more; that she'd explained how before donations we'd spend some time first as carers, about the usual sequence of donations, the recovery centres and so on – but I'm pretty sure she didn't.' (Ishiguro 2005: 80)

The avoidance of protest provokes the reader habituated by dystopian films and fiction to associate individuality with resistance. At the opening of Chapter Four, Kathy tells us, 'I won't be a carer any more come the end of the year, and though I've got a lot out of it, I have to admit I'll welcome the chance to rest – to stop and think and remember' (Ishiguro 2005: 37). That 'chance to rest' means her becoming a 'donor', though the first-time reader will not quite see it yet. It is relief – 'it feels just about right to be finishing at last come the end of the year' (Ishiguro 2005: 4) – at the beginning of a process that will lead to her death.

The limitations placed on the narrator's understanding are there in the earnest clichés she uses. Kathy uses phrases such as 'I've got a lot out of it' and 'I have to admit', which are the commonplace phrases with which a person makes the best of things. Kathy H.'s clichés often have this quality of commonsensical resignation, her language untormented by her knowledge of what will happen to her. Talking about how the 'guardians' merge the students' sex education with a subtle adjustment of their expectations about their future 'donations', for instance, she wonders if they were trying 'to smuggle into our heads a lot of the basic facts about our futures' (Ishiguro 2005: 81). Immediately a clichéd concession withdraws the thought. 'Now to be fair, it was probably natural to run these two subjects together.' 'To be fair': the banality of the phrase expresses just the narrator's ingenuousness. From the first page Kathy is unsuspecting in her ready use of cliché. 'I know for a fact [. . .] it means a lot to me [. . .] a complete waste of space' (Ishiguro 2005: 1). She does not exactly have an impoverished lexicon: she easily uses words such as 'langorous', 'ambivalent', and 'trammelled'. She has read Victorian novels including *Daniel Deronda* (Ishiguro 2005: 120). She recalls how she and her fellow students like to talk about poetry and philosophy, Kafka, Proust, and Picasso (Ishiguro 2005: 117–118), yet all this is kept away from the record of her experience. Characteristically, when she tells us about reading George Eliot's novel it is to piece together another anecdote about the small jars and intimacies of adolescence. She remembers her irritation that Ruth had insisted on outlining the plot to her, 'just as I knew she would' (Ishiguro 2005: 120). The fact that the novel is about a man who tries to discover his true parentage, about the hunger to know your origins, never breaks surface.

For all her earnest reading, Kathy H.'s narrative voice feels deprived of resources. Its ineloquence is signalled by her own struggles with narration. 'This might all sound daft' (Ishiguro 2005: 66); 'All I can say is . . .' (Ishiguro 2005: 193); 'What I'm saying is . . .' (Ishiguro 2005: 274). Like *The Remains of the Day* (1989), *Never Let Me Go* is narrated as if it were being spoken rather than written. The stilted circumlocutions of that earlier novel belonged in a narration that kept reminding the reader, in its very affectation of formality, that it might be supposed to be speech: 'I should say [. . .] that is to say [. . .] as I say [. . .] as I was saying' (all these qualifying clauses appear in its Prologue; Ishiguro 1989: 3–20). Kathy H.'s narration is similarly characterized by the redundant qualifications that we associate with speech. 'Like I say [. . .] Anyway [. . .] As I say [. . .]' (Ishiguro 2005: 125). 'Anyway, my point is [. . .]' (Ishiguro 2005: 131). It is difficult to think of a novel where so many paragraphs begin with 'Anyway [. . .]', that colloquial indication of a speaker pulling him- or herself back to the point after wandering away. 'Anyway, the point is [. . .]' (Ishiguro 2005: 65): the narrator is like a speaker who keeps drifting into elaboration or digression, and keeps having to recover her thread. Telling us about Harry, with whom she almost has sex at school, she mentions that she has seen him recently at a 'recovery centre in Wiltshire. He was being brought in after a donation [. . .] In a wheelchair' (Ishiguro 2005: 99). Kathy wonders if he did not recognize her, and whether later, as the medication wore off, he might have done: 'he'd have tried to place me and remembered' (Ishiguro 2005: 100). The paragraph ends there, with that wistful thought, and then a new one begins: 'Anyway, I was talking about back then [. . .]' (Ishiguro 2005: 100). The material of memory is being organized as we listen. When Kathy H. begins to tell us about the song that gives the novel its title, she starts getting ahead of herself. 'What I've got today isn't the actual cassette, the one I had back then at Hailsham, the one I lost. It's the one Tommy and I found in Norfolk years afterwards – but that's another story I'll come to later. What I want to talk about is the first tape, the one that disappeared' (Ishiguro 2005: 64).

'What I want to talk about.' This narrator is not just sure that she is speaking, she is sure that she is speaking to someone. The addressee, 'you', is there from the first page: 'I know carers, working now, who are just as good and don't get half the credit. If you're one of them, I can understand how you might get resentful – about my bedsit, my car, above all, the way I get to pick and choose who I look after' (Ishiguro 2005: 3). The 'you' to whom she imagines herself speaking is someone like herself, a 'carer', a former 'student', another clone: 'I don't know if you had "collections" where you were' (Ishiguro 2005: 38). Kathy H. wonders how singular or unique has been her upbringing, but she assumes nevertheless that her auditor is the same kind of being as herself, reared for the same end. The assumption is striking, and suggests something of the limitations of the clones' contact with 'real' humans. 'I don't know how it was where you were, but at Hailsham we had to have some form of medical almost every week' (Ishiguro 2005: 13). The fact is irrelevant to the anecdote that she is about to relate – which is an incident that occurs in the queue for this ritual – but then the narrator does not quite know how much she needs to tell her imagined listener, to whom some of the necessary background is surely familiar. 'I'm sure somewhere in your childhood, you too had an experience like ours that day' (Ishiguro 2005: 36). This too is reminiscent of *The Remains of the Day*, where Stevens engages directly with a listener he imagines sharing his interests. 'And let me tell you, if you were to have come into the servants' hall on any of those evenings, you would not have heard mere gossip' (Ishiguro 1989: 18). This 'you' becomes a listener as preoccupied as the narrator with the exact obligations of the English butler. 'You will not dispute, I presume, that Mr Marshall of Charleville House and Mr Lane of Bridewood have been the two great butlers of recent times' (Ishiguro 1989: 34). But Ishiguro does indeed make his narrator 'presume' something incredible – as if he could only imagine telling his story to another butler, or as if, at some deeper level, our recognition and sympathy as readers reveals that we are all butlers (and clones). Kathy H.'s assumption about her listener is, in contrast, logical as well as narrow-minded. She has known only others like herself. She cannot imagine a different kind of being.

Failures to imagine a different reality are native to her narrative language. Her failure to challenge what is to be done to her is linguistic as much as psychological or political. Without protest, she takes on the euphemisms used to label the artificially created humans and to describe, or avoid describing, their fate. On the novel's first page she is talking about being a 'carer', and what it takes to be a 'good carer'. The resonance of 'carer', which is used eight times in the first two pages of the novel, is the stronger because, in our now accepted usage, it is a word of rather recent significance. A 'person whose occupation is the care of the sick, aged, disabled, etc.; one who looks after a disabled or elderly relative at home' is the definition offered by the OED, which records the earliest example of this sense in 1978. 'Carer' is already one of our caring, congratulatory words for those obliged or paid to look after those who cannot look after themselves. It expresses a kind of official admiration for what may well be resentfully undertaken, or done just for money. It is a nice word, then, for Kathy H. to hold on to. She talks proudly but modestly of her skills in 'caring', like anyone talking of a job she has begun to master ('maybe I *am* boasting now'). The exact meaning of the euphemism will be unclear to the first-time reader, its unclearness a consequence of the narrator's own failure to worry at it. In fact, the 'carer' is an accomplice, we eventually understand. The 'carer' is appointed, by some invisible agency, to tend a 'donor' as he or she recovers from an operation. The 'carer' calms and reassures in the wake of surgery, though recovery is merely preparation for further operations – all for the benefit of those who need the transplanted organs.

'Donor' (with the attendant 'donation') is the other familiar yet odd-sounding word that keeps snagging our attention in the opening couple of pages. Kathy H. also uses this word ingenuously, her reliance on it bringing alive its potential for deceit. A 'donor', we are used to thinking, is a voluntary contributor, a generous giver – the opposite of what is the case here. In her first paragraph Kathy H. is proud that she manages to keep her donors from becoming 'agitated' (she puts the word in inverted commas because it is evidently an official term of classification), 'even before fourth donation' (Ishiguro 2005: 3). The reader will later realize – but the re-reader will already know – that this 'fourth donation' is always fatal, and that it is a stage that the weaker or less determined donors do not even reach. Kathy H. is employed to usher her charges down this path to premature death – or 'completion', as she dutifully names it. She is also making herself ready to follow this path, ease with the euphemisms being essential to her preparation. She is not alone. Ruth tells Tommy that their fellow 'student' Chrissie 'completed during her second donation' and he applies the news to himself in just the wrong way. '"I heard that as well," said Tommy. "It must be right. I heard exactly the same. A shame. Only her second as well. Glad that didn't happen to me"' (Ishiguro 2005: 221). What is 'a shame' is not staying the course, not managing to achieve your four 'donations'. This is the mentality, you might protest, of someone who cannot see his own enslavement. Tommy's response might have been devised exactly to provoke those readers who are exasperated by the failure of these characters to imagine escaping their doom.

The characters in this novel – those who are 'students' or 'carers' or 'donors', at least – have limits placed on their imaginations that are invisible to them, and this is true of the novel's narrator, too. Kathy H. is defined by what she does not tell us and what she cannot say. She is not exactly, however, that personage with whom we have been familiar since named by Wayne C. Booth: the 'unreliable narrator' (Booth 1961: 211–234). There is certainly a carefully contrived discrepancy between what she tells us and what we believe the author 'knows' about her world. Yet she is not, like most unreliable narrators, partial or self-deluded or dishonest. A common sign of her will to truth is her very readiness to doubt her own recollections. Frequently she questions the reliability of her memories and the stories she repeats. In the opening chapter, for instance, she tells us about watching Tommy with Ruth from the sports pavilion where she and her friends would go to gossip. She is one of those who gathers to watch him 'get humiliated yet again' (Ishiguro 2005: 7). 'Or maybe I'm remembering it wrong', she suddenly thinks. She ends the chapter recalling how she approached Tommy to interrupt the rage into which his persecution had thrown him, only to begin the next chapter, 'This was all a long time ago so I might have some of it wrong' (Ishiguro 2005: 13). She tells us of having 'to go over these earlier memories quite carefully' (Ishiguro 2005: 37), and her care is signalled by places where her account is uncertain of itself. Memory is uncertain, disputable, haggled over. Kathy H. tells us that she and Tommy or Ruth have disagreed about their recollections of the events she narrates. 'I said we'd been ten at the time; he thought it was later, but in the end came round to agreeing with me. I'm pretty sure I got it right' (Ishiguro 2005: 38). 'When Ruth and I discussed it while I was caring for her down in Dover, she claimed it had been just a matter of two or three weeks – but that was almost certainly wrong' (Ishiguro 2005: 49).

There have been many novels that have made the uncertainties of memory part of the texture of a first-person narration, but none where memory has quite the significance that it does for Ishiguro's narrator. When nothing of a person extends back before them, memory is all they have. Milton's Satan fantasized about being self-begot, and this is what Kathy H. and her fellow 'students' are cursed to be. Their past is entirely their own, to be reclaimed or to disappear, or perhaps to be created. She tells us about the dying donor who wants to hear about Hailsham so that it can become his own false memory. 'What he wanted was not just to hear about Hailsham, but to *remember* Hailsham, just like it had been his own childhood' (Ishiguro 2005: 5; emphasis in the original). Kathy H. recalls her own anger when Ruth seems to her to be 'pretending to forget things about Hailsham' (Ishiguro 2005: 186–187), something one of the 'guardians' used to say, or some detail about a path in the grounds. When Ruth cannot remember some incident, Kathy H. supplies more details, 'trying to clinch it for her memory' (Ishiguro 2005: 198). She chivvies her to remember a magazine advertisement from years earlier, which showed a picture of an office: 'Oh, come on. You remember. We found it in a magazine in some lane. Near a puddle. You were really taken by it. Don't pretend you don't remember. [. . .] Remember how you used to go on about it? How you'd one day work in an office like that one?' (Ishiguro 2005: 225). What is obvious, though not to the narrator, is that Ruth, debilitated by her first 'donation' and on the path to her death, is unwilling to entertain again the fantasies of her youth. 'Ruth was exhausted – that last conversation on the roadside seemed to have drained her' (Ishiguro 2005: 230). Less obvious is the need that has made Kathy H. tactlessly press this memory on her friend. At the end of the novel we find her obstinately disagreeing with 'one of my donors' who has complained 'how memories, even your most precious ones, fade surprisingly quickly' (Ishiguro 2005: 280). 'I don't go along with that. The memories I value most, I don't see them ever fading. I lost Ruth, then I lost Tommy, but I won't lose my memories of them' (Ishiguro 2005: 280). This is close to a sentimental formula in which someone looks for consolation after another's death. Yet it is made unsettling by the narrative's emphasis. The narrator's memories really do make her only connections with others like herself.

Remembering others and understanding others are synonymous for this narrator. Throughout the novel Kathy H. works away on her memories to catch what has really gone on between her and her 'friends'. As she recalls their exchanges, the word 'something' keeps being used for what she remembers, but cannot quite specify. When she narrates the episode where she meets Ruth and Tommy in the churchyard, the word recurs like an anxious tic.

> Maybe I should have picked up something in the way that they greeted me [. . .] It was some time before it occurred to me that something wasn't right [. . .] there had to be something behind her words [. . .] I could see too something dark and troubling gathering behind his eyes [. . .] I should have found something to say [. . .] I could have done something [. . .] That's something that came to me years later [. . .] Something in me just gave up. (Ishiguro 2005: 190–193)

Tommy has been telling Ruth his 'theory', which is that there might be some 'special arrangement' to 'defer their donations' for those who are 'truly in love', and who are shown to be so by the art that the guardians collect from them (Ishiguro 2005: 173). Ruth mocks this hope by telling Tommy that Kathy H. has herself laughed at his strange drawings of animals. All these somethings tell us of the unstated despair of the characters, and of how difficult the narrator finds it to be sure of her understanding of others. When she remembers, she tries to sense what human understanding might be, and we are made to feel her effort to do so. Take this example, when she travels back with Tommy from their meeting with Miss Emily and Madame, who have told them that there can be no postponement of their fate. Miss Emily has explained how her purpose at Hailsham was simply to shelter them from what 'lay in store', and how conflict had arisen with Miss Lucy, who had believed that they 'should be given as full a picture as possible' (Ishiguro 2005: 262–263). Tommy suddenly says, 'I think Miss Lucy was right. Not Miss Emily' (Ishiguro 2005: 268). 'I can't remember if I said anything to that. If I did, it certainly wasn't anything very profound. But that was the moment I first noticed it, something in his voice, or maybe his manner, that set off distant alarm bells' (Ishiguro 2005: 268). This 'something' is Tommy's fury at his destiny. Kathy H. stops the car and Tommy disappears into the darkness; she follows and finds him in a field 'raging, shouting, flinging his fists and kicking out' (Ishiguro 2005: 269). It is not quite rebellion, but his outbursts – 'Me being an idiot,' as he describes it – are the closest to it that these cloned humans come. And 'something' that Kathy H. cannot really understand.

She is not so much an unreliable narrator, as an inadequate narrator. She is not, like the narrator of Ishiguro's *The Remains of the Day*, keeping most natural feelings hidden or denied behind the peculiar speech habits of the narration. (Mr Stevens is both an inadequate and an unreliable narrator.) She is rather puzzling candidly over feelings that have been made obscure to her. Much that she recalls is puzzling, as if her past were a tissue of mysteries. Some of the novel's mysteries are unsolved and perhaps just false leads, puzzles that would characterize any memories of adolescence. Why were certain paths in the school grounds forbidden? What of the legends of students dying in the woods beyond those grounds? Other mysteries have missing explanations that the reader can supply. Why does Miss Lucy disappear? Why are there such frequent medical checks on the students (Ishiguro 2005: 13)? What is the 'training' for which each eventually embarks? Why is smoking thought so bad? Why is Kathy interested in pornographic magazines (which she always examines too quickly)? In what is a desolate story, the supply of missing explanations sometimes has an unexpected effect of bleak comedy. The guardians' opposition to smoking is a parody of care. These adolescents' organs must be kept pure because they are to be used by someone else. Why are the guardians so interested in their students' artworks and poetry? 'Why train us, encourage us, make us produce all of that?' (Ishiguro 2005: 254) asks Kathy. The eventual explanation is cruelly quaint. Like traditional English philanthropists, the ladies running Hailsham believed that some wider public will feel more humanely towards these 'poor creatures' if they can be shown to make art. It is a nice and nasty irony: as children the clones have all been persuaded of the importance of being 'creative'.

We could almost think we recognize some of Kathy H.'s puzzlement, especially about her relationships with others. 'Looking back now, I can see we were pretty confused about the whole area around sex. That's hardly surprising, I suppose, given we were barely sixteen' (Ishiguro 2005: 93). 'Hardly surprising' is the expressive clumsiness of that clichéd circumlocution: 'the whole area around sex'. But this is not ordinary teenage perplexity. She and her fellow students are sterile. They came from nowhere and they cannot reproduce. Her own talk about sex is expressionless, as if, for her, intimacy itself is necessarily incomplete: 'Anyway, the point is, I'd had a few one-nighters shortly after getting to the Cottages. I hadn't planned it that way. My plan had been to take my time, maybe become part of a couple with someone I chose carefully' (Ishiguro 2005: 125). She takes it that her sexual appetites are themselves proof of something peculiar about her genesis, for in the logic of this narrative feelings must turn back on themselves. Thus Kathy H.'s weird and touching trawl through the pornography she finds in search of what she imagines as the lustful, brazen women from whom she must have been 'copied' (Ishiguro 2005: 179). The hunger for intimacy is turned back on itself, and more proof of the solitariness that is her condition.

'Poor creatures. I wish I could help you. But now you're by yourselves' (Ishiguro 2005: 267), says Madame, when Kathy H. and Tommy find her again. Isolation is the very condition of Kathy H.'s narrative of recollection. As, in the narrative's present, she drives the miles between her donors, the busy island seems unpeopled. She visits only service stations; notices only those who might once have been fellow students. They have been reared in seclusion, and the narration itself seems sealed off from wider influences. 'Any place beyond Hailsham was like a fantasy land' (Ishiguro 2005: 66). It sounds like the ordinary hyperbole of a memoir, but is exactly true to the segregation ingrained in Ishiguro's narrator. Thus the strange and memorable episode when Kathy H. recalls gazing with her friends through the window of an office in Cromer, watching for just a moment as people unlike themselves get on with life (Ishiguro 2005: 156–157). Hailsham itself, so exactly and lovingly remembered, is in some uncertain no-place in the English countryside. The adult Kathy keeps thinking that she has glimpsed it again on her travels round England, but she never has done. The non-clones whom she remembers are the distant guardians and their functionaries – 'gardeners and delivery men joke and laugh with you and call you "sweetheart"' (Ishiguro 2005: 36). And how sinister does that endearing term become!

Kathy H. herself cannot hear this. She is not enabled to know what those who do not share her destiny might be like. Ishiguro has invented a person who is related to no one. It is a beautifully maintained, technically exact narrative experiment. He has painstakingly crafted the voice that speaks for this person. He is a novelist known, and sometimes criticized, for the thoroughness with which he fulfils his experimental hypotheses. In *Never Let Me Go*, the experiment is also humane. The novel imagines the speculative attachments that might grow in the place of all natural connection to others. It is a telling fictional enquiry in a culture that is preoccupied, in any number of popular forms, with the 're-discovery' of genealogy. Kathy H. does not have lost parents or unknown siblings. She has no possibility or fantasy of a biological relationship with another person. Yet she is another human being (I share the characters' embarrassment about even using the word 'clone'). Her inadequate attempts to make a story of herself and others who might be like her takes us to the elementary principles of human sympathy. Experimentally, but movingly.

'I'm Sorry I Can't Say More': An Interview with Kazuo Ishiguro

SEAN MATTHEWS

The following is an edited transcript of a public conversation that took place during the conference, 'Kazuo Ishiguro and the International Novel', Liverpool Hope University, 2 June 2007.

Sean Matthews: One of the most dramatic changes, over recent years, in the experience of contemporary writers has been the emergence of a new kind of 'Cult of the Author', evident in an explosion of 'Author Events' and 'Author Interviews'. You have found yourself, increasingly, a part of this circuit of readings, conversations, and profiles. Around the time of the publication of *The Remains of the Day* you did a tremendous number of public appearances, all over the world, which you talked about finding exhausting, even quite traumatic. In *The Unconsoled*, the main character is in many ways trapped in a touring artist's nightmare. Could you tell us something about this aspect of your life as a writer?

Kazuo Ishiguro: Author events are called 'Readings' but increasingly they're not readings at all. When I first started to do them, authors were expected to just read from their work, but over the years people have come to want a discussion, and a question-and-answer session. Author events have turned into an art form in their own right. In a sense we are now coming to a point where books are bypassed altogether. People can actually become very knowledgeable about the literary scene simply by attending author events: they have a direct line to the author without ever encountering the books, or doing any hard work. I'm exaggerating, of course, but it is something that troubles me. There is a healthy aspect to it, I suppose, in that it stops authors becoming too introverted, it reminds us that we're writing for real human beings, but even that has a more problematic side. When you travel around the world to promote your books, you can become a little too sensitive to your foreign readership. I once spent two days in Norway, and I was asked a number of questions about particular cultural references in my work. Now, I find that when I'm writing in my study, I often find myself addressing a particular Norwegian in my head because at some point I know I will have to explain this book to a Norwegian, and many cultural references would not survive the Norwegian translation. Thus, the result of having to spend two solid days facing those Norwegians is that they are now looking over my shoulder when I'm back in the solitude of my study. This is how globalization touches the author. You do this for the Japanese, you do this for farmers in the American mid-West, and unless you're careful, you lose all sense of your own identity. You might actually even lose contact with your own language.

Coming at it from another angle, some of my readers speculate, on the grounds of my biography, about the meanings of my writing, particularly in terms of my relation to Japan and the preponderance of characters who seem to be outsiders. I don't know if there is a deep connection there. I'm not even sure that my characters are really outsiders as much as people say. Someone like the main character in my second novel, *An Artist of the Floating World*, is very much part of that society and generation, and that to a certain extent *is* his tragedy, that he wasn't remarkable enough to stand outside of that generation and moment, during the war. He's just being swept along with the tide. To some extent there is a similar situation in *Never Let Me Go*. The characters do belong to a rather odd community, but they are nonetheless very much part of that community, and they cannot stand outside it. This is why they're so passive about what they're being told to do; they cannot stand outside their situation as individuals. Many of my characters tend to go with the flow, and even an outsider like Stevens in *The Remains of the Day* to some extent isn't an outsider. He's deeply somebody who thinks like a member of his class, and he can't quite get out of that. I started writing *The Remains of the Day* because of my suspicion that to some extent we are all in some sense butlers; at an ethical and political level, most of us are butlers. We don't stand outside of our milieu and evaluate it. We don't say, 'Wait, we're going to do it this way instead'. We take our orders, we do our jobs, we accept our place in the hierarchy, and hope that our loyalty is used well, just like this butler guy. So my characters may be isolated figures personally, but I do try to make them like everyman characters. I suppose I personally don't feel that I'm a kind of an outsider either, for that matter.

S. M.: That kind of speculative, bio-critical reading is often something that academics and literary critics and teachers, who make their living by telling people about how to investigate the imaginary worlds of Kazuo Ishiguro, can be guilty of. Do 'professional' readers of this kind also, as you put it, hover at your shoulder while you write?

K. I.: Like many writers, I *am* very aware of what happens in the book world. When you publish a book and there's a review somewhere, you rush out, read the review and, depending on the review, spit on it. I'm not aware in the same way of what people are saying and writing about me in the universities. Every now and again, it comes into my orbit, and usually I simply feel deeply flattered that all these people are taking my work so seriously.

There needs to be more contact between universities and writers like myself. I think it's increasingly important – important for writers, and for writing – to have some place where modern and contemporary literature can be discussed away from the pressures of commercialism. When I first began to write books, there was what you would call the 'high-brow' end of publishing. This had many drawbacks, but it did tend proudly to make a stand against the domination of commercial aspects in the publishing of literary fiction. You had very serious discussions about literature. Nowadays this has almost vanished, despite the proliferation of creative writing courses. For a young writer starting out today, there are enormous commercial pressures, regardless of whether they're trying to be Dan Brown or Samuel Beckett. Publishers look at books and say: 'How many copies can I sell of the debut novel?' If they expect to sell a certain number of copies, they are published: literary merit is hardly of any value. There needs to be a counterbalance to this situation, and perhaps universities can function as a shelter from that rampant commercialism; they can provide a place where people can discuss what makes a good book and what the values we want to carry on in a literary tradition are.

S. M.: It is interesting that you use the term 'literary tradition'. Do you have any conscious ideas about the literary tradition to which your own work might relate? Are you conscious of authors and works to which you have a particular relation?

K. I.: That's a difficult question. In a broad spectrum, I would like to be thought of in the same vein as the more serious writers. You thought I was going to say Tolstoy . . . I would like to be thought of ultimately, yes, as writer who has a serious purpose.

I want my books to be entertaining, of course, with no overly hard work on a page-to-page basis, but I'm also trying to have a serious conversation with my readers. I hope we are talking about the serious things in life, about what makes our life worthwhile.

There have, however, been significant influences on my work, which I would readily acknowledge. I had a 'Japanese phase' in my early twenties when I was hungry for everything about Japanese culture. I found that Japanese filmmakers, such as [Akiro] Kurosawa and [Yasujiro] Ozu, had a profound effect on me, and they probably influenced me enormously as a writer. These movie makers were often called the 'humanist tradition' of film, particularly Kurosawa. In contrast, the novelists that I came across at the time, [Yukio] Mishima and [Yasunari] Kawabata, I found very negative, even nihilistic. I don't want to pronounce any judgement on them, but I felt they were a very alien literature. I couldn't quite understand what was going on, they seemed to revel in a negative vision of life, as though having an artistic sensibility and having a negative sensibility were one and the same. So I could get fairly little out of them. I never see myself in relation to someone like Mishima, who was a very right-wing sort of nutter – well, how else can you describe him? – perhaps he was a great writer, but he was a kind of neo-fascist and if it wasn't for the fact that he was Japanese I would never think of myself in relation to him.

The current generation of Japanese writers, by the way, people like Haruki Murakami (who is one of my favourite writers), I see them in a different tradition altogether. These are writers I can relate to, very readily. I think Murakami is popular everywhere. If you go to Italy and France, he is probably *the* international writer: in every language he has a significant presence. He's a world away from that nihilistic tradition.

The other literary tradition, if that's the word in this case, with which I'm most often aligned is 'Postmodernism', but I've never really thought of myself in those terms, either. When I was a student of literature and creative writing the 'postmodern' label was very trendy, it was almost like an ethical position. As a writer of a new generation you *had* to write in a postmodern way, otherwise you were somehow encouraging imperialism. I'm not sure what the logic was. So there was a little phase, I suppose, when I wanted to be called postmodern, but to be absolutely honest, the writers who were presented to me as models of postmodernism, writers such as Bartheleme or Calvino, they were not the writers who were as useful to me as a developing writer. When push comes to shove, we were learning from Dickens, Dostoevsky, Jane Austen, and, yes, Tolstoy. I found that there was nothing much I could use from postmodernism.

Thinking further about the characteristics of postmodern writing, I'm personally not interested in 'metafiction', in writing books about the nature of fiction. I've got nothing against such books, but for me there are more urgent questions than the nature of fiction. So in that sense I am not interested in writing about storytelling, but I *am* interested in storytelling in the sense of what a community or a nation tells itself about its past and by implication therefore where it is at the moment and what it should be doing next. If you want to draw a parallel between how individuals come to terms with their past and decide what to do next, and how a nation or a community approaches such things, then the issue of storytelling is an important one. The stories that people tell each other within a community, they could literally be stories, but in the modern age it would tend to be TV programmes, journalism, all of that commentary that follows every event and dresses it up for us, interprets it for us, and tells us what it might actually meant. What are the tools by which we tell these stories? What exactly are these stories that we tell ourselves? When we tell ourselves stories as a nation about why we did something, what is the motivation? What drives the process? Are we trying to be honest or are we trying to deceive, or comfort ourselves?

These are very much the same questions that apply to the function of religion in society. So I'm interested in stories and storytelling in that sense, but I don't like books that simply contemplate the nature of fiction.

S. M.: This concern with storytelling seems to involve the author's responsibility towards the way in which he or she represents people, places, events, and history. There is, however, a tension in your work between, on the one hand, universality – your stories travel well, they can be read everywhere, in Norway and in Japan – and, on the other hand, specificity – they take place in very particular historical moments, such as during the Suez crisis, and in precise places, such as in Nagasaki. Could you say something about this sense of responsibility towards the representation of place and history in your work?

K. I.: This is a question which has troubled me throughout my career. I have always had an uneasy relationship to settings and history. I often feel that I've used history as just another source for my fiction. I'm not like Primo Levi or, more recently, like Irène Nemirovsky [a Jewish Ukranian writer (1903–1942) who worked in France, died in Auschwitz, and who was rediscovered in the late 1990s], who writes about the German invasion of France. They are writers who feel the need to bear witness to the events that are happening at particular moments in history.

In contrast to such writers, I have my own stories and themes, and, to some extent, I've turned to history almost for dramatic effect. The settings often come quite late in the writing process because I look for a location that allows me to orchestrate my story the best way possible. I never started *The Remains of the Day* with the idea of writing about the 1930s. Other considerations came first. Then I thought about setting it in a specific period where all these ideas would reverberate in the best way. The 1930s is associated with questions about democracy, so it's better to do it there than in the 1970s. However, this leaves me with the nagging feeling that I use history and exploit deep and sometimes tragic experiences that real people have had as a kind of backdrop or thematic dressing. But I try to be responsible about this and to not misrepresent events. I'm not the person to come to for the truth about a particular era, I'm afraid.

The question of where to set a novel is a similar process to that of choosing the period in which to set it. Deciding on a location is inevitable: you have to set a novel somewhere. I'm writing a novel now, and it took me a long while to decide where to set it precisely for this reason. I have often written about individuals who struggle with their past and their conscience, but now I wanted to write a novel about how people – not just individuals – but communities and countries remember and forget their own history. There are perhaps times when a nation *should* forget and when you *can* cover things up, and leave things unresolved because it would stir up all kinds of trouble. For a long time I've been struggling with the setting. If I set it, say, during the Bosnian wars in the 1990s, it becomes a book about the Bosnian wars in the 1990s. If I do author events, I will get lots of questions about Bosnia, and that would be perfectly understandable. I could just as easily move it to the United States and talk about how America has not quite confronted its relationship with the slavery and segregation eras, but then it becomes about that. So, do I write something weird, about a strange, abstract kind of place, with alien types of being behaving strangely? No: a novel has to be set somewhere.

This is a very practical problem for a novelist. There's always the tension between the setting you choose and the fact that you want to use that location for universal metaphors, for stories that can be applied to all sorts of human situations. You've got to say to your readers that the novel is set in a particular time and place, but hopefully they'll be able to see that it's also about things that are happening over and over again. The balance is quite difficult, but it is why great books can yield so many different kinds of readings.

S. M.: Do these questions of responsibility and seriousness involve also choices about form, particularly in terms of narrative voice? You have often made use of 'unreliable' first-person narrators, certainly first-person narration has predominated in your writing, but more recently you seem to be employing an objectifying, third-person voice?

K. I.: The distinction between first- or third-person narration is no big deal. The book I'm writing now is not narrated in the first person, but it might as well be, for large sections at least. More important is where the consciousness is located in a novel.

There is, however, a deeper question. One of the reasons that I'm moving away from the first person is that doing things only one way can become artistically crippling – is one doing it for artistic reasons, or just from habit? There is something about a certain kind of first-person narrative, exemplified in a book like *The Remains of the Day*, in which the first-person narrative works to hide certain things, even from the narrator himself. Stevens is struggling to come to terms with uncomfortable memories and finally admitting those things is very cathartic, the climax is when the narrator comes to understand something about himself.

This is a perfectly good narrative model, but as I get older and the world around me keeps changing, I feel less and less comfortable about that narration. That model was an easy fit when I was younger, but such a repressed kind of narration doesn't quite fit now. Emotional repression isn't the problem in our times, as it was in the fifties. We suffer from almost the opposite. Everyone is just spilling out their feelings everywhere.

The repressed voice of the first person is not suitable to express what it's like to live today. It's not so much that we are holding down our darker urges; these days it's almost hard to hold on to the centre, as there is always, tauntingly, some other person you could be, some other person you could be married to, some other career you might have, some other lifestyle you might have, if only you'd join the gym. We're living in a world where the horizon is forever taunting us to be somebody else. We have role models hurled at us from every direction. It's almost like the antithetical problem: it's hard to hold onto any sense of your self, because we're being told you can be anything you want, if you just put your mind to it.

So the form of the novel, the voice, relates to the time the writer lives in. I'm conscious, looking back on when I was writing *The Remains of the Day*, I think what you can very loosely call Freudian ideals, sorry, ideas, had a big effect on writers of my generation. In fact, I had been working in social work in London and in that world particularly there was a therapy-ish kind of personal growth counter-culture, so without actually being a Freud-nut, I imbibed a lot of reflexes from those loosely Freudian ideas. When the film came out this was really highlighted: the film more than the book was about repression. My agent, Deborah Rogers, made a very astute remark; she said, 'The film is about emotional repression, the book is about self-denial.' I think that's an important distinction. The Antony Hopkins part was a study of emotional repression and this was partly why the film was such a big hit in America – I know, I got many letters about it. It's only looking back that I see these ideas about repression, even about how human beings are put together, emotionally and psychologically, were in the air at the time, and some of these assumptions have now been eroded or questioned – or have become mere conventions – and so I'm revising my ideas about how to draw a character in a novel. It's gone to almost a cartoon level in some work. I remember seeing, back to back, biopics of Johnny Cash and Ray Charles, and there is now a typical way in which characters are made up. You see an artist in torment in the present day and they have these key flashbacks to events they experienced when they were three, and this explains why they are drug addicts. In popular fiction and popular drama, this has become a lazy way to build a character. You just have a little moment when someone comes up with a revelation about their trauma and then you have a fully formed character. So-called literary authors such as me are guilty of this as well, albeit in a slightly more sophisticated way. You tend to think that to build a character and a rather interesting person then you have to explain it by things in the past, then you have 'done' that character. Whereas in real life people are much more mysterious. You can know someone for years and years and there are large chunks that you just cannot explain. You've had a perfectly nice child and, suddenly, 'Why are you like that?' Or the other way around. People are much more complex and complicated than that model allows. People's potential to change their lives or to change themselves somewhere in the middle of their lives, that has been underestimated. You can date a certain novelist or a certain generation by their assumptions about character, and how you write full characters and how you basically build on that Freudian novel. Maybe it's time that we moved on, accepted more the unpredictable, unaccountable nature of human being, and that will be apparent at the level of form and voice and structure in the novel.

S. M.: It almost sounds like you are beginning to regret some of your earlier writing. Would you want to go back and revise some things?

K. I.: I would never want to go back and rewrite my previous work. Some writers have started to do this. They issue paperback editions of something they published thirty years before and change bits. Henry James wrote prefaces to his collected works. I find this alarming. What I wrote then is what I wrote then, with all its flaws and failures. It represents who I was then, and what I wanted to say then. Sometimes you come across a photograph of yourself twenty years ago, with flares and a stupid hair style. You have to be a very strange kind of person to want to alter that picture, to photoshop it. That's who you were, that isn't honest.

S. M.: In the light of this, do you keep those photos – with the flares and stupid hair – for posterity? More to the point, are you storing all the notebooks, scrap paper, and draft versions for posterity? Future generations will, I am sure, want to study in the Kazuo Ishiguro Archive.

K. I.: No. I find this really a very vexing question. Up to *The Remains of the Day* I used to religiously throw away everything. I wanted people to see the final novel and nothing else. I didn't keep a shred of paper; emotionally I was shredding everything. Then a book collector phoned me and said this was a mistake, that I could get huge amounts of money selling this material. In the future, he said, I should store everything and sell it to some mug in Texas. I wish I hadn't had this phone call. Now I can't throw anything away. On any given day I produce an enormous amount of stuff on paper, and at the end of the day I have to put it in a cardboard box and take it up to the loft. I don't know what this going to achieve. Certainly a lot of money, but deep in my heart I don't understand why this stuff would be valuable to anyone. It may be interesting for some people to trace the processes of creation and writing, but it doesn't have the same value one gets from reading a novel. It might be a separate area of interest within academia, but I personally can't say whether my experience of reading my favourite authors would be greatly enhanced if I knew particular background details, and trawled through their paraphernalia. I don't know if I will value *Crime and Punishment* more as a result, or less, perhaps, because I can see all the mechanics behind the text. What is important is to look at writing as a dialogue between author and serious readers, and to understand the satisfaction and fascination that comes from appreciating a work of art.

S. M.: Nonetheless, critics are interested in tracing the creative process by analyzing a work of art in the different stages of its creation. Through such analysis they may be able to say something about the nature of creativity, and how craftsmanship may shape inspiration. It's interesting in terms of your own writing to think about how the short stories, or the films, relate to novels.

K. I.: Anyone who knows my work will know I'm not very prolific. Since 1982, I have only published six novels, but I do actually *write* a lot. Behind these novels, I write lots of experiments. In the past I have used the short story form as a way to work out ideas for my novels. It's another thing that worries me: I'm conscious about not only abusing history, but the short story form as well. Rather than invest in a whole novel that would take years to write, I often just give an idea a go in a short story to see if it would come off. However, very often I write things that aren't really short stories in a way that Alice Munro or Chekhov wrote short stories. These are just pieces that end quite quickly, and sometimes these things find their way into my novels.

As for films, they are very important to who I am, for a couple of reasons. First, I think the hazard of being a novelist is that there is a singular vision in the book where you are everything, costume designer, set designer, the director, but over the years it's sometimes difficult to keep getting inspired. If you interview a musician, say a jazz musician, by this point in the conversation, the musician would have mentioned seven or eight people that he or she had played with in the past. So the history of my development as a jazz musician is the history of who I played with. This is so for the theatre, and for many other art forms. With painting and with novels, there is danger that you just become very insular, that you don't move to the next stage when you should. I've seen this happen to a lot of writers and I feel that had they been involved in a collaborative art form they would have come to know things about themselves as they got older and responded to change in different ways. But sometimes you don't have that incentive. It's partly to compensate for this that I do like to work in other art forms, above all film, where the writer is very low down in the creative hierarchy. You're up against much more immediate technical and commercial decisions, practical decisions, about what it is possible to film. I think that sort of collaboration is something I value very much.

It's not, in the end, *my* vision as a writer that is at stake. I see cinema as the director's medium. I'm helping the director. In fact, *The White Countess* was a story that James Ivory and I concocted together. It was really the case of us sitting together and saying 'What do we really want to make a film about?' Then we formed the story, saying 'Why don't we do it this way?' It was done like that. It's very much a collaborative thing. If you look at it from the point of view of a novelist, I would find it incredibly frustrating, to be a screenwriter. I would be angry about how little they're valued in relation to the work which is actually put in. But because it's a side thing, I've managed to come out relatively unscathed and, as I say, I really value the collaborative experience.

On another level, just watching films and being a fan of films, and sometimes being involved in films, it does have a big effect on the way I write.

When I try to imagine a scene, as a writer, it's almost like I'm seeing a kind of cinematic scene. But I can't say that the actual experience of working in the film industry has helped me much, practically, with my novels. Only in this very general sense that working with other people and making your imagination and your artistic ego blend into other artistic egos. It is an indirect effect and you come back and you've slightly expanded, you've taken something else into yourself.

S. M.: How did you get involved in films in the first place?

K. I.: It's not a recent thing. After my first novel, the reason why I was able to become a full time writer was because I wrote a couple of pieces for Channel 4, television plays although they were technically made on film. So I began earning a living by writing screenplays. Since then I have been trying to have two careers going at once. For years and years, maybe twenty years, I had a film in development, called *The Saddest Music in the World*. It was finally released in 2004. This is once again the nature of film. You can do it, and people might not notice that you're doing it. But I rather like having both things going, though to be honest film writing is now a kind of a hobby, it's not something I see as my main thing.

S. M.: Coming at this from the other direction, as it were, what did you feel when you saw the film that had been made of *The Remains of the Day*?

K. I.: A film has to be related to the book, like a cousin. Film is a very practical form and there are many considerations in play as to, say, who should play Stevens. Given that this is going to be a Hollywood film, which English actors can open a film in the United States, in 1990? At that time there were only three actors: Jeremy Irons, Bob Hoskins, and Antony Hopkins. I think John Cleese was actually offered the part because he had become big box office material with *A Fish called Wanda* and people felt he was someone who could open this film. What I'm saying is that decisions in the film world are often made according to things like that. You're not necessarily looking for the person who would be the perfect embodiment of the author's vision. Anthony Hopkins did a superb job. He was different to the Stevens I had in my head, he created another version, another kind of Stevens, to the point where I imagined Stevens being like him. The film isn't a simple, direct translation of the book, it's another kind of work altogether. That's how it often goes. The same thing applies to what happened to the story. Many, many non-artistic factors come into why a story ends up a certain way in the film. With books, because you can go over it, if you feel like it, you can weed out all these non-artistic reasons, if you've got the patience.

S. M.: Turning to your most recent work, *Never Let Me Go*, it seems to demonstrate the pressure of many of the things that you've been talking about in terms of the narrative voice, the form, and the underlying seriousness of your work.

K. I.: I think that's true. In all my works, to some extent, I try to create a situation where the characters are emotionally slightly eccentric, and that goes for Kathy, too. You say to Stevens, for instance, 'Why don't you step out of this and just ask this lady for a date?' It's a kind of technique: you withhold the most obvious thing that you want a character to do. I suppose the big thing about *Never Let Me Go* is that they never rebel, they don't do the thing you want them to do. They passively accept the programme in which they are butchered for their organs. I wanted a very strong image like that for the way most of us are, in many ways we are inclined to be passive, we accept our fate. Perhaps we wouldn't accept this to *that* extent, but we are much more passive than we'd like to think. We accept the fate that seems to be given to us. We accept the conditions that are given to us. I suppose, ultimately, I wanted to write a book about how people accept that we are mortal and we can't get away from this, and that after a certain point we are all going to die, we won't live forever. There are various ways to rage against that, but in the end we have to accept it and there are different reactions to it. So I wanted the characters in *Never Let Me Go* to react to this horrible programme they seem to be subjected to in much the way in which we accept the human condition, accept ageing, and falling to bits, and dying.

In many ways, my work is no more complicated than that, I'm concerned with serious, but straightforward truths. I've been asked about, for instance, the significance of Kathy's reading of George Eliot's *Daniel Deronda*, but I have to admit there is no real significance to it. I just wanted her to be reading a certain kind of Victorian novel and not a blindingly obvious one, like *Bleak House* or so. It says something about her relationship to literature, she doesn't just read *Middlemarch*, she reads *Daniel Deronda*. I read *Daniel Deronda* years ago and I can't remember what it is about, I don't remember enough about it to use it in that way. I personally don't like to use allusions in my books, but if someone's reading a book I've got to give it a name, much like I have to put them in a place and time. So I try to choose a book that's appropriate but I don't expect people to go and read that book in order to find echoes. Having said which, if people want to do that, that's fine with me. There are writers like that, someone like T. S. Eliot does nothing else, but I personally don't like to do that.

It's related to the use of symbols: again, it's not something I like to do. In the scene in *Never Let Me Go* where they find that boat, in the field, I hadn't intended it to be some kind of huge symbol. It doesn't represent death or something. I just needed a scene like that. It seemed to be emotionally right. I had actually seen a boat gone to ground, somewhere in the marshes in Norfolk, and it was a kind of haunting sight. I just wanted them to experience something like that, as what would be a kind of cultural event in their lives, rather than going to Glastonbury. It seemed to me, totally, that it was right. There was something about an old fishing boat, years since it ever went out to sea, the ground all dried up around it, and these kids talk about it and see it and think about their lives. And they say, 'Well, we've seen it,' and then they go away. That felt like what I wanted.

I used to want to be a musician and I still play. A scene like that, my answer is almost the answer a musician might give, like 'Why did you play that solo in that way?' or, 'Why did you write that passage like that?' I can't quite give you a logical answer. I can only speak in the way a musician speaks. It sounds good to me, tonally, emotionally. That's what I wanted. There are many decisions I make as a writer which I can't really back up with simple answers like, 'That's supposed to be a metaphor,' or, 'That's what it's supposed to be,' or, 'It's an echo of T. S. Eliot.' Often I find myself sketching something out and it's just got to be a certain way, and nothing else will do. I can't tell you why. It's very similar to a musician who says that it should be played this way, because it sounds right this way, otherwise it wouldn't be right. I just wanted that boat because of the atmosphere it gave. I'm sorry I can't say more.

References
Works Cited by Contributors

Introduction: 'Your Words Open Windows for Me': The Art of Kazuo Ishiguro, Sebastian Groes and Sean Matthews

Ishiguro, K. (1982), *A Pale View of Hills*. London: Faber and Faber.
—(1986), *An Artist of the Floating World*. London: Faber and Faber.
—(1989), *The Remains of the Day*. London: Faber and Faber.
—(1993), *The Gourmet. Granta*, 43, 89–128.
—(1995), *The Unconsoled*. London: Faber and Faber.
—(2000), *When We Were Orphans*. London: Faber.
—(2005), *Never Let Me Go*. London: Faber and Faber.
—(2005), *The White Countess*. Released 21 December, dir. James Ivory, prod. Ismail Merchant for Merchant Ivory Productions.
—(2009), *Nocturnes: Five Stories of Music and Nightfall*. London: Faber and Faber.
Leavis, F. R. (1948), *The Great Tradition*. London: Chatto and Windus.
—(1955), *D. H. Lawrence: Novelist*. London: Chatto and Windus.
Lukacs, G. (1957), 'The Ideology of Modernism', in Lukacs, G. (ed.; 1963), *The Meaning of Contemporary Realism*, trans. John and Necke Mander. London: Merlin Press.
McEwan, I. (2005), 'Save the Bootroom, save the Earth', 19 March, *The Guardian*, http://www.guardian.co.uk/artanddesign/2005/mar/19/art1 [accessed 1 September 2009].
Oe, K. and K. Ishiguro (1991), 'The Novelist in Today's World: A Conversation', *Boundary 2*, 18, 109–122; Repr. as 'Wave Patterns: A Dialogue', in *Grand Street*, 10, 75–91. Repr. in B. W. Shaffer and C. F. Wong (2008), 52–65. Originally published in (1989) *Kokusai Koryu*, 53, 100–108.
Thompson, E. P. (1968 [1963]), *The Making of the English Working Class*. Harmondsworth: Penguin.

Chapter One: 'Somewhere Just Beneath the Surface of Things': Ishiguro's Short Fiction, Brian W. Shaffer

Beckett, S. (1956), *Waiting for Godot*. London: Faber and Faber.
Booth, W. (1983), *The Rhetoric of Fiction*. Chicago: University of Chicago Press. [Second edition.]

Freud, S. (1955), 'The Uncanny', in *Standard Edition of the Complete Psychological Works of Sigmund Freud*, Vol. 17. London: The Hogarth Press and The Institute of Psychoanalysis, 217–252.

—(1989), 'Creative Writers and Daydreaming,' in *The Critical Tradition: Classic Texts and Contemporary Trends*, David H. Richter (ed.). New York: St. Martin's Press, 650–656.

Ishiguro, K. (1981a), 'A Strange and Sometimes Sadness', in *Introduction 7: Stories by New Writers*. London: Faber and Faber, 13–27.

—(1981b), 'Waiting for J', in *Introduction 7*, 28–37.

—(1981c), 'Getting Poisoned', in *Introduction 7*, 38–51.

—(1982), *A Pale View of Hills*. London: Faber and Faber.

—(1983a), 'The Summer after the War', *Granta* 7, 121–137.

—(1983b), 'A Family Supper', in *Firebird 2*, T. J. Binding (ed.). Harmondsworth: Penguin, 121–131; also in *The Penguin Collection of Modern Short Stories*, M. Bradbury (ed.). Harmondsworth: Penguin, 1987, 434–442; and *Esquire*, March 1990, 207–211.

—(1986), *An Artist of the Floating World*. London: Faber and Faber.

—(1989), *The Remains of the Day*. London: Faber and Faber.

—(1995), *The Unconsoled*. London: Faber and Faber.

—(2000), *When We Were Orphans*. London: Faber and Faber.

—(2001), 'A Village after Dark', in *The New Yorker*, 21 May.

—(2005). *Never Let Me Go*. London: Faber and Faber.

Kamine, M. (1989), 'A Servant of Self Defeat', *The New Leader*, 13 November, 22.

King, B. (2004), *The Internationalization of Literature: The Oxford English Literary History, Vol. 13: 1948–2000*. Oxford: Oxford University Press.

Lewis, B. (2000), *Kazuo Ishiguro*. Manchester: Manchester University Press.

Mason, G. (1989), 'An Interview with Kazuo Ishiguro', *Contemporary Literature* 30 (3), 335–347.

McEwan, I. (1975), 'Conversation with the Cupboard Man', in *First Love, Last Rites*. London: Jonathan Cape, 75–87.

—(1978), *The Cement Garden*. London: Jonathan Cape.

—(1998), *Amsterdam*. London: Jonathan Cape.

Oe, K. and K. Ishiguro (1991), 'The Novelist in Today's World: A Conversation', *Boundary 2*, 18 (3), 109–122.

Sexton, D. (1987), 'David Sexton meets Kazuo Ishiguro', *The Literary Review*, January, 16.

Sinclair, C. (1987), 'The Land of the Rising Son', *The Sunday Times*, 'Magazine', 11 January, 36–37.

Stevenson, R. L. (2007), *Strange Case of Dr. Jekyll and Mr. Hyde*. London: Penguin. First published in 1886.

Vlitos, P. (2003), 'Kazuo Ishiguro', in *World Writers in English, Vol. I: Chinua Achebe to V. S. Naipaul*, J. Parini (ed.). New York: Scribner's, 177–193.

Sim, W. (2005), 'Kazuo Ishiguro', *Review of Contemporary Fiction*, 25 (1), 80–115.

Chapter Two: Strange Reads: Kazuo Ishiguro's *A Pale View of Hills* and *An Artist of the Floating World* in Japan, Motoyuki Shibata and Motoko Sugano

Costigan, E. (1991), 'Patterns of Retrospect: A Reading of the Novels of Kazuo Ishiguro', *Studies in Language and Culture*, 17, 19–36.

Fujikawa, Y. (1988), 'Review of Kazuo Ishiguro's *Ukiyo no Gaka*', *Marie Claire*, Japan edition, June, 224.

Hamilton, C. (2007), 'Interview with Kazuo Ishiguro', 'Hamilton on Sunday', BBC Radio Merseyside, First broadcast 3 June.

Ishiguro, K. (1991 [1982]), *A Pale View of Hills*. London: Faber. The Japanese translation by Takeshi Onodera was first published in 1984.

—(1986), *An Artist of the Floating World*. London: Faber and Faber.

—(1988), *Ukiyo no gaka*, Shigeo Tobita (trans.). Tokyo: Chuokoronn.

—(1996 [1989]), *The Remains of the Day*. London: Faber and Faber. The Japanese translation by Masao Tsuchiya first appeared in 1990.

Lewis, B. (2000), *Kazuo Ishiguro*. Manchester: Manchester University Press.

Mason, G. (1989a), 'An Interview with Kazuo Ishiguro', *Contemporary Literature*, 30 (3), 334–347.

—(1989b), 'Inspiring Images: The Influence of the Japanese Cinema on the Writings of Kazuo Ishiguro', *East West Film Journal*, 3 (2), 39–52.

McLeod, J. (1998), '(Un)popular Postmodernism: Reading Kazuo Ishiguro's *An Artist of the Floating World*', *Diegesis: Journal of the Association for Research in Popular Fictions*, 2, 31–35.

Miura, M. (1988), 'Senchū no Shinnen wo tou [Interrogating his faith during the war]', *Asahi Shimbun*, 4 April, Morning edition, 12.

Rubin, J. (2002), *Haruki Murakami and the Music of Words*. London: Harvill.

Sim, W. (2006), *Globalisation and Dislocation in the Novels of Kazuo Ishiguro*. New York: Edwin Mellen Press.

Tobita, S. (1988), 'Translator's Afterword', *Ukiyo no Gaka*, Kazuo Ishiguro (ed.). Tokyo: Chuokoron, 280–286.

—(1992), 'Translator's Afterwords', *Ukiyo no Gaka*, Kazuo Ishiguro (ed.). Tokyo: Chuokoron, 315–319.

Chapter Three: 'Like the Gateway to Another World': Kazuo Ishiguro's Screenwriting, Sebastian Groes and Paul-Daniel Veyret

Ackroyd, P. (1993 [1985]), *Hawksmoor*. London: Penguin.

Carter, A. (1994 [1993]), *Nights at the Circus*. London: Vintage.

Ishiguro, K. (1981), 'A Strange and Sometimes Sadness', in *Introduction 7: Stories by New Writers*. London: Faber and Faber, 13–27.

—(1983), 'The Summer after the War', *Granta* 7, 121–137.

—(1986), *An Artist of the Floating World*. London: Faber and Faber.

—(1991 [1982]), *A Pale View of Hills*. London: Faber and Faber.

—(1993), *The Gourmet. Granta*, 43, 89–128.

—(1995), *The Unconsoled*. London: Faber and Faber.

—(2001 [2000]), *When We Were Orphans*. London: Faber.

—(2005), *Never Let Me Go*. London: Faber and Faber.

—(2009), *Nocturnes: Five Stories of Music and Nightfall*. London: Faber and Faber.

Krider, D. O. (1998), 'Rooted in a Small Space: An Interview with Kazuo Ishiguro', *Contemporary Literature*, 30 (3), 335–347.

Luckhurst, R. (2002), 'The Contemporary London Gothic and the Limits of the "Spectral Turn"', *Textual Practice*, 16 (3), 527–546.

Robinson, R. (2006), 'Nowhere, in Particular: Kazuo Ishiguro's *The Unconsoled* and Central Europe', in *Critical Quarterly*, 48 (4), Winter, 107–130.

Rushdie, S. (1988), *The Satanic Verses*. New York: Viking.

Sinclair, I. (1975), *Lud Heat: a book of the dead hamlets*. London: Albion Village Press.

Todd, R. (1996), 'Fantasies of London: Past and Present', in *Consuming Fictions*. London: Bloomsbury, 164–197.

Wood, M. (1995), 'The Discourse of Others', in *Children of Silence: Studies in Contemporary Fiction*. London: Pimlico, 171–181.

Filmography

Screenplays written by Kazuo Ishiguro

(1984). *A Profile of Arthur J. Mason*, unpublished manuscript. Broadcast in the UK, Channel 4, 18 October, dir. M. Whyte, prod. A. Skinner for Skreba/ Spectre.

(1993). *The Gourmet. Granta*, 43, 89–127. Broadcast in the UK, Channel 4, 8 May 1986, dir. M. Whyte, prod. A. Skinner for Skreba/Spectre.

(2003). *The Saddest Music In The World*. Released in UK, 25 October; released in USA, 14 February 2004, dir. Guy Maddin, prod. N. Finchman for IFC.

(2005). *The White Countess*. Released 21 December, dir. James Ivory, prod. Ismail Merchant for Merchant Ivory Productions.

Adaptations of Ishiguro's work

(1993). *The Remains of the Day*. Released 12 Novermber, dir. James Ivory, adapted by Ruth Prawer Jhabvala, for Merchant Ivory Productions.

(2010). *Never Let Me Go*. Dir. Mark Romanek, adapted by Alex Garland, A. DNA Films.

Chapter Four: History, Memory, and the Construction of Gender in *A Pale View of Hills*, Justine Baillie and Sean Matthews

Butler, J. (1990), *Gender Trouble*. London and New York: Routledge.

Carter, A. (1979), *The Sadeian Woman: An Exercise in Cultural History*. London: Virago.

Hutcheon, L. (1989), *The Politics of Postmodernism*. London and New York: Routledge.

Ishiguro, K. (1983 [1982]), *A Pale View of Hills*. Harmondsworth: Penguin.

Krider, D. O. (1998), 'Rooted in a Small Space: An Interview with Kazuo Ishiguro', *Kenyan Review*, 20(2), 146–154.

Kristeva, J. (1986a [France 1977]), 'Stabat Mater', trans. L. S. Roudiez, in *The Kristeva Reader*, T. Moi (ed.). Oxford: Blackwell, 161–186.

—(1986b [France 1979]), 'Women's Time', trans. A. Jardine and H. Blake, in *The Kristeva Reader*, 188–213.

Lyotard, J. (1988), from *The Differend: Phrases in Dispute*, trans. G. Van Den Abbeele, in I. Gregson (2004), *Postmodern Literature*. London: Arnold, 161–163.

—(1992 [1982]), 'Appendix: Answering the Question: What is Postmodernism?', trans. R. Durand, in *The Postmodern Condition: A Report on Knowledge* trans. G. Bennington and B. Massumi, first published in France in 1979 before the addition of Lyotard's appendix. Manchester: Manchester University Press, 71–82.

Oe, K. and K. Ishiguro (1991), 'The Novelist in Today's World: A Conversation', *Boundary 2*, 18/3, 109–122.

Rushdie, S. (1991 [1989]), 'Kazuo Ishiguro', in *Imaginary Homelands: Essays and Criticism 1981–1991*, 244–246.

Waugh, P. (1992), 'Modernism, Postmodernism, Gender' in *Practising Postmodernism/Reading Modernism*. London: Edward Arnold, 119–135.

Wong, C. F. (2000), *Kazuo Ishiguro*. Tavistock: Northcote House.

Chapter Five: Artifice and Absorption: The Modesty of *The Remains of the Day*, David James

Bigsby, C. (2008), 'In Conversation with Kazuo Ishiguro', repr. in *Conversations with Kazuo Ishiguro*, Brian W. Shaffer and Cynthia F. Wong (eds). Jackson, MI: University of Mississippi Press, 15–26. Originally published in 1987 in the *European English Messenger*, Zero Issue, 26–29.

Ishiguro, K. (1989), *The Remains of the Day*. London: Faber and Faber.

—(1995), *The Unconsoled*. London: Faber and Faber.

Krider, D. O. (1998), 'Rooted in a Small Space: An Interview with Kazuo Ishiguro', *Kenyon Review*, 20 (2), 146–155.

Mason, G. (1989), 'An Interview with Kazuo Ishiguro', *Contemporary Literature*, 30 (3), 335–347.

Robinson, J. (2005), *Deeper than Reason: Emotion and Its Role in Literature, Music and Art*. Oxford: Oxford University Press.

Rushdie, S. (1992 [1991]), *Imaginary Homelands: Essays and Criticism 1981–91*. London: Granta.

Wilson, A. (1983), *Diversity and Depth in Fiction: Selected Critical Writings*, ed. Kerry McSweeney. London: Secker & Warburg.

Chapter Six: 'To Give a Name, Is That Still to Give?': Footballers and Film Actors in *The Unconsoled*, Richard Robinson

Adelman, G. (2001), 'Doubles on the Rocks: Ishiguro's *The Unconsoled*', *Critique*, 42 (2), 166–179.

Barthes, R. (1989), 'The Reality Effect', *The Rustle of Language*, R. Howard (trans.). Berkeley and Los Angeles: University of California Press, 141–148.

Chaudhuri, A. (1995), 'Unlike Kafka', *London Review of Books*, 8 June, 30–31.

Collini, S. (ed.). (1992), *Interpretation and Overinterpretation*. Cambridge: Cambridge University Press.

Derrida, J. (1995), *On the Name*. Stanford, CA: Stanford University Press.

Edel, L. and L. H. Powers (1987), *The Complete Notebooks of Henry James*. New York and Oxford: Oxford University Press.

Elsaesser, T. (2000), *Weimar Cinema and After: Germany's Historical Imaginary*. London and New York: Routledge.

Freud, S. (1982), *The Psychopathology of Everyday Life*, trans. A. Tyson. Harmondsworth: Penguin.

Ishiguro, K. (1995), *The Unconsoled*. London: Faber and Faber.

Joyce, J. (1939), *Finnegan's Wake*. London: Faber and Faber.

Kracauer, S. (1947), *From Caligari to Hitler: A Psychological History of the German Film*. Princeton: Princeton University Press.

Krider, D. O. (1998), 'Rooted in a Small Space: An Interview with Kazuo Ishiguro', *Kenyan Review*, 20, 146–154.

Lewis, B. (2000), *Kazuo Ishiguro*. Manchester and New York: Manchester University Press.

Lodge, D. (1992), *The Art of Fiction*. Harmondsworth: Penguin.

Mason, G. and K. Ishiguro (1989), 'An Interview with Kazuo Ishiguro', *Contemporary Literature*, 30 (3), 335–347.

McHale, B. (1987), *Postmodernist Fiction*. London: Methuen.

Škrabánek, P. (2002), *Night Joyce of a Thousand Tiers*, ed. Louis Armand and Ondřej Pilný. Prague: Litteraria Pragensia.

Swift, G. (1989), 'Interview with Kazuo Ishiguro', *Bomb*, Issue 29 (Fall).

Filmography

(1930). *Der Blaue Engel*, dir. Josef von Sternberg.

(1968). *2001: A Space Odyssey*, dir. Stanley Kubrick.

Chapter Seven: *When We Were Orphans*: Narration and Detection in the Case of Christopher Banks, Hélène Machinal

Auden, W. H. (1948), 'The Guilty Vicarage: Notes on the Detective Story, by an Addict', *Harpers*, May, 406–412.

Barthes, R. (2000 [1953]), *Mythologies*, trans. A. Lavers. London: Vintage.

Ishiguro, K. (1989), *The Remains of the Day*. London: Faber and Faber.

—(1995), *The Unconsoled*. London: Faber and Faber.

—(2001 [2000]), *When We Were Orphans*. London: Faber and Faber.

Richards, L. (2000), 'January Interview: Kazuo Ishiguro', *January Magazine*, http://www.januarymagazine.com/profiles/ishiguro.html [accessed 19 June 2009].

Williams, R. (1984), *The English Novel from Dickens to Lawrence*. London: Hogarth Press. First published 1970, 16–17.

Chapter Eight: Controlling Time: *Never Let Me Go*, Mark Currie

Augustine, St. (1961), *Confessions*. Trans. R. S. Pine-Coffin. Harmondsworth: Penguin Books.

Ishiguro, K. (2005), *Never Let Me Go*. London: Faber and Faber. Paperback edition.

Wakeford, J. (1969), *The Cloistered Elite: A Sociological Analysis of the English Public Boarding School*. London: Macmillan.

Afterword: On First Reading *Never Let Me Go*, John Mullan

Booth, W. C. (1961), *The Rhetoric of Fiction*. Chicago: University of Chicago Press.

Ishiguro, K. (1989), *The Remains of the Day*. London: Faber and Faber.

—(1995), *The Unconsoled*. London: Faber and Faber.

—(2005), *Never Let Me Go*. London: Faber and Faber.

Oxford English Dictionary, http://www.askoxford.com/concise_oed/carer?view=uk [Accessed 12 June 2009].

Further Reading

Editorial annotations are enclosed in brackets where suitable.

I. Works by Kazuo Ishiguro

Novels

(1982). *A Pale View of Hills*. London: Faber and Faber.
(1986). *An Artist of the Floating World*. London: Faber and Faber.
(1989). *The Remains of the Day*. London: Faber and Faber.
(1995). *The Unconsoled*. London: Faber and Faber.
(2000). *When We Were Orphans*. London: Faber and Faber.
(2005). *Never Let Me Go*. London: Faber and Faber.

Short stories

(1981a). 'A Strange and Sometimes Sadness', in *Introduction 7: Stories by New Writers*. London: Faber and Faber, 13–27.
(1981b). 'Getting Poisoned', in *Introduction 7*, 38–51.
(1981c). 'Waiting for J', in *Introduction 7*, 28–37.
(1983a). 'A Family Supper', in *Firebird 2*, T. J. Binding (ed.). Harmondsworth: Penguin, 121–131; also in *The Penguin Collection of Modern Short Stories*, M. Bradbury (ed.). Harmondsworth: Penguin, 1987, 434–442; and *Esquire*, March 1990, 207–211.
(1983b). 'The Summer after the War', *Granta* 7, 121–137.
(2001). 'A Village after Dark', *The New Yorker*, 21 May, 86–91.
(2009). *Nocturnes: Five Stories of Music and Nightfall*. London: Faber and Faber.

Screenplays

(1984). *A Profile of Arthur J. Mason*, unpublished manuscript. Broadcast in the UK, Channel 4, 18 October, dir. M. Whyte, prod. A. Skinner for Skreba/Spectre.
(1993). *The Gourmet*, Granta, 43, 89–127. Broadcast in the UK, Channel 4, 8 May 1986, dir. M. Whyte, prod. A. Skinner for Skreba/Spectre.
(2003). *The Saddest Music In The World*. Released in UK, 25 October; released in USA, 14 February 2004, dir. Guy Maddin, prod. N. Finchman for IFC.

(2005). *The White Countess*. Released 21 December, dir. James Ivory, prod. Ismail Merchant for Merchant/Ivory.

Film adaptations of Ishiguro's work

(1993). *The Remains of the Day*. Released 12 November, dir. James Ivory, adapted by Ruth Prawer Jhabvala, Merchant Ivory Productions.
(2010). *Never Let Me Go*. Dir. Mark Romanek, adapted by Alex Garland, A. DNA Films.

Other

(1983). 'I Became Profoundly Thankful for Having Been Born in Nagasaki', in *The Guardian*, 8 September, 9.
(1986). 'Introduction' to Yasunari Kawabata's *Snow Country and Thousand Cranes*, trans. E. G. Seidensticker. Harmondsworth: Penguin, 1–3.
(1993). 'Letter to Salman Rushdie', in *The Rushdie Letters: Freedom to Speak, Freedom to Write*, S. McDonogh (ed.). London: Brandon, 79–80.

II. Critical Material

Book-length studies

Fluet, L. (2008), 'Ishiguro's Unknown Communities', *Novel: A Forum on Fiction*, 40 (3), Summer 2007. [A special edition of the journal devoted to Ishiguro's work containing five essays.]
Gallix, F., V. Guignery, and P. Veyret (eds). (2004), *Kazuo Ishiguro, Etudes Britanniques Contemporaines, Revue de la Société d'Etudes Anglaises Contemporaines*, 27, 127–141. [An excellent publication containing an interview, bibliography, and nine essays on Ishiguro's work.]
Lewis, B. (2000), *Kazuo Ishiguro*. Manchester: Manchester University Press.
Parkes, A. (2001), The Remains of The Day: *A Reader's Guide*. New York: Continuum Contemporaries.
Peters, S. (2000), *York Notes Advanced:* The Remains of The Day. London: York Press.
Petry, M. (1999), *Narratives of Memory and Identity: The Novels of Kazuo Ishiguro*. Frankfurt: Peter Lang.
Porée, M. (1999), *Kazuo Ishiguro*: The Remains of the Day. Paris: Didier Érudition-CNED.
Shaffer, B. W. (1998), *Understanding Kazuo Ishiguro*. Columbia: University of South Carolina Press.
Shaffer, B. W. and C. Wong (eds). (2008), *Conversations with Kazuo Ishiguro*. Jackson, Miss.: University of Mississippi Press. [This collection contains a selection of insightful interviews with Ishiguro.]

Veyret, P. (2002), *Kazuo Ishiguro: Au risque de la mémoire*. Bordeaux: Presses Universitaires de Bordeaux. [Publication in French on the relationship between truth and memory in Ishiguro's work.]

Wong, C. (2000), *Kazuo Ishiguro*. Tavistock: Northcote House.

Book chapters

Bradbury, M. (1987), 'The Floating World', in *No, Not Bloomsbury*. London: Andre Deutsch, 363–366.

—(1993), *The Modern British Novel*. London: Secker and Warburg, 423–425.

Childs, P. (2005), *Contemporary British Novelists: British Fiction since 1970*. New York: Palgrave Macmillan, 123–140.

Connor, S. (1996), 'Outside In', in *The English Novel in History: 1950–1995*. London: Routledge, 83–127.

Doring, T. (2006), 'Sherlock Holmes – He Dead: Disenchanting the English detective in Kazuo Ishiguro's *When We Were Orphans*,' in *Postmortems: Crime Fictions from a Transcultural Perspective*, C. Matzke, C. and S. Muhleisen (eds). Amsterdam: Rodopi, 59–86.

Doyle, W. (1993), 'Being an Other to Oneself: First Person Narration in Kazuo Ishiguro's *The Remains of The Day*', in *L'Altérité dans la littérature et la culture du monde Anglophone*, Labbé, E. (ed.). Le Mans: University of Maine Press, 70–76.

Foster, J. W. (2006), '"All the Long Traditions": loyalty and service in Barry and Ishiguro', in *Out of History: Essays on the Writings of Sebastian Barry*, C. H. Mahony (ed.). Dublin: Catholic University of America Press, 99–119.

Goody, I. (2005), '"Fin de siècle, fin du globe: Intercultural Chronotopes of Memory and Apocalypse in the Fictions of Murakami Haruki and Kazuo Ishiguro', in *Intercultural Explorations*, E. Eoyang (ed.). Amsterdam: Rodopi, 95–203.

Gordon, G. (1998), *Philosophy of The Arts: An Introduction to Aesthetics*. London & New York: Routledge, 121–127.

Griffiths, M. (1993), 'Great English Houses: New Homes in England? Memory and Identity in Kazuo Ishiguro's *Remains of the Day* and V. S. Naipaul's *The Enigma of Arrival*', *Span*, 36, 488–503.

Hall, L. (1995), 'New Nations, New Selves: The Novels of Timothy Mo and Kazuo Ishiguro', in *Other Britain, Other British: Contemporary Multicultural Fiction*, Robert Lee (ed.). London: Pluto Press, 90–110.

Hitchens, C. (1993), 'Kazuo Ishiguro', in *For the Sake of Argument: Essays and Minority Reports*. London: Verso, 320–322.

Holmes, F. M. (2005), 'Realism, Dreams and the Unconscious in the Novels of Kazuo Ishiguro', in *The Contemporary British Novel since 1980*, J. Acheson and S. E. Ross (eds). New York: Palgrave Macmillan, 11–22.

King, B. (1991), 'The New Internationalism: Shiva Naipaul, Salman Rushdie, Buchi Emecheta, Timothy Mo and Kazuo Ishiguro', in *The British and Irish Novel since 1960*, J. Acheson (ed.). New York: St Martins Press, 192–211.

Lodge, D. (1992), 'The Unreliable Narrator', in *The Art of Fiction*. New York: Viking, 154–157.

Luyat, A. (1994), 'Myth and Metafiction: Is Peaceful Co-Existence Possible? Destruction of the Myth of the English Butler in Kazuo Ishiguro's *The Remains of The Day*', in *Historicité et métafiction dans le roman contemporain des îles Britanniques*, M. Duperray (ed.). Aix-en-Provence: University of Provence, 183–196.

Massie, A. (1990), *The Novel Today: A Critical Guide to The British Novel 1970–1989*. London/New York: Longman, 64.

Newton, A. Z. (1997), 'Telling Others: Secrecy and Recognition in Dickens, Barnes and Ishiguro', in *Narrative Ethics*. Cambridge: Harvard University Press, 241–285.

Page, N. (1991), 'Speech, Culture and History in the Novels of Kazuo Ishiguro', in *Asian Voices in English*, Mimi Chan and Roy Harris (eds). Hong Kong: Hong Kong University Press, 161–168.

Petry, M. (1999), *Narratives of Memory and Identity: The Novels of Kazuo Ishiguro*. Frankfurt: Peter Lang.

Rennison, N. (2005), *Contemporary British Novelists*. London: Routledge, 91–94.

Salecl, R. (1996), 'I Can't Love You Unless I Give You Up', in *Gaze and Voice as Love Objects*, R. Salecl and S. Zizek (eds). Durham: Duke University Press, 179–207.

Spark, G. (2008), 'The Mysterious Case of the Disappearing Empire: History and the Golden-Age Detective Genre in Kazuo Ishiguro's *When We Were Orphans*', in *Sub/versions: Cultural Status, Genre and Critique*, P. Macpherson, C. Murray, G. Spark, and K. Corstorphine (eds). Newcastle upon Tyne: Cambridge Scholars Press, 124–134.

Stanton, K. (2006), 'Foreign Feeling: Kazuo Ishiguro's *The Unconsoled* and the New Europe', in *Cosmopolitan Fictions: Ethics, Politics, and Global Change in the Works of Kazuo Ishiguro, Michael Ondaatje, Jamaica Kincaid, and J.M. Coetzee*. Abingdon: Routledge.

Stevenson, R. (1993), *A Reader's Guide to the Twentieth Century Novel in Britain*. Lexington: University of Kentucky Press, 130–136.

Sutherland, J. (1998), 'Why Hasn't Mr. Stevens Heard of the Suez Crisis?', in *Where was Rebecca Shot?: Puzzles, Curiosities and Conundrums in Modern Fiction*. London: Weidenfeld and Nicholson, 185–189.

Weiss, T. (2003), 'Where is Place? Locale in Ishiguro's *When We Were Orphans*', in *Anglophone Cultures in Southeast Asia: Appropriations, Continuities, Contexts*, R. Ahrens, D. Parker, K. Stierstorfer, and K-K. Tam (eds). Heidelberg: Universitatverlag, 271–294.

Wood, M. (1995), 'The Discourse of Others', in *Children of Silence: Studies in Contemporary Fiction*. London: Pimlico, 171–181.

Journal articles

Adelman, G. (2001), 'Doubles on the Rocks: Ishiguro's *The Unconsoled*', *Critique: Studies in Contemporary Fiction*, 42 (2), Winter, 166–179.

Appiah, K. A. (2001), 'Liberalism, Individuality, and Identity', *Critical Inquiry*, 27 (2), 305–332.

Arai, M. (1990), 'Ishiguro's Floating Worlds: Observations on his Visions of Japan', *General Education Review*, 22, 29–34.

Ash, J. (1994), 'Stick it up *Howard's End*', *Gentleman's Quarterly*, 8, 43.

Bain, A. M. (2007), 'International Settlements: Ishiguro, Shanghai, Humanitarianism', *Novel: A Forum on Fiction*, 40 (3), 240–264.

Bigliazzi, S. (2007), 'Inside (Counter-)Factuality: Reassessing the Narrator's Discourse in Kazuo Ishiguro's *The Remains of the Day*', *Rivista di Letterature Moderne e Comparate*, 60 (2), 219–244.

Birch, D. (2008), 'A Brief History of the Future', *Times Literary Supplement*, 30 January.

Britzman, D. P. (2006), 'On Being a Slow Reader: Psychoanalytic Reading Problems in Ishiguro's *Never Let Me Go*', *Changing English: Studies in Culture and Educations*, 13 (3), 307–318.

Cardullo, B. (1995), 'The Servant', *Hudson Review*, 47 (4), 616–622.

Capri, D. (1997), 'The Crisis of the Social Subject in the Contemporary English Novel', *European Journal of English Studies*, 1 (2), 165–183.

Cheng, C. (2005), 'Making and Marketing Kazuo Ishiguro's Alterity', *Post-Identity*, 4 (2), [no pagination].

Chertoff, D. and L. Toker (2008), 'Reader Response and the Recycling of Topoi in Kazuo Ishiguro's *Never Let Me Go*', *Partial Answers: Journal of Literature and the History of Ideas*, 6 (1), 163–180.

Cunningham, H. C. (2004), 'The Dickens Connection in Kazuo Ishiguro's *When We Were Orphans*', *Notes on Contemporary Literature*, 34 (5), 4–6.

Davis, R. G. (1994), 'Imaginary Homelands Revisited in the Novels of Kazuo Ishiguro', *Miscellanea*, 15, 139–154.

—(1995), '*The Remains of the Day*: Kazuo Ishiguro's Sonnet on his Blindness', *Cuadernos de Investigacion Filologicia*, 21–22, 57–67.

Ekelund, B. G. (2005), 'Misrecognizing History: Complicitous Genres in Kazuo Ishiguro's *The Remains of the Day*', *International Fiction Review*, 32 (1–2), 70–90.

Finney, B. (2002), 'Figuring the Real: Ishiguro's *When We Were Orphans*', *Jouvert: A Journal of Postcolonial Studies*, 7 (1), http://english.chass.ncsu.edu/jouvert/v7is1/ishigu.htm, [accessed 23 June, 2009].

Fluet, L. (2003), 'The Self-Loathing Class: Williams, Ishiguro and Barbara Ehrenreich on Service', *Key Words: A Journal of Cultural Materialism*, 4, 100–130.

—(2007), 'Ishiguro: Unknown Communities', *Novel: A Forum on Fiction*, 40 (3), 205–304.

—(2007), 'Immaterial Labours: Ishiguro, Class and Affect', *Novel: A Forum on Fiction*, 40 (3), 265–288.

Forsythe, R. (2005), 'Cultural Displacement and the Mother-Daughter Relationship in Kazuo Ishiguro's *A Pale View of Hills*', *West Virginia University Philological Papers*, 52, 99–108.

Francois, P. (2004), 'The Spectral Return of Depths in Kazuo Ishiguro's *The Unconsoled*', *Commonwealth Essays and Studies*, 26 (2), 77–90.

Griffiths, M. (1993), 'Great English Houses – New Homes in England? Memory and Identity in Kazuo Ishiguro's *The Remains of the Day* and V.S. Naipaul's *The Enigma of Arrival*', *Span*, 36, 488–503.

Guth, D. (1999), 'Submerged Narratives in Kazuo Ishiguro's *The Remains of the Day*', *Forum for Modern Language Studies*, 35 (2), 126–127.

Hama, M. (1991) 'A Pale View', *Switch*, 8 (6), 76–102.

Hassan, I. (1990), 'An Extravagant Reticence', *The World and I*, 5 (2), 369–374.

Henke, C. (2003), 'Remembering Selves, Constructing Selves: Memory and Identity in Contemporary British Fiction', *Journal for the Study of British Culture*, 10 (1), 77–100.

Ingersoll, E. G. (2001), 'Desire, the Gaze, and Suture in the Novel and the Film: *The Remains of the Day*', 28 (1–2), 31–47.

—(2007), 'Taking Off the Realm of Metaphor: Kazuo Ishiguro's *Never Let Me Go*, *Studies in the Humanities*, 34 (1), 40–59.

Janik, D. I. (1995), 'No End to History: Evidence from the Contemporary English Novel', *Twentieth Century Literature*, 22 June, 160–189.

Jirgens, K. E. (1999), 'Narrator Resartus: Palimpsestic Revelations in Kazuo Ishiguro's *The Remains of the Day*', *Q/W/E/R/T/Y: Arts, Litteratures & Civilisations du Monde Anglophone*, 9, 219–230.

Lang, J. (2000), 'Public Memory, Private History: Kazuo Ishiguro's *The Remains of the Day*', *CLIO: A Journal of Literature, History and the Philosophy of History*, 29 (2), 143–165.

Lee, H. (1990), 'Quiet Desolation', *New Republic*, 22 January, 36–39.

Luo, S.-P. (2003), '"Living the Wrong Life": Kazuo Ishiguro's Unconsoled Orphans', *Dalhousie Review*, 83 (1), 51–80.

Ma, S.-M. (1999), 'Kazuo Ishiguro's Persistent Dream for Postethnicity: Performance in Whiteface', *Post Identity*, 2 (1), 71–88.

Mallett, P. J. (1996), 'The Revelation of Character in Kazuo Ishiguro's *The Remains of the Day* and *An Artist of the Floating World*', *Shoin Literary Review*, 29, 1–20.

Mason, G. (1989), 'Inspiring Images: The Influence of the Japanese Cinema on the Writing of Kazuo Ishiguro', *East West Film Journal*, 3 (2), 39–52.

McCombe, J. P. (2002), 'The End of (Anthony) Eden: Ishiguro's *The Remains of the Day* and Midcentury Anglo-American Tensions', *Twentieth Century Literature: A Scholarly and Critical Journal*, 48 (1), 77–99.

McDonald, K. (2007), 'Days of Past Futures: Kazuo Ishiguro's *Never Let Me Go* as "Speculative Memoir"', *Biography: An Interdisciplinary Quarterly*, 30 (1), 74–83.

Nunokawa, J. (2007), 'Afterword: Now They are Orphans', *Novel: A Forum on Fiction*, 40 (3), 303–304.

O'Brien, S. (1996), 'Serving a New Order: Postcolonial Politics in Kazuo Ishiguro's *The Remains of the Day*', *Modern Fiction Studies*, 42 (2), 787–806.

Patey, C. (1991), 'When Ishiguro Visits the West Country: An Essay on *The Remains of the Day*', *Acme*, 44 (2), 135–155.

Pégon, C. (2004), 'How to Have Done With Words: Virtuoso Performance in Kazuo Ishiguro's *The Unconsoled*', in *Etudes Britanniques Contemporaines, Revue de la Société d'Etudes Anglaises Contemporaines*, 27, 83–95.

Reitano, N. (2007), 'The Good Wound: Memory and Community in *The Unconsoled*', *Texas Studies in Literature and Language*, 49 (4), 361–386.

Robbins, B. (2001), 'Very Busy Just Now: Globalisation and Harriedness in Ishiguro's *The Unconsoled*', in *Comparative Literature*, 53(4), Autumn, 426–442.

—(2007), 'Cruelty is Bad: Banality and Proximity in *Never Let Me Go*', *Novel: A Forum on Fiction*, 40 (3), 289–302.

Robinson, R. (2006), 'Nowhere, in Particular: Kazuo Ishiguro's *The Unconsoled* and Central Europe', *Critical Quarterly*, 48 (4), Winter, 107–130.

Rothfork, J. (1996), 'Zen Comedy in Postcolonial Literature: Kazuo Ishiguro's *The Remains of the Day*', *Mosaic*, 29 (1), 79–102.

Rushton, R. (2007), 'Three Modes of Terror: Transcendence, Submission, Incorporation', *Nottingham French Studies*, 46 (3), 109–120.

Sarvan, C. (1997), 'Floating Signifiers and *An Artist of the Floating World*', *Journal of Commonwealth Literature*, 32 (1), 93–101.

Sauerberg, L. O. (2006), 'Coming to Terms – Literary Configurations of the Past in Kazuo Ishiguro's *An Artist of the Floating World* and Timothy Mo's *An Insular Possession*', *EurAmerica: A Journal of European and American Studies*, 36 (2), 175–202.

Scanlan, M. (1993), 'Mistaken Identities: First Person Narration in Kazuo Ishiguro', *Journal of Narrative and Life History*, 3 (2/3), 145.

Seaman, M. J. (2007), 'Becoming More (than) Human: Affective Posthumanisms, Past and Future', *Journal of Narrative Theory*, 37 (2), 246–275.

Sim, W. (2005), 'Kazuo Ishiguro', *Review of Contemporary Literature*, 25 (1), 80–115.

Slay, J. (1997), 'Ishiguro's *The Remains of the Day*', *Explicator*, 55 (3), 180–182.

Su, J. J. (2002), 'Refiguring National Character: The Remains of the British Estate Novel', *MFS: Modern Fiction Studies*, 48 (3), 552–580.

Sumners-Bremner, E. (2006), '"Poor creatures": Ishiguro's and Coetzee's Imaginary Animals', *Mosaic: A Journal of the Interdisciplinary Study of Literature*, 39 (4), 145–160.

Suter, R. (1999), '"We're Like Butlers": Interculturality, Memory and Responsibility in Kazuo Ishiguro's *The Remains of the Day*', *Q/W/E/R/T/Y: Arts, Litteratures & Civilisations du Monde Anglophone*, 9, 241–250.

Tamaya, M. (1992), 'Ishiguro's *The Remains of the Day*: The Empire Strikes Back', *Modern Language Studies*, 22 (2), 45–56.

Terestchenko, M. (2007), 'Servility and Destructiveness in Kazuo Ishiguro's *Remains of the Day*', *Partial Answers: Journal of Literature and the History of Ideas*, 5 (10), 77–89.

Teverson, A. (1999), 'Acts of Reading in Kazuo Ishiguro's *The Remains of the Day*', *Q/W/E/R/T/Y: Arts, Litteratures & Civilisations du Monde Anglophone*, 9, 251–258.

Trimm, R. S. (2005), 'Inside Job: Professionalism and Postimperial Communities in *The Remains of the Day*, *Lit: Literature Interpretation Theory*, 16 (2), 135–161.

Veyret, P. (2005), 'The Strange Case of the Disappearing Chinamen: Memory and Desire in Kazuo Ishiguro's *The Remains of the Day* and *When We Were Orphans*', *Etudes Britanniques Contemporaines: Revue de la Société d'Etudes Anglaises Contemporaines*, 29, 159–172.

Vinet, D. (1999), 'The Butler's Woman, a Strategy of Avoidance in Kazuo Ishiguro's *The Remains of the Day*', *Etudes Britanniques Contemporaines: Revue de la Société d'Etudes Anglaises Contemporaines*, 16, 63–80.

—(2000), 'The Avatars of the Father in *The Remains of the Day*', *Etudes Britanniques Contemporaines, Revue de la Société d'Etudes Anglaises Contemporaines*, 19, 53–67.

—(2004), 'Fugal Tempo in *The Unconsoled*', *Etudes Britanniques Contemporaines, Revue de la Société d'Etudes Anglaises Contemporaines*, 27, 127–141.

—(2005), 'Revisiting the Memory of Guilt in Ishiguro's *When We Were Orphans*', *Etudes Britanniques Contemporaines: Revue de la Société d'Etudes Anglaises Contemporaines*, 29, 133–144.

Wain, P. (1992), 'The Historical-Political Aspect of the Novels of Kazuo Ishiguro', *Language and Culture*, 23, 177–205.

Walkowitz, R. L. (2001), 'Ishiguro's Floating Worlds', *ELH*, 68 (4), 1049–1076.

Walkowitz, R. L. (2007), 'Unimaginable Largeness: Kazuo Ishiguro, Translation, and the New World Literature', *Novel: A Forum on Fiction*, 40 (3), 216–239.

Wall, K. (1994), '*The Remains of the Day* and its Challenges to Theories of Unreliable Narration', *Journal of Narrative Technique*, 24 (1), 18–24.

Watson, G. (1995). 'The Silence of the Servants', *Sewanee Review*, 103 (3), 480–486.

Westermann, M. (2004), 'Is the Butler Home? Narrative and the Split Subject in *The Remains of the Day*', *Mosaic: A Journal for the Interdisciplinary Study of Literature*, 37 (3), 157–170.

Whyte, P. (2007), 'The Treatment of Background in Kazuo Ishiguro's *The Remains of the Day*', *Commonwealth Essays and Studies*, 30 (1), 73–82.

Winsworth, B. (1999), 'Communicating and not Communicating: The True and the False Self in *The Remains of the Day*', *Q/W/E/R/T/Y: Arts, Littératures & Civilisations du Monde Anglophone*, 9, 259–266.

Wong, C. (1995), 'The Shame of Memory: Blanchot's Self Dispossession in Ishiguro's *A Pale View of Hills*', *Clio*, 24 (2), 127–145.

Wroe, N. (2005), 'Living Memories', *The Guardian Review*, 19 February, http://www.guardian.co.uk/books/2005/feb/19/fiction.kazuoishiguro [accessed 5 July 2008]

Yoshioka, F. (1988), 'Beyond the Division of East and West: Kazuo Ishiguro's *A Pale View of Hills*', *Studies in English Literature*, 71–86.

Zinck, P. (2005), 'The Palimpsest of Memory in Kazuo Ishiguro's *When We Were Orphans*', *Etudes Britanniques Contemporaines: Revue de la Société d'Etudes Anglaises Contemporaines*, 29, 145–158.

Reviews

A Pale View of the Hills

Bailey, P. (1982), 'Private Desolations', *Times Literary Supplement*, 19 February, 179.

Campbell, J. (1982), 'Kitchen Window', *New Statesman*, 19 February, 25.

King, F. (1982), 'Shimmering', *Spectator*, 27 February, 25.

Lively, P. (1982), 'Backwards and Forwards', *Encounter*, 58/59 (6/1), 86–91.

Milton, E. (1982), 'In a Japan Like Limbo', *New York Times Book Review*, 9 May, 12–13.

Spence, J. (1982), 'Two Worlds Japan Has Lost Since the Meiji', *New Society*, 9 May, 266–267.

Thwaite, A. (1982), 'Ghosts in The Mirror', *Observer*, 14 February, 33.

An Artist of the Floating World

Chisholm, A. (1986), 'Lost Worlds of Pleasure', *Times Literary Supplement*, 14 February, 162.

Dyer, G. (1986), 'On Their Mettle', *New Statesman*, 4 April, 26.

Garland, A. (1998), 'On the Shelf: *An Artist of the Floating World*', *Sunday Times: Books*, 10 May, 9.

Hunt, N. (1987), 'Two Close Looks at Faraway', *Brick*, 31, 36–38.

Morton, K. (1986), 'After the War was Lost', *New York Times Book Review*, 8 June, 19.

Parrinder, P. (1986), 'Manly Scowls', *London Review of Books*, 6 February, 16.

Stuewe, P. (1986), 'Genuine Japanese . . . Slush-Pile Saviour . . . for God and Greed', *Quill and Quire*, 52 (12), 31.

Wasi, J. (1987), 'Book Reviews', *Indian Horizons*, 36 (1&2), 52–54.

The Remains of the Day

Annan, G. (1989), 'On the High Wire', *New York Review of Books*, 7 December, 3–4.

Coates, J. (1989), 'Deceptive Calm', *Chicago Tribune Books*, 1 October, 5.

Dyer, G. (1989), 'What the Butler Did', *New Statesman and Society*, 26 May, 34.

Gray, P. (1989), 'Upstairs Downstairs', *Time*, 30 October, 55.

Gurewich, D. (1989), 'Upstairs Downstairs', *New Criterion*, 8 (4), 77–80.

Hutchings, W. (1990), 'English: Fiction', *World Literature Today*, 64 (3), 463–464.

Iyer, P. (1991), 'Waiting upon History', *Partisan Review*, 58 (3), 585–589.

Kamine, M. (1989), 'A Servant of Self-Deceit', *New Leader*, 13 November, 21–22.

King, F. (1989), 'A Stately Procession of One', *Spectator*, 27 May, 31–32.

Rafferty, T. (1990), 'The Lesson of The Master', *New Yorker*, 15 January, 102–104.

Rubin, M. (1989), 'A Review of *Remains of the Day*', *Christian Science Monitor*, 13 November, 13.

Rushdie, S. (1991 [1989]) 'What the Butler Didn't See', *The Observer*, 21 May, 53. Reprinted as 'Kazuo Ishiguro', in *Imaginary Homelands: Essays and Criticism 1981–1991*. London: Granta, 244–246.

Strawson, G. (1989), 'Tragically Disciplined and Dignified', *Times Literary Supplement*, 19 May, 535.

Thwaite, A. (1989), 'In Service', *London Review of Books*, 18 May, 17–18.

The Unconsoled

Brooke, A. (1995), 'Leaving Behind Daydreams for Nightmares', *The Wall Street Journal*, 11 November, A12.

Brookner, A. (1995), 'A Superb Achievement', *The Spectator*, 24 June, 40–41.

Chaudhuri, A. (1995), 'Unlike Kafka', *London Review of Books*, 8 May, 30–31.

Cunningham, V. (1995), 'A Pale View of Ills without Remedy', *The Guardian*, 7 May, 15.

Cusk, R. (1995), 'Journey to the End of the Day', *The Times*, 11 May, 38.

Eder, R. (1995), 'Meandering in a Dreamscape', *Los Angeles Times Book Review*, 8 October, 3; 7.

Gray, P. 'Bad Dreams: After *The Remains of The Day*, a Weird Non-Sequitur', *Time*, 2 October, 81–82.

Hughes-Hallet, L. (1995), 'Feeling No Pain', *Sunday Times Books*, 14 May, 7; 9.

Innes, C. (1995), 'Fiction without Frontiers', *Los Angeles Times*, 5 November, 11.

—(1995), 'Dr. Faustus Faces the Music', *Nation*, 6 November, 546–548.

Iyer, P. (1995), 'The Butler Didn't Do It, Again', *Times Literary Supplement*, 28 April, 22.

Janah, M. (1995), 'A Dreamscape of Music and Memory', *San Francisco Chronicle*, 8 October.

Kakutani, M. (1995), 'A New Annoying Hero', *New York Times*, 17 October.

Kauffmann, S. (1995), 'The Floating World', *New Republic*, 6 November, 42–45.

Kaveney, R. (1995), 'Tossed and Turned', *New Statesman and Society*, 12 May, 39.

Kiely, R. (1995), 'In an Unknown City to an Unknown Destination', *Boston Book Review*, 1 October, 32.

Menand, L. (1995), 'Anxious in Dreamland', *New York Times Review*, 15 October, 7.

Passaro, V. (1995), 'New Flash from an Old Isle', *Harper Magazine*, 10 October, 71–75.

Rorem, N. (1996), 'Fiction in Review', *Yale Review*, 84 (2), 154–159.

Rorty, R. (1995), 'Consolation Prize', *Village Voice Literary Supplement*, 10 October, 13.

Rubin, M. (1995), 'Probing the Plight of Lives "Trapped" in Others' Expectation', *Christian Science Monitor*, 4 October, 14.

Shone, T. (1995), 'Chaos Theory', *Harper's Bazaar*, 1 October, 132.

Simon, L. (1996), 'Remains of the Novelist', *Commonwealth*, 22 March, 25–26.

Smith, J. (1995), 'Lost Worlds: Memories form the Basis of His Brilliant Writing', *San Francisco Chronicle*, 12 November.

Steinberg, S. (1995), 'A Book about Our World', *Publisher's Weekly*, 18 September, 105–106.

Sweet, N. (1995), 'Kafka Set to Music', *Contemporary Review*, 10 October, 223–224.

Todd, T. (1995), 'Down and Out in Central Europe', *Austin Chronicle*, 7 June, 32.

Wilhelmus, T. (1996), 'Between Cultures', *Hudson Review*, 49 (2), 316–322.

Wood, J. (1995), 'Ishiguro in the Underworld', *Guardian*, 5 May, 5.

Wood, M. (1995), 'Sleepless Nights', *New York Review of Books*, 21 December, 17–18.

When We Were Orphans

Anastas, B. (2000), 'Keeping It Real', *Village Voice*, 3 October.

Barrow, A. (2000), 'Clueless in Shanghai', *Spectator*, 25 March, 44–45.

Bouldrey, B. (2000), 'A Life in Pieces', *San Francisco Chronicle*, 24 September, http://www.sfgate.com/cgi-bin/article.cgi?file=/chronicle/archive/2000/09/24/RV63071.DTL [accessed 4 June 2008].

Carey, J. (2000) 'Few Novels Extend the Possibilities of Fiction. This One Does', *Sunday Times: Culture*, 2 April, 45.

Francken, J. (2000), 'Something Fishy', *London Review of Books*, 13 April, 45.

Gray, P. (2000), 'The Remains of Shanghai', *Time*, 18 September, http://www.time.com/time/magazine/article/0,9171,997979,00.html [accessed 8 June 2007].

Gorra, M. (2000), 'The Case of Missing Childhood', *The New York Times*, 24 September.

Hensher, P. (2000), 'It's The Way He Tells It . . .' *The Observer*, 19 March, http://www.guardian.co.uk/books/2000/mar/19/fiction.bookerprize2000 [accessed 2 September 2007].

Jaggi, M. (2000), 'In Search of Lost Crimes', *The Guardian*, 1 April, 8.

Jones, R. C. (2000), 'Shanghai Search', *The Times*, 2, 6 April, 15.

Kakutani, M. (2000), 'The Case He Can't Solve: A Detective's Delusions', *New York Times*, 19 September, http://query.nytimes.com/gst/fullpage.html?res=9E04E3DF173BF93AA2575AC0A9669C8B63 [accessed 5 April 2008].

Leith, S. (2000), 'Shanghai Sherlock', *The Daily Telegraph: Arts and Books*, 25 March, 4.

McWilliam, C. (2000), 'Painful, Lovely, Limpid in Freezing Fog', *Financial Times: Weekend*, 8 April, 4.

Oates, J. C. (2000), 'The Serpent's Heart', *Times Literary Supplement*, 31 March, 21–22.

Sutcliffe, W. (2000), 'History Happens Elsewhere', *Independent on Sunday*, 'Review', 2 April, 56–58.

Never Let Me Go

Atwood, M. (2005), 'Brave New World', *Slate*, 1 April 2005, http://slate.msn.com/id/2116040 [accessed 14 December 2008].

Browning, J. (2005), 'Hello Dolly', *Village Voice*, 22 March, http://www.villagevoice.com/2005-03-22/books/hello-dolly/ [accessed 8 August 2009].

Deb, S. (2005), *The New Statesman*, 7 March, 55.

Desai, A. (2005), 'A Shadow World', *New York Review of Books*, 52 (14), 22 September, http://www.nybooks.com/articles/article-preview?article_id=18261 [accessed 4 May 2009].

Dyer, G. (2005), '*Never Let Me Go*, by Kazuo Ishiguro', *Independent*, 27 February, http://www.independent.co.uk/arts-entertainment/books/reviews/never-let-me-go-by-kazuo-ishiguro-746712.html [accessed 14 December 2008].

Freeman, J. (2006), *Poets and Writers*, 5 June, 41.

Giles, G. (2005), *Newsweek*, 4 April, 52.

Grossman, L. (2005), 'Living on Borrowed Time', *Time*, 11 April, http://www.time.com/time/magazine/article/0,9171,1044735,00.html [accessed 6 August 2009].

Harrison, M. J. (2005), 'Clone Alone', *The Guardian*, 26 February, http://www.guardian.co.uk/books/2005/feb/26/bookerprize2005.bookerprize [accessed 15 January 2008].

Hensher, P. (2005), 'School for Scandal', *The Spectator*, 26 February, 32, http://www.spectator.co.uk/books/21309/school-for-scandal.thtml [accessed 30 May 2008].

Hill, T. (2005), 'England's Dreaming', *'Never Let Me Go'*, *The Times*, 31 August, http://entertainment.timesonline.co.uk/tol/arts_and_entertainment/books/article518560.ece [accessed 13 June 2008].

Inverne, J. (2005), 'Strange New World', *Time International*, 28 March, 68.

Jennings, J. (2005), *Artforum International*, 4 March, 1.

Kakutani, M. (2005), 'Sealed In a World, That's Not as It Seems', *The New York Times*, 4 April, http://www.nytimes.com/2005/04/04/books/04kaku.html [accessed 9 October 2007].

Kipen, D. (2005), 'Love Among Clones', *San Francisco Chronicle*, 14 February, http://www.sfgate.com/cgi-bin/article.cgi?f=/chronicle/reviews/books/NEVER_LET_ME_GO.DTL [accessed 6 July 2007].

Kermode, F. (2005), 'Outrageous Game', *London Review of Books*, 21 April, 21.

Kerr, S. (2005), 'When They were Orphans', *The New York Times*, 17 April, 16.

Menand, L. (2005), 'Something about Kathy', *The New Yorker*, 28 March, 78.

Messud, C. (2005), 'Love's Body', *The Nation*, 16 May, http://www.thenation.com/doc/20050516/messud [accessed 6 October 2009].

Moore, C. (2005), 'Meanings Behind Masks', *The Daily Telegraph*, 6 March, http://www.telegraph.co.uk/arts/main.jhtml?xml=/arts/2005/03/06/boish06.xml&sSheet=/arts/2005/03/06/bomain.html [accessed 6 June 2007].

O'Neill, J. (2005), 'New Fiction', *Atlantic Monthly*, May, http://www.theatlantic.com/doc/200505/oneill [accessed 23 January 2008].

Sandhu, S. (2005), 'Raw Emotional Intensity', *The Daily Telegraph*, 26 February, 1.

Schiefer, N. (2005), *London Free Press*, 16 April, D8.

Siddhartha, D. (2005), 'Lost Corner', *The New Statesman*, 7 March, 55.

Wood, J. (2005), 'The Human Difference', *The New Republic*, 12 May, http://www.powells.com/review/2005_05_12.html [accessed 14 December 2008].

Yardley, J. (2005), 'Never Let Me Go', *Washington Post*, 17 April, 2.

Nocturnes

Coe, J. (2009), 'Nocturnes', *Financial Times*, 16 May, http://www.ft.com/cms/s/2/65193848-40db-11de-8f18-00144feabdc0.html [accessed 27 June 2009].

Fleming, T. (2009), 'Heartbreak in Five Movements', *The Observer*, 10 May, http://www.guardian.co.uk/books/2009/may/09/kazuo-ishiguro-nocturnes [accessed 21 May 2009].

Kermode, F. (2009), 'Exercises and Excesses', *London Review of Books*, 31 (9), 14 May, 33.

Mukherjee, N. (2009), 'Unhappy Endings', *Time*, 15 May, http://www.time.com/time/magazine/article/0,9171,1902710,00.html [accessed 19 May 2009].

Robson, L. (2009), 'Nocturnes', *New Statesman*, 14 May, (5), http://www.newstatesman.com/books/2009/05/ishiguro-laugh-novel-world [accessed 1 July 2009].

Tayler, C. (2009), 'Scenes from an Italian Café', *The Guardian*, 16 May, http://www.guardian.co.uk/books/2009/may/16/nocturnes-music-nightfall-kazuo-ishiguro [accessed 26 June 2009].

Interviews and profiles

Adams, T. (2005), 'For Me, England is a Mythical Place: Interview with Kazuo Ishiguro', *The Observer*, 20 February, http://www.guardian.co.uk/books/2005/feb/20/fiction.kazuoishiguro [accessed 5 December 2006].

Bates, K. G. (2005), 'Interview with Kazuo Ishiguro', broadcast on NPR Radio on May 4, transcript published in B. W. Shaffer and C. Wong (2008), 199–203.

Bigsby, C. (1987), 'In Conversation with Kazuo Ishiguro', 'An Interview with Kazuo Ishiguro', *European English Messenger*, Zero Issue, 26–29. Repr. B. W. Shaffer and C. F. Wong (2008), 15–26.

Bradbury, D. (2000), 'Making up a Country of His Own', *Times*, 2, 6 April, 12–13.

Bradbury, M. (1995), 'Breaking Loose', *W Magazine*, 1, 34–37.

Chira, S. (1989), 'A Case of Cultural Misperception', *New York Times*, 28 October, 13.

Clee, N. (1989), 'The Butler in Us All', *Bookseller*, 14 April, 1327–1328.

Crummet, G. and C. F. Wong (2006), 'A Conversation about Life and Art with Kazuo Ishiguro', in B. W. Shaffer and C. F. Wong (2008), 204–220.

De Jongh, N. (1982), 'Life after the Bomb', *The Guardian*, 22 February, 11.

Field, M. (1988), 'This Britisher is Japanese', *Sydney Morning Herald*, 12 March, 74.

Freeman, J. (2005), 'Never Let Me Go: A Profile of Kazuo Ishiguro', *Poets and Writers Magazine*, May–June. Repr. in B. W. Shaffer and C. F. Wong (2008), 194–198.

Frumkes, L. B. (2001), 'Kazuo Ishiguro', *The Writer*, 114 (5). Repr. B. W. Shaffer and C. F. Wong (2008), 189–193.

Gallix, F. (2000), 'Kazuo Ishiguro: The Sorbonne Lecture', *Etudes Britanniques Contemporaines*, 18 June. Repr. B. W. Shaffer and C. F. Wong (2008), 135–155.

Hawley, J. (1988), 'Grousebeating with Royals', *Sydney Morning Herald*, 5 March, 72.

Hensher, P. (1995), 'Books', *Harper's and Queen*, June, 21.

Hogan, R. (2000), 'Kazuo Ishiguro', *Beatrice.com*. Repr. B. W. Shaffer and C. F. Wong (2008), 156–160.

Howard, P. (1989), 'A Butler's Tale Wins Booker for Ishiguro', *The Times*, 27 October, 24.

—(1993), 'A Comedy of Authors' *Times: Supplement*, 21 September, vi.

Iyer, P. (1996), 'A New Kind of Travel Writer', *Harper's Magazine*, February, 30–32.

Jaggi, M. (1995), 'Dreams of Freedom', *The Guardian*, 29 April, 28.

—(1995), 'Kazuo Ishiguro Talks to Maya Jaggi', *Wasafiri*, 22, 20–24.

—(2004), 'Kazuo Ishiguro with Maya Jaggi' [1994], in *Writing Across Worlds: Contemporary Writers Talk*, S. Nasta (ed.). London: Routledge, 159–170. Repr. in Shaffer, B. W. and C. F. Wong (2008), pp. 110–119.

Kellaway, K. (1995), 'The Butler on A Bender', *The Observer Review*, 16 April, 6–7.

Kelman, S. (1991), 'Ishiguro in Toronto', *The Brick Reader*. Repr. in B. W. Shaffer and C. F. Wong (2008), 42–51.

Krider, D. (1998), 'Rooted in a Small Space: An Interview with Kazuo Ishiguro', *Kenyon Review*, 20 (2), Spring, 146–154. Repr. in B. W. Shaffer and C. F. Wong (2008), 125–134.

Mackenzie, S. (1996), 'Into the Real World', *The Guardian*, 15 February, 12.

—(2000), 'Between Two Worlds', *The Guardian: Weekend*, 25 March, 10–11; 13–14; 17.

Mason, G. (1989), 'An Interview with Kazuo Ishiguro', *Contemporary Literature*, 30 (3), 335–347.

Morrison, B. (1989), 'It's a Long Way from Nagasaki', *Observer*, 29 October, 35.

Mullan, J. (2006), 'Kazuo Ishiguro Talks to John Mullan', *The Guardian*, 23 March, http://www.guardian.co.uk/culture/culturevultureblog/2006/mar/23/guardianbookc2 [audio interview, 39 minutes].

Newsweek (2005), 'Like Lambs to The Slaughter: An Interview with Kazuo Ishiguro', 4 April.

Oe, K. and K. Ishiguro (1991), 'The Novelist in Today's World: A Conversation', *Boundary 2*, 18, 109–122; Repr. as 'Wave Patterns: A Dialogue', in *Grand Street*, 10, 75–91. Repr. in B. W. Shaffer and C. F. Wong (2008), 52–65. Originally published in (1989) *Kokusai Koryu*, 53, 100–108.

Ohno, B. (1996), 'Who is The Unconsoled?: A Profile of Kazuo Ishiguro', *Mars Hill Review*, 5, 137–142.

Oliva, P. (1996), 'Chaos as Metaphor: An Interview with Kazuo Ishiguro', *Filling Station Magazine*, Winter, 9. Repr. in B. W. Shaffer and C. F. Wong (2008), 120–124.

Patterson, C. (2005), 'The Samurai of Suburbia', *The Independent*, 'Books', 4 March, http://www.independent.co.uk/arts-entertainment/books/features/kazuo-ishiguro-the-samurai-of-suburbia-527080.html [accessed 7 April 2006].

Sandhu, S. (2005), 'The Hiding Place', *The Telegraph*, 6 March, http://www.telegraph.co.uk/arts/main.jhtml?xml=/arts/2005/03/06/boishiguro.xml [accessed 5 December 2007].

Sexton, D. (1987), 'Interview: David Sexton Meets Kazuo Ishiguro', *Literary Review*, January, 16–19.

Shaffer, B. (2001), 'An Interview with Kazuo Ishiguro', *Contemporary Literature*, Spring, 1. Repr. in B. W. Shaffer and C. F. Wong (2008), 161–174.

Sinclair, C. (1987a), 'The Land of the Rising Son', *The Sunday Times*, 'Magazine', 11 January, 36–37.

—(1987b), 'Kazuo Ishiguro in Conversation', *The Roland Collection* (video), 34 minutes.

Smith, J. L. (1995), 'A Novel Taste of Criticism: Kazuo Ishiguro', *The Times*, 3 May, 17.

Swaim, D. (1990), 'Don Swaim Interviews Kazuo Ishiguro', in B. W. Shaffer and C. F. Wong (2008), 89–109.

Swift, G. (1989), 'Kazuo Ishiguro', *Bomb*, Autumn, 22–23. Repr. in B. W. Shaffer and C. F. Wong (2008), 35–41.

Tonkin, B. (2000), 'Artist of His Floating World', *Independent*, 'Weekend Review', 1 April, 9.

Tookey, C. (2005), 'Sydenham, mon amour', *Books and Bookmen*, March, 33–34.

Vorda, A. and K. Herzinger (1991), 'An Interview with Kazuo Ishiguro', *Mississippi Review*, 20, 131–154. Reprinted as 'Stuck on The Margins: An Interview with Kazuo Ishiguro', in *Face to Face: Interviews with Contemporary Novelists*, Allan Vorda (ed.). Houston, Texas: Rice University Press, 1993, 1–36. Repr. in B. W. Shaffer and C. F. Wong (2008), 66–88.

Wachtel, E. (ed.). (1996), 'Kazuo Ishiguro', in *More Writers and Company*. Toronto Alfred A. Knopf, 17–35.

Wilson, J. (1995), 'The Literary Life: A Very English Story', *The New Yorker*, 6 March, 96–106.

Wong, C. (2001), 'Like Idealism is to the Intellect: An Interview with Kazuo Ishiguro', *Clio*, 30, 309–325. Repr. in B. W. Shaffer and C. F. Wong (2008), 174–188.

Websites

http://www.contemporarywriters.com/authors/?p=auth52 [Biography and Critical Overview by James Proctor].

http://www.litencyc.com/php/speople.php?rec=true&UID=2318 [Profile and Critical Perspective by Sebastian Groes].

http://en.wikipedia.org/wiki/Kazuo_Ishiguro [Biography and some useful websites].

http://www.faber.co.uk/author/kazuo-ishiguro/ [With audio interview].

Index

Lightning Source UK Ltd.
Milton Keynes UK
UKHW020024040719
345549UK00004B/140/P